MW00465334

COMING HOME

BRITTNEY GRINER

COMING HOME

with Michelle Burford

ALFRED A. KNOPF
NEW YORK
2024

THIS IS A BORZOI BOOK PUBLISHED BY ALFRED A. KNOPF

Copyright © 2024 by Brittney Griner

All rights reserved. Published in the United States by Alfred A. Knopf,
a division of Penguin Random House LLC, New York, and distributed in Canada
by Penguin Random House Canada Limited, Toronto.

www.aaknopf.com

Knopf, Borzoi Books, and the colophon are registered trademarks of
Penguin Random House LLC.

A cataloging-in-publication record has been established for this book
by the Library of Congress.
LCCN: 2024930872
ISBN: 978-0-593-80134-5 (hardcover)
ISBN: 978-0-593-80135-2 (ebook)

Front-of-jacket photograph by Dana Scruggs
Back-of-jacket photograph by Miguel Negron, U.S. Army South
Jacket design by John Gall

MANUFACTURED IN CANADA
10 9 8 7 6 5 4 3 2 1
FIRST EDITION

FOR RELLE—
You will forever be my home.

CONTENTS

BEFORE

February 15, 2022

My eyelids slide open. *Tuesday. Already. Fuck.* Me and Relle lie in a tumble of sheets, the Arizona sun pouring into our bedroom. I groan. This trip overseas, this final stretch, it came so fast. "When's your flight again?" my wife asks. "Ten twenty-five," I mumble. I glance at my phone. *Seven a.m.* I'm a stickler for time. My dad was military, law enforcement. If I'm on time, I'm late. Not today, Pops. Haven't even finished packing. I'm still on yesterday. I'm still on Relle and me.

Yesterday. A Valentine's Day with my wife that almost didn't happen. My season has been the whirlwind they all are. Hooping for the Phoenix Mercury from May to October. Playing in Russia, October to April. Three one-week breaks to fly home and see my baby, three short-ass trips that make me miss her more. Before this break I get Covid. My team, UMMC Ekaterinburg, are reigning champs of the EuroLeague. I'm on the practice court, preparing to throw down in Spain, when I suddenly feel like death. I test positive, and so does half the team. *Game over, break here.*

"You need a negative PCR test to get into America," the team doc tells me. Google disagrees. A search reveals the rules have just changed, and I insist on the less-sensitive antigen test. The team has its reasons for wanting us to stay. Might get home and be too sick to return. Might miss games. Might jeopardize our shot at another title. Great reasons, but I have better ones: my back, my knees, my ankles, all in throbbing pain, yet nothing compared to my heart. It aches for Relle, for this season to be done. I've quietly decided it's my last.

I test negative and cough my way to Phoenix through a mask. Seven days at home, only six given the time difference, four spent feeling like crap. I'm finally on my feet the night before our special day. I'm going big this year, bigger than I have since we met. Our paths first crossed at Baylor in Waco, Texas. I was a sophomore and star baller; she was brand-new and fine as hell. I stopped by the SUB food court for my usual chocolate shake, and as soon as I picked it up, I felt a tap on my shoulder. I turned and saw this girl, cute and classy, with a scarf on her neck and curves for days.

"Excuse me, I think that's mine," she said, pointing at my cup. This was my shake, no doubt about it, but one look at her and I let that go. "My bad," I said, handing it to her. She took it and smiled. "And I think it's rude you don't remember my name," she said. I stared at her. Had we met? "I know your name," I said, trying to be slick. "So what is it?" she clapped back. *Busted.* "Okay, I don't remember your name," I said, "but if you tell me, I promise I'll never forget." We cracked up. "Actually, we haven't met," she said, extending her hand. "I'm Cherelle Watson." Thirteen years of love and friendship later, Relle still claims I stole her shake. Wrong. But I don't argue 'cause I clearly came out ahead. I found my person and my place all at once.

I had no real place before I met Relle. When you're six foot nine and wear size 17 men's sneakers, you don't fit. Not in cars. Not in chairs. Not in beds. Not in crowds. And definitely not in a world that mistakes you for what it most fears: a Black man.

Your presence is a threat. Your Blackness intimidates. Your height and swagger add to the alarm. You walk through the world on high alert, scanning your surroundings and holding your breath. Lower your guard for even a second and boom, you might get taken out. Many have. More will. We're home but not home free. We're seen, but through a warped lens.

That was why I started hooping. It made me feel truly visible. It also made me feel less like an outsider, a giant with no titties. When you're still flat chested by eighth grade, people talk. Girls in the locker room point and whisper, "Is she a boy, a dyke, a freak? Why is her voice so low? Is she tucking—hiding a penis in her underwear?" The stares, the taunts, they hurt like hell, much like the sorrow I carried around: *What's wrong with me, and when will I be normal?*

Basketball was my normal. On court, I wasn't a weirdo. I was an athlete above all, a starter always. Forty minutes of acceptance, four quarters of sanity. At fifteen, I found my sport, my identity. At sixteen, I dunked my way to fame with a YouTube video that went viral. In the world, I was a riddle. But in the arena, I was a star. I soared. I slammed. I sold tickets. I was applauded, affirmed, celebrated. I'd never felt at home in my skin. Basketball brought me the closest.

And then I met Relle. That freedom I experienced while hooping, I felt it all the time with her. At Baylor and beyond, we had our ups and downs, and we were best friends when I asked her to marry me. In 2018, we wed, no fuss or fanfare, just the two of us with a promise: we do, we will, forever. By then our love had been tested by my long stints in China, in Russia, on the road. That continued. Relle was in law school in North Carolina, living between there and our home in Phoenix. Zoom kept us close; the distance kept things exciting. That's the upside of distance. You meet your lover fresh each time you come together, and then while you're apart you support each other's grind. The downside is the longing, the absence of touch. As we watched *Grey's Anatomy* together on FaceTime, I'd imagine holding Relle in my arms.

That got old. I was tired of missing home, missing holidays, missing us. I was also legit exhausted. Your body takes a beating in this sport, and I'd been pounding mine for fifteen years. When that YouTube dunk caught fire in 2007, so did my career. Next thing I knew, I was meeting Shaq, who'd seen the video. Life sped up. Three-time All-American. Number one overall WNBA draft pick. WNBA All-Star. A historic Nike deal. Two Olympic golds, four EuroLeague titles, honors on and on. One blessing after another, with big battles behind the scenes: A cracked back so painful I couldn't sleep. Zero cartilage in my knees. Life under the microscope and on the road, with no steady home, no stability. Every sport has an off-season, but pro women hoopers often work year-round. We earn about 250 times less than NBA players and have a hard cap on our salaries. In the WNBA that year I made around $220,000. Overseas, I earned a million plus. That pay gap is why I was in Russia in the first place.

A few months before my Valentine's Day visit, my agent and I had negotiated a Thanksgiving break. It was the first time in years I'd been home on the actual holiday, and my wife threw down in the kitchen. Ham, mac and cheese, mashed potatoes, and my favorite, homemade honey-bun cake. Mom and my nephew E.J. flew in from Houston. Relle, a preacher's kid from Arkansas, gave me the tradition I craved. On that break, something in me said, *This is it. I can't go back.*

I take pride in being a breadwinner, promised Relle I'd always provide. That was why I teared up when I told her, "Baby, I'm done." She hugged me. She'd already sensed it. "You're not the only source of income," she reminded me. She'd soon have her law degree. Also, we'd find other ways for me to earn. I honestly wanted to quit right then, but I had to honor my contract. Dad drilled that into me growing up: Finish what you start. So we decided I'd complete this one last season before leaning into the next one. We'd find a church. We'd grow our family. We'd be together. Finally.

For Valentine's Day, I go all out. Relle has been working her butt off in school, making us both proud. So I book a spa day at the Biltmore, a luxury resort. She thinks I'm coming with her. That's the surprise. "This day is all about you," I tell her. "I want you to get pampered. Take your time." I chauffeur her there and kiss her goodbye, promise to pick her up later. While I play golf, she relishes the experience: facial, massage, the works. When I return, she is glowing, as gorgeous as she was when we first met. Out to dinner, we exchange sweet nothings between bites of steak and potatoes. At home I have one last surprise: a massive bouquet of roses. "Babe, you've been holding back on me!" she squeals. "This isn't a bouquet, it's a *garden*!" That evening, in the dark, as I hold Relle close, I think, *I've just gotta make it to April.*

And then.

Just as my blessings come with battles, my *afters* flow from *befores*. Before, I am BG, No. 42, a daddy's girl from Texas. Before, I am hopeful, more than ever, with a future so bright it burns my eyes. I'm on my way to Russia, a place I've called my second home. For eight seasons I've played there, won there, lived there for long stretches, greeted the schoolgirl fans always lined up near my locker room. I'll go back now and grind my way to playoffs, earn this last round of cash for my family. I'll finish strong, with dignity, the way Pops taught me to. Before, I have no clue what's coming. That is the gift of that Valentine's Day.

A short time later and a world away, I wake up in an *after* I'd wish on no one. My horror begins in a land I thought I knew, on a trip I wish I hadn't taken. It's the memory of what I left behind and the gut-wrenching truths I encountered. It's the diary of my heartaches, my regrets, my questions about what a Black life is worth. It's my gratitude to the millions who rallied for my rescue. It's how I endured a nightmare, the most frightening ordeal of my life. And it's the story of us, of Relle and me, and how our love finally brought me home.

PART I

HOSTAGE

The system put a mark on us. You're not the same as everyone else. And nobody ever asked who we were. As Black and brown people, it's as if we were born guilty.

—Yusef Salaam of the Exonerated Five

BG

Hey baby I got stopped by security at customs

If you don't hear from me for like one hour or more get my agent on the phone

Wake up plz

Fuck

Baby text me plz I'm freaking out

Baby

Yo

Baby

Hello

This is it for me

*Brittney's first texts on February 17, 2022,
from the Moscow airport to her wife, Cherelle,
then asleep at 2:02 a.m. at their home in Phoenix*

1

FLIGHT TO HELL

That whole day was strange. On the morning of my Russia flight, my wife and I lingered in bed till the last minute because something in me kept whispering, *Don't go.* "Babe, we gotta get out of here," Relle finally said around 8:30 a.m. *Oh snap. Two hours till takeoff.* Relle was planning to ride with me to the airport and then go to brunch with a friend. She threw on a sundress as I dragged myself out of bed. From then on, everything went sideways.

Relle usually packs for me. I hold the WNBA record for most dunks, and I can practically block a shot in my sleep, but please don't ask me to organize anything. Not a closet. Not a pantry. Not a schedule. And for damn sure not a suitcase. That's my wife's territory and also her talent. I do the hooping, she does the planning. I do the driving, she does the shopping. I open doors, she walks through them. Our skills and desires are complementary, which is what makes us a perfect team. Also, we're both Southerners, old-school traditional. Several months before this trip, however, we'd switched things up. She was in her third year of law school, juggling two jobs and running on fumes. "Our support has to look different," she said. *Of course.* "Babe, don't worry," I told her. "I got this." In principle, that was true. In practice, I was a mess.

Even with our new understanding in place, my baby had my back ahead of this trip. Every time I'd fly in on break, she'd do a Target run to stock up on the American foods and seasonings I couldn't get in Russia: candy, cookies, brown sugar, pancake mix, Worcestershire sauce, Sweet Baby Ray's barbecue sauce, and of course my Tony Chachere's Original Creole Seasoning. My mom's from Louisiana, Cajun country, so I don't play when it comes to my spices. I love to eat, always have, and my food needs to taste right. Before our Valentine's Day celebration, Relle had organized all those items into hard-shell roller suit-cases, my two checked bags. That left me with my carry-ons to pack: a small roller bag and my Louis Vuitton backpack, the NBA edition. I carry that backpack everywhere.

Soon as I got up, I pulled out my roller. I shoved in my Nintendo Switch, my headphones, all my electronics, a jumble of cables and cords. I then grabbed my backpack, unzipped the large compartment, and slid in my huge MacBook Pro. I didn't pack many clothes. Just a few pairs of underwear and sweats. I had an apartment in Russia, provided by my team, and most of my stuff was already there. If my wife had packed my carry-ons, she would've started by making sure they were empty. She would've unzipped the pockets, one at a time, and turned the bags over to dump them out. She then would've rolled and zip-tied every cord and stacked them neatly inside the case. I did none of that. No time. My stuff was all over the place, just randomly scattered in the bag. The one thing I was careful about was my passport. If someone stole that, I was in trouble. That was why I always kept mine in my hoodie pocket. In ten minutes flat, I finished packing and pulled on my Cross Colours hoodie, the Black Lives Matter edition. "You're done that quick?" Relle asked. "Yep," I said, "I'm ready to roll."

My iPhone wasn't. As we were leaving, I couldn't find it anywhere. We tore up the house in search of that phone, kept calling it to see if we'd spot it. Nothing, plus I had it on Silent mode. I'm known to lose things—wallet, keys, headphones—and since I always have on gym clothes, stuff falls out of my pockets when I sit down. Not my fault. Something goes missing, but it's usually not *lost* lost, because a minute later I'll be like, "Oh, I'm sitting on it." I wasn't so fortunate on this day, and I couldn't go to Russia without my phone. At 8:45, I was worried. By 9:00, I was manic and sweating. Finally, at 9:20, an hour before my flight, we found it behind our bed's headboard. It takes twenty minutes to get to the Phoenix airport from our place, and I drove our white Audi like I'd stolen it. Relle gripped the seat the whole way. At 9:45 I screeched up to the curb. We said our "I love yous" with the car still running, and she sped off.

The curb agent waved me toward him. Normally, I couldn't have checked bags so close to flight time, but there was nothing normal about that Tuesday. Even my route was different. I usually flew Phoenix to LA and then on to Moscow, with a final connection into Ekaterinburg, aka Ekat, the city where my team was based. But this time I'd go from Phoenix to New York's JFK before going on to Russia, and if I missed this first flight, I'd throw off my whole itinerary. Lucky for me, the agent rushed my bags through to Ekat. He also escorted me through security and to my gate just so I'd make the flight. That was how late I was.

After the agent had walked off, I felt something in my pocket. *Damn.* I called Relle, who was halfway to brunch. "Do not turn off the car," I told her. "Turn around and come back because I still have the keys." Relle chuckled. She knew who she married, and this was right on brand for me. With my flight already boarding, I couldn't run out to the curb. So I spotted an airport worker walking by and said, "Bro, I need your help. I'm going overseas and I messed up." I held up the key fob. "Can you please take these out to my wife?" He quickly agreed. I'm sure it helped that he recognized me and that I handed him all the cash I had on me, about $250. I snapped a pic of the dude and sent it to Relle so she'd know who to look for. Minutes later she had the keys and I was headed to New York.

Things went sideways again at JFK. My carry-ons were screened, zero issues, but when I presented my Covid test, the agent said, "This is no good." *What?* For my results to be considered valid, she explained, the test had to be taken within forty-eight hours of my scheduled arrival in Russia. I'd miss that cutoff by twenty minutes based on my time stamp. I was pissed. I rushed to a site at the airport to take the dumb test, the one where they shove a swab up your nose and scratch out your skull. I waited for the results by email, refreshing every second and finally calling Relle to say, "Babe, I'm probably gonna miss this." I did. Big time. So I checked myself into an airport hotel and rang my team with the news. I may lose things, but I'm never late. I'm usually the nerd who's at the airport four hours before my flight. So they understood, no big deal, and rebooked me for the next day on Aeroflot Russian Airlines.

On Wednesday evening I returned to the international terminal, no hassles, no hiccups, no bags flagged. I texted Relle. "Hey, honey, about to take off," I wrote. "I'll call you when I get there. I love you." My plane departed as scheduled, at 7:25 p.m. New York time. I settled in for the nine-hour flight, ate some dinner, listened to music. Later I pulled out my laptop and booted up *Grey's Anatomy*. I nodded off after four episodes, and when I woke up, we were starting our descent. It was noon in Moscow when we landed. My Ekat flight was at three. *One last layover*, I thought as I put away my computer. One short sprint to the end of my final season.

....

The air felt different. I'd traveled to Russia dozens of times in eight years and never had this eerie feeling. I went through passport control, got my stamp, and took an escalator down to security for my transfer to the domestic terminal. Two large glass doors slid open. The scene on the other side proved something was off.

The place was crawling with workers. It was usually pretty empty, maybe a couple of screeners, and then you'd sail right through to your connecting flight. This checkpoint was fully staffed: five, six workers near the metal detectors, another bunch huddled by the trays, a screener guy seated behind the X-ray machine. Everyone was in uniform, and a few had on blue military camos. *What the hell is going on?* A blond, skinny police lady walked alongside the passengers, her dog sniffing every bag. The canine smelled the luggage of the person in front of me. All clear. Same thing when the dog sniffed my bags. No reaction. He immediately moved on to the next passenger, but the woman tapped me on the shoulder. She said something in Russian, God knows what, and motioned for me to step aside.

I wasn't the only one pulled from the line. Most of the Russians flew through the metal detectors, but us foreigners were being flagged for additional search. I glanced around at the passports. There was a guy from Pakistan, several from Ukraine, a few from Uzbekistan. I don't know what that dog did when he sniffed their bags, but I was one hundred percent sure how it reacted to mine: totally chill, a day at the beach, absolutely nothing to see here, folks. My father was a cop, a Vietnam vet, and I grew up with police-trained Rottweilers, Malinois, all of them. I know what dog signals look like. When they sniff something suspicious, they normally sit, bark, make weird movements. This dog didn't even whimper. I wasn't nervous when I got yanked, just annoyed at the hassle. I had no reason to be scared. My carry-ons were clean.

I placed my bags on the conveyor and watched them roll away. Before they were even inside the scanner, the screener got up and leaned all the way into the machine. *Strange.* I stepped through the metal detectors, no alarm, then came around to my bags. There stood the screener's teammate, a customs agent. Bald, early forties, hard-nosed, in a tight-knit sweater and chinos. If you're standing in a customer service line, he's the guy you don't want to go to. No smile, no emotion, no nothing.

He gestured for me to unzip my bags. I studied his face to be sure I understood, since in America you don't touch your bags. You stand your butt back while the agent rummages through them. That clearly wasn't the case in Russia, because he signaled again for me to open them. I started pulling stuff out left and right, showing him every item, unzipping small compartments he didn't even know existed. I wanted to get this search over with and move on to my last flight.

I'd worked my way through the backpack when I opened one last zip. I slid in my hand and felt something inside. The agent stared as I slowly lifted out a cartridge with cannabis oil. *Fuck.* I'm a licensed cannabis user in the United States, with a medical marijuana card issued by my doctor. He prescribed cannabis years ago, to help me cope with my debilitating sports injuries. In Arizona cannabis is legal. In Russia it's forbidden. I knew that. Honest to God, I just totally forgot the pen was in my bag. The moment I felt it in that pocket, my stomach sank.

The agent took the cartridge and held it up. "What this substance?" he said in broken English. My tongue was frozen, but my brain was scrambling, trying to find a way out of this. "Um, it's CBD," I finally said. Although cannabis was prohibited, I'd heard CBD was a lesser offense. Not true, I already knew in that moment, but I tried. "What this?" the agent asked again in even choppier English. *This dude doesn't know what I'm saying.* I pulled out my phone, typed "CBD" into Google Translate, and showed him my screen. He looked at the phone and then back at me. Silence. A moment later he reopened my roller as I stood by, stone-faced. First he pulled out my Nintendo Switch. Next he pulled out the heap of cords, as tangled as my insides. And last he lifted a pair of sweats. A cartridge fell from the pocket and tumbled onto the tabletop. *Fuck. Fuck. Fuck.*

Fear takes many forms. There's the kind you feel when life sneaks up from behind and frightens you half to death. Some people freeze. Others run. I'm usually the one who fights like hell. When I saw those cartridges, not one but two, a different type of fear shuddered through me. There was no instinct to fight, flee, or freeze. Instead, my body went into a major free fall, as if I'd stumbled off a cliff and plunged into the ocean. Down and down I spiraled, through the depths, in the dark, sinking further and further but never reaching the floor. *Whoosh*. As I dropped I felt empty, disconnected, alone. I was there but not there, alive but numb, lost in a watery underworld.

The agent picked up the cartridge and glared at me. I couldn't speak, think, breathe. I was still falling, still flailing, desperate to slow the spiral. Even after the second cartridge was discovered, I was hoping he'd let it slide, give me a strong warning, allow me to just throw that shit away. Both of the vape pens were practically empty, with not even enough cannabis oil to get you high. Clearly I wasn't a smuggler. If I was truly trying to sneak in drugs, I wouldn't have them in the front zip of a backpack. *Come on, bro.* I'd seen too many episodes of *Locked Up Abroad* to be that foolish. Also, I definitely wouldn't have helped the agent search my bag. Hell no. I was literally pulling stuff out like, "You want to see this?" I cleared pockets, unscrewed bottles. Obviously I wasn't Pablo Escobar. I just fucking forgot the cartridges were in my bag, end of story. And yet the horror was just beginning. Meanwhile, others were breezing through security, all of them appearing to be Russian. Especially since that dog hadn't whimpered at my luggage, I began wondering if I'd been singled out.

The agent pointed at a nearby row of chairs. "You wait," he said, or I think that's what I heard. I collapsed into the seat. When he walked off with the cartridges, I started blowing up Relle's phone. It was just after 2:00 a.m. in Phoenix, and she was dead asleep, with the ringer off. "Hey, nine-one-one, wake up, wake up, wake up, wake up!" I said on her voicemail. "Yo, babe, I need you to answer." I left her a dozen messages like that before getting super real on the last one. "Babe, I think I'm about to get locked up," I said with a crack in my voice. "I really need you to call me. Please." *Click.* My hands were trembling so badly that I almost dropped the phone. I drew in a breath, tried to gather myself, and sent Relle a text. Then another. And another. And then ten more. Row after row of desperation, each message more distraught than the last. "This is it for me, Babe," I finally wrote. I could no longer feel my fingers but managed to hit send.

When I didn't hear from Relle, I reached out to family. "Hey, I love you," I wrote to my mom. My parents are divorced but still in touch, live close to each other in Houston. I was purposely vague with both Mom and Pops because I didn't want to alarm them. Same thing with my brother, DeCarlo; my sisters, SheKera and Pier; and my nephew E.J., then in tenth grade. We're close. "Shit has gone sideways," I wrote, "but I can't say much. I don't want you to worry about me. Everything is going to be okay." If I'd received that cryptic-ass message from a loved one, I would've been *more* worried, not less. But I wasn't doing the typing, the calling, the pleading. Panic had taken over. I also called my local translator, provided by the team. I gave him the lowdown and told him to contact Max Ryabkov, the team's GM. *Help might be close.*

The screener returned. With him was a young guy, hair slicked back, who introduced himself as Anton. I understood that only because he spoke English. Sort of. At least a bit better than anyone else there. He held up the cartridges. "We take this to forensics," he said in a thick accent. "Forensics?" I asked. I'd heard him. But I repeated the word because I couldn't believe this was happening. "You wait," said the screener. I hadn't caught this first guy's name, thought he was just a random airport employee. He wasn't. Anton explained they were sending the pens for testing. This "screener" was apparently Anton's supervisor, a head honcho in the Russian Federal Customs Service (FCS). *Crap.* "You wait," Anton said. "How long is it going to be?" I asked. He stared at me blankly. So much for his knowing English. I typed my question into Google and held up the translation. Neither of them even looked at the screen. "Wait, wait, wait" is all they would say. I waved the screen in front of Anton again. Same thing. No acknowledgment. They pointed at my passport, grabbed it from my hand. They also took my Ekat boarding pass and walked away

I waited. I worried. I was too shaken up to weep. I fell deeper into despair by the hour, prayed Relle would soon wake up. Noon turned into 2:00 p.m., which meant I'd probably miss my flight to Ekat at 3:00. As I sat there these two customs guys darted all over that security checkpoint, shouting in Russian and holding up the cartridges, leaving and returning with the pens. *I thought they were taking them to forensics?* I had no idea what was happening, when it might end, or if it would. The words I'd texted Relle looped through my head. *This is it for me. This is it for me. This is it for me.* I'd watched enough documentaries on Russian prisons to know how inmates were treated. They were tortured. Starved. Stripped of everything. As I slid down in my chair and imagined the worst, my heart pounded away. Fear is one thing. But uncertainty, the unknown, a free fall into mystery—that's much stronger than fear; it's terror. This sitch was going south, spinning out of control fast, and I had no way of stopping it. That scared me most of all.

My phone lit up at 2:30 p.m. *Relle. Thank God.* She'd set her alarm for 4:30 a.m. Phoenix time so she could prepare for a Zoom court session later that morning. She'd awoken to my flurry of messages and went right into lawyer mode: "Who are these people, why do they have you, and what exactly are they saying?" I gave her the full picture in my shaky voice, and she was firm from the beginning: I had nothing to hide. "Babe, you aren't some drug smuggler," she said. "You had two pens in your bag, both of them medically licensed with cannabis legally purchased. Don't freak out. You've done nothing wrong."

That relaxed me a little. Relle worked at a firm specializing in criminal defense. She and her colleagues handled drug and homicide cases all the time, knew this territory well. That was why she felt so strongly that we should hush our mouths and let the truth do the talking. She promised to call my agent, Lindsay Kagawa Colas, who was probably still asleep at her home in Portland, Oregon. "Don't you say a word to anyone, don't you write anything down," Relle warned. "We've got this, baby. We'll get through it together. We'll be in contact soon, so keep your phone close. I love you." She sounded strong, so brave on my behalf, but I heard the same fear in her voice as in my own. After our call she left messages for Lindz and we continued our convo on text. Again she led with her legal instincts.

RELLE: What are the agents saying?

ME: Nothing right now. They told me they're going to test the pens for drugs.

RELLE: Even when the results come back, say nothing until you've heard from an attorney. You didn't misplace any cartridges in your checked luggage, correct?

ME: Right. Nothing.

RELLE: You may get arrested upon results, my love. I'm not sure what their process is there.

ME: I'm sure I will. I knew I should've stayed with you and never come back here. I'm sorry for having you in this with my dumb ass. I just want to come home.

RELLE: It's okay, babe. You made a simple mistake. We'll get through this together and discreetly. I have my Zoom so I'll be busy for a while, but I'll be quick with court and available to you. I love you. This moment in time doesn't change that. I'm still proud to be your wife. Keep your head up, your confidence up, your faith in God up. This, too, shall pass.

With all my heart I wanted to believe Relle, prayed this crisis would somehow end. But as time dragged on with no sign of the agents, any hope I had left began slipping away. My baby had studied the law in the United States, knew our Constitution inside out. Yet while due process runs the show in the land of the free, this was Russia. This was Putin's house. This was hell.

2

DAYBREAK

The customs agents finally returned with both cartridges around 4:00 p.m. *Guess they never took them to forensics. Guess I'm still screwed.* Anton was holding what looked like an evidence bag, as well as some kind of document in Russian.

"You sign here," he said, pointing at a line near the bottom.

I studied the paper. "What is this?" I asked.

"Sign," he repeated, shoving the paper toward me.

I pushed it away. "I'm not signing anything," I said. "*Nyet, nyet, nyet.*" I hadn't learned much Russian in my time there, but I knew how to say no.

Neither of them responded. They just stood there gazing at me, as if they had no idea what I was saying. I looked up "lawyer" on Google Translate. "*Advocat,*" I said over and over. Anton pushed the document toward me again and repeated, "Sign here!" with his nostrils flaring. I said "I don't know" in every way I could think of, in Russian, with gestures, with a hunch of my shoulders. They had to know what the hell I meant because a shrug is universal. Their silence, it seemed, was a blatant dismissal, a raised finger in my face.

This back-and-forth continued until they brought over a lady from a nearby duty-free shop. They spoke to her in Russian before she turned to me and said, "They want you to sign." *Are they kidding me? This woman is a cashier, not a translator!* "I don't know what this is," I said, "and I'm not signing." I remembered Relle's warning and kept refusing, and the lady and the men got louder and more insistent. Round and round we went for several minutes until finally, under pressure, I buckled. *Whatever. Maybe if I sign this, I can go.* The agent then put the vape pens in the bag, folded it over, sealed it, and left me there with the same stupid order: "You wait." It seemed they needed my signature to officially put the vape pens into evidence. *Not sure.*

A half hour later the agents came back. I stood when I spotted them, searched their faces for signs they'd come to free me. "You go with us," Anton said. *Go where?* "We go to office," he said. *What kind of office?* I hesitated for a moment, thought about resisting, but what real choice did I have? I'd already been pushed to sign a document I couldn't even read, much less understand. This was no different. I had to go with them, even if I had no clue where they were taking me. The head guy pointed at a nearby corridor and started walking. I pulled on my backpack, grabbed the handle of my roller, and followed. They didn't handcuff me. They didn't need to. They'd confiscated my passport. My flight to Ekat was long gone. I was already their prisoner. Shackles were not necessary.

The hallway led to an exit. When the door swung open, a burst of cold hit my face. February in Russia is no joke, often below freezing. I hadn't packed a coat in my carry-on, hadn't thought I'd need one. If my day had gone as planned, my driver would've picked me up and taken me straight to my apartment. *If. If. If.* The agents walked toward a parking lot. I stopped for a moment to pull on my hood and gazed up at the Moscow sky. Gray like always, grayer on this evening, the sun fading as dusk set in. We weaved in and out of several cars until the head guy stopped and unlocked a trunk. *Whose car is this?* It was a banged-up sedan, the Russian version of a '98 Honda Civic, and definitely not one that looked official. He lifted the trunk and motioned for me to put in my roller, which I did. He then opened a rear door and turned to see the question on my face: *Where are you taking me in your shitty personal car?* "Get in" was his only answer. I lumbered into the back seat, crouching my head low just so my tall ass could fit. He slammed my door and then he and Anton got in up front.

We looped around to a fenced area next to the airport. As we approached, the gates rolled open to reveal a redbrick building that looked like a mini prison. *Could be customs headquarters.* An armed guard stood out front. He and Anton spoke briefly before the guard waved us in. We walked upstairs to an office, where the agents sat behind a desk across from me in a chair. Another guy came in, blue camo uniform, didn't speak, just sat by the door, maybe a guard. Meanwhile, Anton started talking my ear off. Sometime between our duty-free showdown and now, his English had magically improved. How convenient.

"So what do you think of LeBron?" he said with a grin. "Is he as good as Michael Jordan?" "No idea," I muttered. He kept talking, all lighthearted, not caring that I'd clearly caught on to his tactic. This dude was trying to get me comfortable so I'd slip up and say something stupid. He threw out random topics to see if I'd take the bait. "How do you feel about Trump?" he asked. I flipped the script. "How do *you* feel about Trump?" I asked. He and the others laughed. "I think Trump's great," he said. On and on this went, with Anton asking me about sports, politics, even my WNBA salary, which he'd pulled up on the Internet. I said little, mostly stared at my phone. Every few minutes he'd throw in a question like, "Do your teammates smoke weed too?" I shrugged. "I don't know what they do," I said. "Weren't you bringing drugs to somebody?" he asked. I repeated the truth: "I didn't know I had the pens." "So you don't know any drug dealers here?" he pressed. "*Advocat,*" I said over and over. Since this had become an interrogation, I needed a lawyer, anyone, at my side. I prayed I'd hear from home.

Heaven must've heard me 'cause my screen lit up. It was

Lindsay, my agent, reaching out on WhatsApp. In Portland, she'd awoken to a call from her colleague Tracy, who was also on the text that Relle had sent. I had signed on with Lindz from jump, since becoming the top WNBA draft pick in 2013. Easy choice since she has repped so many greats, including Sue Bird, Diana Taurasi, Maya Moore, and Seimone Augustus. The world knows her as an executive vice president at Wasserman, the massive talent agency with offices on six continents. I know her as a badass who has always had my back.

On WhatsApp, Lindz created a text thread for me, her, the team. She then had me turn on disappearing messages to keep our convo private. Like Relle, she got straight to the point. "Where exactly are you?" she asked. "I need you to drop a pin." As I did she pulled up Google Maps and spotted the redbrick building. Even before Lindz reached me, she'd started rallying the troops at Wasserman and beyond. She'd pulled in Wasserman's chief legal counsel, Mike Pickles, who was fluent in Russian and had practiced law in Moscow. She'd also called her many contacts in Ekat, the Russian Basketball Federation, USA Basketball, the WNBA, and the NBA. She'd also networked her way to Alex Boykov, a Moscow attorney who was standing by to help me. "Alex is on his way to you," she told me. She gave me his number, added him to our text thread, and sent him my pin. *Major exhale.*

Alex called me when he arrived. The guard wouldn't let him upstairs to see me, he said, so he was waiting down at the entrance, in the cold. On Google Translate, I typed in "My lawyer is here" and showed Anton the screen. He wrinkled his face. "You wait," he said. "Why?" I shot back. He shrugged. I continued pushing and eventually pieced together the reason for the holdup. My cartridges had actually been taken to forensics for testing. The "investigation"—whatever that meant in a country where a duty-free cashier could serve as a customs translator—was still underway. Alex could meet with me only if and when I was charged. Translation: wait, wait, wait. My bladder, however, couldn't.

"Toilet," I said loudly. Anton motioned for the guard to take me to the restroom. I thought he'd just stand at the outside door, but this dude actually stood right next to my stall and listened to me piss. *Really? Come on, bro.* Forget the intrusion. I just needed a minute alone to wrap my head around the nightmare I was living. When I returned, I asked for my lawyer again. Anton declined, so I changed my request: "Yo, can I get a cigarette?" Surprisingly, he said, "Sure," and handed me one from his pack. I've never been much of cigarette smoker, but I'd also never been this stressed. "You can smoke in the bathroom," he said as he gave me a lighter. The guard didn't escort me this time, no idea why. *So I can smoke alone but not piss alone? Backward.* I leaned against the bathroom wall and slid down into a deep squat. Every part of me felt broken. My back. My knees. My hands. My spirit. I lit up, inhaled deeply, and started coughing my ass off. It'd been five, six months since I'd last smoked, so that first drag almost killed me. Wouldn't have mattered. My insides felt dead already. Forty-eight hours earlier I'd been with Relle, surprising her with roses on Valentine's Day. That now seemed like a lifetime ago, in a homeland a galaxy away.

At 8:00 p.m. Anton started arguing in Russian on the phone. He hung up and turned to me. "Checked bags?" he said. "Yeah, two," I said. They'd just realized I had more luggage, which was idiotic since that was noted on my boarding pass. The three of us got back in the car and went to the checkpoint where this big mess started. I described my luggage to Anton: two black hardcase rollers with my name on the tags. An hour later this fool returned with a rinky-dink green canvas bag. Not mine. "Open it," he ordered. I backed up. "I'm not putting my handprints on that," I said. He left and stayed gone long enough for the other agent to hit on a flight attendant who waltzed by. Her lips were so big they looked like they'd been stung by a bee . . . Russian women love their lip injections. The agent made eyes at her and struck up a chat. I was like, *Yo, can you please stop trying to get ass while you're fucking me in mine?* Crazy.

Anton returned with the correct bags. When I unzipped the first one, he glanced around at my pile of containers but didn't inspect a single one. Also, he never even opened the second roller. He just shoved a document at me and said, "Sign here." I was too exhausted to resist. I could've had kilos of drugs stashed in those containers, like actual smugglers do when they hide cocaine in shampoo bottles. But these agents didn't care what might be mixed with my barbecue sauce. They already had all the evidence they needed for their so-called investigation.

....

Back in redbrick purgatory, a customs investigator finally arrived with the forensic results hours after I'd sat there sweating. I glanced at my phone. *Two a.m.* He read from a document as Anton translated, said the vape pens contained cannabis oil. No surprise. The real blow came when I heard my charge, Article 229.1, part 2 in the Russian criminal code. I'd been accused of smuggling a significant amount of narcotics into the country. *Significant amount?* They'd found 0.2 grams in one cartridge, 0.5 in the other—a total of 0.7 grams, such little oil that it'd be gone as soon as the pens were warmed up. In America, that's not enough weed to raise a brow even in the handful of states yet to legalize it. But in Russia it's considered a "significant amount," punishable by five to ten years and a fine of up to a million rubles—just over ten grand in U.S. dollars. And that was just the initial charge. As the investigation progressed, additional allegations could be added. As Anton spoke, my mind wandered to that security checkpoint. *Why was I stopped in the first place? And now suddenly I could be facing a decade in prison?* Maybe that search wasn't arbitrary. Maybe I'd been targeted.

Around 3:00 a.m., they finally let Alex come upstairs. When I hear the words *Russian lawyer,* someone old, dry, and stoic comes to mind. Alex was the opposite: young, cool, shoulder-length hair, a Russian hippie with a photo of the rocker Gregg Allman as his WhatsApp profile pic. He greeted me warmly, and we stepped into the hall to speak privately, candidly, finally.

I had a thousand questions and even more fears, but my heart raced so fast I could hardly get them out. "Yo, so what's, like, the worst-case scenario?" I asked. He cleared his throat. "Well, right now it's just one charge," he said. "We have to let the investigation finish." *Forget that.* "But for real . . . how many years could I get?" I asked. He drew in a breath. "I mean, it could be a year or two," he said. He paused. "Or it could be the whole ten." *Whoosh. Whoosh. Whoosh.*

Alex didn't seem surprised I'd been asked to sign a document before seeing a lawyer; that wasn't unusual in the (shady) Russian legal system. Still, he seemed hopeful that I wouldn't get anywhere close to the maximum sentencing because I had no criminal record. I'd later learn that in 2021, the year before I was detained, thirty-six people were sentenced with my same charge in the Russian criminal code. In ten of those cases, the defendants received less than three years in prison; in five, up to five years; and in two cases, five to eight years. The remaining nineteen of those thirty-six defendants—more than half—had their sentences suspended. By those numbers, the odds seemed in my favor. But in that moment I felt doomed.

Back inside, the head customs investigator stepped up his interrogation. Why was I in Russia? Who was I bringing drugs to? Why were the cartridges in my luggage? Alex sat next to me and guided me through the questioning. I answered robotically, the way I had for the last ten hours: "I didn't know I had the pens." *Period. Done and done. Please let me fly home to my wife.* They seemed determined to get me to admit I was a smuggler, some undercover drug lord supplying half the country. Ridiculous. I was in that chair, insisting on the truth, but my mind was all over the place. I thought of my teammates, my family and friends, imagined how they'd react when they heard the charge. I mostly thought of Relle, the big plans we'd made, all of that now in limbo. I truly felt my life was over that night. If only I'd known what was coming.

After the grilling, Alex and I met in the hall again. He said, "You'll be taken to Khimki City Police Station," a temporary detention center, like county jail in America. I welled up. "This will all be okay," he said when he noticed my tears. *Will it?* Alex was trying to comfort me, in a moment when no one could've. As much as I hoped he was right, my heart told me that he wasn't. There I stood in a foreign country, under arrest in the wee hours. I was on my way to jail with no clue as to how long I'd be there or what conditions I might face. Even if everything *became* all right, it definitely wasn't as I cried in that hall. "I'll come see you as soon as they'll allow me," Alex said. On that point I believed him.

The agents confiscated most of my belongings. Backpack. Carry-on suitcase. The two large rollers. They gave it all to Alex, who promised he'd deliver everything to my Ekat apartment. They also seized my most valuable possession: my phone, my lifeline, my only connection to home. They didn't give that to Alex. They needed to keep it as part of their "investigation," they said. Relle and Lindz had stayed in constant touch as the horror unfolded. My previous call with my wife had been hours earlier, as I awaited my fate at the security checkpoint. My baby and I had traded sentiments, me tearful, her consoling. From the customs building, I used Alex's phone to call Lindz, who put me through to Relle. "I love you," she said. *Me too. Always.*

At around 6:00 a.m., two local cops arrived, one of them holding handcuffs. I'd grown up playing with my dad's cuffs, a shiny steel pair with a double lock. The cuffs this cop held looked nothing like Pops's. They were dented and rusty, with a single lock, operated with an ancient-looking skeleton key. The officer gestured for me to hold my hands together so he could cuff me at the front. *Click.* As he turned the key and tightened the cuffs, the metal cut into my flesh. I cringed. Alex noticed that the cuffs were gouging my large wrists and intervened. "You need to loosen them," he said. The cop rolled his eyes and recuffed me as I stared straight ahead. More spiraling, more numbness. Faster, deeper, endless.

On February 15, I left Phoenix in a frenzy, my heart full of Relle, my bags stuffed with seasonings. Three hellish days later, just before dawn, I lost my freedom, my peace, my life as I'd known it. As the cops led me away in cuffs through the crisp morning air, Alex walked beside me. He carried a small plastic bag with the few items I'd be allowed to take: three pairs of underwear, a couple of T-shirts and sweatpants, a flannel hoodie, and a book of sudoku puzzles burrowed between the folds. The time was around 7:00 a.m. The future was unimaginable.

3

CAGED

I didn't go straight to hell. The cops in plain clothes first drove me all over town in their personal vehicle, no siren lights, partition, or legroom. We made three stops.

In the dim light of daybreak, we pulled away from the red-brick building and onto a boulevard. Moscow was already stirring. As I watched the world go by from my back seat window, my reality sank in. *I am a prisoner.* Locals roamed the streets, chatting on their phones, smoking. Forty-eight hours earlier that had been me, walking around with no big cares, taking my freedom for granted. People gazed as I passed. Strange to see a six-foot-nine foreigner with dreads hunched over in a hatchback. The cops had removed my cuffs once I was in the car, but the ride was still agonizing. When I cracked my back in high school, I was in such pain I had to be carried off the court. I bent over the next day to put on my socks and collapsed. The pain subsided somewhat, but my back never fully recovered, and the spasms returned on that ride. My head grazed the ceiling, my knees were crouched and locked. The cops talked away in Russian as they chain-smoked and ignored me. *I wonder if the people staring know I'm an inmate. I wonder when this ride will end.*

An hour later we pulled up to a shabby clinic. The cops recuffed me for my perp walk through the lot. The clinic lobby was even more run-down than the exterior. An overhead light flickered. A few sketchy-looking men waited in busted chairs. They gaped as the officers led me down a hall to an area draped off with a stained curtain. An old guy—the doc, I guess—came in with a Dixie cup. He looked me up and down. "You drug addict?" he said in choppy English. "No," I snapped, "*not* a drug addict." He laughed. "Yes, yes, yes . . . you drug addict," he said, pushing the cup into my hand. I assumed he wanted me to piss for a drug test, which I did squatting over a hole-in-the-ground toilet. Minutes later I was back in the car for another long ride, the whole time fearing what could be coming.

Stop two was a quick Covid test, a Q-tip rammed up my nose. The last stop took forever to get to because the cops seemed to have the wrong address. They'd pull into a lot, argue on the phone, drive off. We went to three hospitals before they found the right one; the whole ride was three or four hours. My back was hurting so badly by this point that I walked hunched over and teared up as we entered. They kept me cuffed in the lobby, which was crawling with people. That seemed to be the rule: handcuffs on when others were around, off in the car. The first click of those cuffs reorders the world, divides innocents and inmates, the free and the feared. Occasionally, someone crosses the barrier, as one lady did in the hospital waiting room. She noticed me crying and approached, patted my shoulder, and whispered, "Okay, okay." Her kindness surprised me, and the tears fell faster. She said something to the cop, who barked and waved her off. After a long wait I went in for a chest X-ray, a few seconds in front of a rusty machine, clothes on. TB is big over there. I guess they had to make sure I was clear.

Afterward, the cops smoked in front of the hospital, with me standing there cuffed. Everyone who passed gave me a puzzled look, the same question in their eyes as was in my head: *What the hell is going on here?* Ice covered the ground. I exhaled and saw my breath. My head spun. When my lawyer told me I'd be taken to Khimki, or county, as I call it, I didn't know the difference between that and *jail* jail, the Russian prison camps I'd heard about. County would be mixed gender, Alex said. What if I was thrown in a cell with all men, mistaken for male like I usually was? My passport said "female," but what if I got pranked? And if someone attacked me, how would I react? Would I defend myself—*could* I defend myself? When you're tall it's assumed you're fearless, and when you're Black, you're thought to be thick-skinned, but my size and color were no more insulating than my thin hoodie in the cold. I was as terrified as I was frozen.

Another long drive later, with my knees still jammed up to my shoulders, we pulled up to county. I'd lost track of time, but it must've been dusk. We drove through two sets of tall gates, then got out near a courtyard enclosed with crumbling rebar. The cops led me into a waiting room and sat me near two women, young, dark-haired, cuffed. We exchanged glances but no words. A guard eventually came and took me up three flights of stairs and into a hall of steel cages, each with a covered peephole and a light on its door. I couldn't see the prisoners' faces, but I could hear them pounding the walls. Pressing their inside buttons to turn on their outside lights. Flipping open their peepholes, coughing and moaning. Raising hell to get the staff's attention. The guard did not flinch as he led me through. We stopped at an empty cage, and he gestured for me to enter. He handed me a pillow, sheets, and a rolled-up mattress, as well as my bag of items. He bolted me in and left. *Click.*

I glanced around the cold cell. It was small but bigger than I'd imagined, around seven by seven feet. A dim lightbulb hung overhead. So did a camera. The walls were chipped and corroded, one side exposed rebar, another painted and repainted in three colors, spiderwebs in every corner. The place looked like it had been bombed and abandoned. A twin bed frame with metal railings was rammed against a wall. Across from the bed were a rickety table and a chair. I walked over to the barred window and looked out, but it was covered in dust so thick I couldn't see anything. I had a small sink and a "toilet," a hole-in-the-ground commode stained with shit and urine. It reeked. On the sink sat a mini bar of soap. There was also a Dixie cup.

A guard eventually brought me a meal: macaroni noodles in thick milk, with a piece of smelly fish. I bit into the fish and spit it out. *Disgusting.* I'm not a person who turns up my nose at everything. I love to eat too much to be picky. But this food was legit inedible. The fish tasted spoiled. The milk was like sludge. Still, I ate it because I was starving. My last real meal had been on the flight to Moscow. I flushed down the nastiness with hot tea, which a guard brought that evening (and would three times a day for the length of my stay). That was what the Dixie cup was for. I almost declined the water when I saw the calcified kettle it came from. But boiled water was semi-clean water in a place where that was scarce.

After dinner I pulled out my bag of personal items. I'd got-ten the plastic bag in a duty-free airport shop. Just before I was arrested, I'd dumped my chips from the bag and stuffed in what I could fit. *Not much.* I surveyed my things and noticed what was missing. In the stress, I'd forgotten to grab the toothbrush from my carry-on. *Oh well.* Thank God, I had thrown in a pen with my sudoku book. I unrolled the white mattress, which was covered in brown blotches. Same with the pillow. Both were filled with what felt like lumpy wool yarn. With my clothes still on, I sat on the bed mat and tried not to let it touch my skin. Impossible. As I stretched out, the frame creaked under my weight. My calves jutted through the rails of the footboard and dangled over the edge. When I sank into the metal planks, my back went into another spasm. I felt like crying, but no tears came. The point beyond pain is paralysis.

As tired as I was, I could not sleep. During the car ride all over Moscow, the constant motion had been a strange gift. All that back seat crouching, the tests and X-rays, they were hellish but distracting. In the solitude of my cell, my fears and what-ifs demanded a hearing. What if I'd never taken this stupid trip, had stayed in Phoenix like I wanted to? What if I hadn't missed that first flight or had taken my usual route through Los Angeles? If I'd arrived in Moscow just one day earlier, would that security checkpoint have been fully staffed? And why didn't I get my ass up earlier on travel day, with enough time to find those vape cartridges? Because I didn't want my time with Relle to be over. Because my spirit told me to stay, while my honor and work ethic got me up from that bed. Now there I lay in another bed, six thousand miles from the one I belonged in.

The jail was near a train stop, with trains running from 5:30 a.m. till after midnight. That was how I knew the next morning had arrived, by the rattling of the tracks and the screeching brakes. I slid my aching body from the bed to the floor, crawled to the peephole, and looked out. I couldn't see much, but the inmates' pounding continued, just as it had all night. I pressed my buzzer.

Through my peephole and the vents, I heard the guards gathered down the hall, blasting music, ignoring us prisoners. My peephole eventually flipped open, *clink*, and a guard shouted something in Russian. "Shower!" I yelled. While I was desperate to get clean, I mostly wanted to get out of that cage. "*Nyet!*" he spat back, and then I heard laughter. Male voices began speaking, all foreign words until one came through clear. "American," I heard. Back to gibberish. "Basketball," someone said. Another round of chortles. My hole flipped open, and two eyeballs stared in, followed by a second and a third set. As I crawled back to bed, writhing in pain, I knew exactly what I'd just witnessed. I'd become a spectacle, the guards' entertainment, a freak show to liven their shift.

....

In elementary school we visited the Houston aquarium, where white Bengal tigers are on exhibit. No idea why they're at an aquarium, but I know people flock to see them. I will always remember what I felt when I finally spotted one behind a glass barrier: sad. Hundreds gathered to admire the tiger's striking color, the result of a rare genetic mutation. While the world gawked and snapped photos, the tiger was sprawled out and miserable. No one can read an animal's mind, but I somehow felt I could. I've known cages like that tiger's. My life has been one.

I came out of the womb with long-ass limbs, and the curiosities continued. In elementary school I was always a few inches taller than the other girls in my class. By middle school I towered over most of them. While the girls budded tits and giggled in a high pitch, my voice grew deeper by the year. My mother insisted I wear a bra, to "get ready" for my breasts to come in. I'm in my thirties and still waiting. The teasing in school was cruel and endless, a series of humiliations. There was the day in sixth grade when I passed through the hall, spotted a group of girls gathered around the coolest one. The hall fell silent when I walked up, until Ms. It stormed toward me and patted my chest. "See?!" she shouted. "I told you she ain't got no chest! She's a *boy*!" Everyone cracked up, and I backed away, partly out of shock but mostly because the laughter cut me deep.

My parents kept thinking my growth spurt would end, but instead I just got taller. They took me to doctors all over Houston. I got tested for tumors on my pituitary gland, screened for every imaginable cancer and disease. Everything came back clear. One doc decided athletics was the culprit. I started playing volleyball in seventh grade, and she claimed that spiking and pounding delayed my puberty; she said this could have been why I was breastless. Another doc concluded, "This is just a phase." My parents weren't convinced, and who could blame them? In those years a high school football player made headlines when he dropped dead because of a heart condition. Other teen athletes had also collapsed. So I went through another round of crazy tests, including one where dye was pumped through my body. That shit hurt. "No more, please," I said to my folks in ninth grade. They let me move on. While everyone else was puzzled, I was clear by then. This was me, born this way, just like those white tigers.

My realization didn't end the shaming. Though things improved once I started balling, the stares followed me into adulthood. A few years ago at an airport in the States, someone saw me step into the women's restroom and reported it to a couple of workers. They came in and pounded on my stall door. "Sir, you need to come out," one shouted. "This is the women's bathroom." I finished my business and creaked open the door, told them I *was* a woman. They both looked me up and down, with *WTF* splashed across their foreheads. I'd seen this movie many times and knew how to end it quickly. I yanked down my sweats and showed them my privates—*woot!*—a flash to settle the question. "We are so, so sorry," one lady said, while the other cupped her hand over her mouth. Everyone's "so sorry." That does nothing to soothe the ache. Over the years I've endured it all: flashing my chest and crotch, having to show my ID, enduring invasive airport pat-downs, the searches meant for men only. I get mistaken for male so frequently I've learned to just keep it moving. My heart, however, can't always.

My stature doesn't just make me a spectacle. It also puts me in danger. Many Black parents give their sons the Talk, warn them that their color and gender make them a target. The greater your stature, the more threatening you become, particularly to a cop who's frightened and trigger-happy. Years ago, I was speeding and got pulled over. My bad. When I saw the lights and heard sirens, I panicked and swerved into the HOV lane rather than to the side of the road. The officer was angry when he approached my window. He spoke harshly to me as Relle looked on, clutching her seat as his voice rose, fearing the situation would escalate. "Buddy" and "dude," he kept calling me, clearly mistaking me for male. He finally asked for my ID, looked at it, and then stared back at me. His whole demeanor shifted. "Ma'am," he said, "please watch your speed next time." For hours after that incident Relle and I were rattled because we knew how close I'd come to getting shot. If I'd reached for my ID and he'd assumed it was a gun, that encounter might've ended in bloodshed. Some might call that an exaggeration. I call it Breathing While Black. You don't have to be speeding, as I was. If you're a brother in particular, and a person of color in general, what you look like makes you vulnerable. That's not an overstatement. It's a truth that's been proven over and over, with one heartbreaking headline after the next.

In the Russian prison system, I was marked for a different reason. In a nation long at odds with my homeland and the West, I was, to their disgust, an American.

....

The morning after I'd been thrown in jail, Alex still hadn't come. As the hours crept by, I grew physically weak. I tried to keep down food but couldn't. Anything I ate messed up my stomach. But if I declined food, I sat there starving, and I mean that literally. My hunger got so bad I choked down anything the guards brought: grits the consistency of gravel; more of that rank fish; bowls of *grietchka*, a buckwheat grain plentiful there. Eating solved my hunger but created another issue: it kept me over that toilet. I ripped apart my Van tee and used one part as my face towel, the other to clean the rest of me. I had only that tiny soap and no access to a shower. There was one on the premises, but the guards refused to take me. I'd never felt dirtier.

I kept my sudoku book at my side. With no phone or visitors, solving puzzles kept me from going crazy. You don't realize how much you rely on human contact until you lose it. You know you need love and friendship, but you can forget you also need brief interactions: a smile from a cashier, chitchat with neighbors. Those people aren't in the front row of your life, but they're still part of what keeps you sane. They show you that you matter by lighting up when they see you. They make you feel less alone. I missed just hearing someone speak English, and most of all, I missed Relle. In our years together we'd talked every day, would turn on our FaceTime cameras and just be in each other's worlds. I'd watch Relle at her desk, studying for exams, and at some point I'd sign off with, "Good night, babe." We'd blow our kisses and promise to catch up in the morning. I'd now spent several agonizing days without her.

I opened my sudoku book. I've always loved numbers, was pretty good at math and science in school. I'm curious about how things work, enjoy anything hands on. I'd tried sudoku when the craze first hit, and I immediately got hooked. From then on, I always traveled with puzzles, especially on long flights. I'd bought this book in the New York airport, just before life turned left. If I began hyperventilating in my cell, doing a puzzle calmed me. During my first two days I did a bunch of them, and then switched things up on day three. I read every word in that book, down to the copyright, and then started counting the squares. If I lost count I'd start again, turning it into a game. As long as I was counting, reading, anything, that was one minute less of remembering where I was.

Every day I wrote in the margins, scribbled my thoughts and the date. Some pages are filled with entries; others have just a couple. "It's early, or late," I wrote in one entry, dated February 19. "I'm trying, Baby, to be strong for you." Farther down on that page, in messy handwriting, I added a postscript that chills me: "In jail in Moscow and losing my mental. Don't know if I will survive." My book had five hundred puzzles. I prayed I'd make it home before the last.

4

POPS

Alex visited around noon on February 19, a Saturday. When I saw him I teared up out of relief and exhaustion. He brought me a few personal items, including snacks from my luggage and a toothbrush. I'd never been so happy to get a toothbrush. The night before, I'd been lying in the dark, thinking, *Fuck, I ain't got a weapon. I can't make no shank, like they did in* Orange Is the New Black. *I ain't even got a paper clip. All I got are some raggedy drawers, a shirt I done tore up, and my fists.* I had no clue where I'd end up after county, but if I was going to the tank, one of those rat-infested Russian prison camps I'd seen on Netflix, I had to be ready to fight. *And I don't speak the language too?* I thought. *Oh, I'm gonna have to beat somebody's ass.* Thanks to Alex, I was armed.

The toothbrush was Alex's first gift to me. The second was his preparation. With the help of the team Lindz had quickly pulled together, Alex had already completed my paperwork requesting bail and house arrest. My team, UMMC Ekat, had arranged for an apartment to be rented for me near the court-house. They'd also agreed to pay for the rental, a promise they put in writing for the hearing. Soon after Alex arrived, a guard cuffed me and we entered a room not much bigger than my cell for my formal arrest hearing. A middle-aged woman in a black robe, the judge, sat on an elevated podium. A guard led me to a small cage in a corner. That's how proceedings take place in Russia, with the accused already jailed. Alex sat close by, on a bench on the other side of the bars. The investigator, a short, heavyset woman with black hair and a scowl, sat on another bench. In Russian courts, cases are first assigned to an investigator, not a prosecutor like in America. That investigator is the one asking the judge to arrest a defendant. He or she can also request that your detention be extended so there's more time to investigate. Only after that process is complete is your case file kicked over to the prosecutor's office.

The judge spoke first, followed by the investigator. Alex stood and replied. I sat there lost in a swirl of Russian, studying their faces for signs of hope. Moments later, Alex whispered the verdict. My lawyers asked for a bail of 7 million rubles—about $75,000 U.S. dollars—but the judge denied any bail. After the first blow came a harder one. "No house arrest," Alex said. The investigator had argued I was a flight risk, that I'd probably flee the country if they let me leave jail. That meant that even if I'd been granted bail, posting it would've been pointless. Regardless of any money I'd pay, I'd have to remain in custody for at least thirty days.

Thirty days. When Alex said those words, I almost collapsed in that cage. *Why would I be considered a flight risk?* I thought. I wasn't Castro, with some private plane, able to jet off to Colombia. Also, they'd confiscated my passport. Where the hell was I gonna go, and *how?* And if this judge was so worried I'd escape, why didn't she just slap an ankle monitor on me? Because she had other plans. By her order that afternoon, I'd be locked up again briefly at county and then moved to a female detention center. Alex hugged me goodbye and promised we'd fight the ruling. I mumbled "Okay" and stared at the floor. Back in my cage, I collapsed on my bed. My sudoku diary was open to my entry from hours before. "'Bout to go to court," I'd scribbled. "Please, God, let me leave here." Even if heaven answered, it wouldn't be quick. That much was clear. Little else was.

The roar of the train woke me up the next morning, not that I'd actually slept. When you're caught between *before* and a month of tomorrows, your eyes won't close. Uncertainty keeps your lids on alert. A few days in the hole is one thing; thirty days means settling your ass down. It means having hour after hour to remember how you fucked up. It means reviewing all the ways you've failed yourself, your family, your team. It means imagining your pops's disappointment when he hears where you are. Alex had brought me some blank paper for writing letters, and I pulled out a sheet. I scooted near the window in search of light but found none. "Hey Pops," I wrote at the top of the page. That was as far as I got before I broke down.

....

You can't begin to know me unless you first know Raymond Griner. I've told you I'm a daddy's girl, but I'm more like a daddy's son. My father and I joke about that all the time. That man isn't just my Pops. Growing up, he was my hero.

My dad is hard-core, probably because life made him that way. He doesn't talk much about his early years, but I've heard enough to know they were rough. He's the youngest of three, the baby in his family, like me. My aunt Doris was the oldest. My dad's brother, Lemar, drowned as a kid, sometime in the late 1950s. He and my dad were swimming in the woods near their home in Jasper, Texas, when Lemar jumped in a deep creek, hit something underwater, and didn't come up. When he eventually surfaced, Pops dragged his brother from the water, hoisted him on his back, and carried his limp body through the woods toward home. I can only imagine the fear shuddering through my father, the strain of carrying his dead brother on his small shoulders. Tragedy struck again around that time when Dad lost his mother to heart problems. She was young, only in her thirties. Both griefs marked the end of my father's innocence and the start of his next chapter.

Following their mother's passing, Pops and his sister moved to Watts, California, to live with their aunt and uncle. I don't know why my grandfather sent them there. Maybe he was overwhelmed with the heartache of losing his young wife. Or maybe he wanted his now-motherless children to grow up with his sister's nurturing presence. The year was 1960, give or take. Pops was around ten. He settled into a different world, small town versus West Coast, Klan country versus inner city. A few years after he got there, his 'hood went up in flames. On that humid August day in 1965, a white cop pulled over Marquette Frye, a young Black man, for allegedly driving drunk. The ugly confrontation sparked a much wider one, lasting six long days and leaving thirty-four people dead. The world would come to know it as the Watts Riots, the largest rebellion of the civil rights era. My dad simply knew it as one more sorrow in a childhood filled with so many of them.

After graduating from Fremont High School, Dad moved back to Jasper, where the Griners owned a Black funeral home and cemetery; in those days, even death was segregated. He worked in the business for a time, until his family tried to get him to stay. Pops wasn't having it and instead enlisted in the army. Soon after, he got sent to Vietnam, where he witnessed even more tragedy. When Pops talks about enlisting, he says it was both the stupidest thing he ever did and the smartest. He couldn't unsee the horrors of 'Nam. Still, military life gave him discipline and character. He relied on both when he returned to Texas in the early 1970s.

In Huntsville he got into law enforcement, patrolling a state prison by horseback. Next he worked as a traffic cop in Humble, a small town in the Houston area. There he was, one Black cop, with the nerve to be policing a then-all-white area. The racial threats started right away and grew louder by the day. Finally, his captain said to him, "Ray, you can patrol here, but you probably shouldn't live here." Too dangerous. Pops just stared at him. "They can try to come after me," he said, "but it'll be murder." That's Raymond Griner in a nutshell—tough as they come, and stubborn to the core. He did not leave.

Around then Pops married his first wife, Miss Flo. They had two children: my brother, DeCarlo, and my sister SheKera. After Dad and Miss Flo split, Pops met my mom, Sandra, in a grocery store. Dad was working a second job as a security guard for the store when my mother, who was cashiering, caught his eye. Mom was shy and still living with her parents. Dad was assertive and several years older. As opposite as they were, they somehow clicked; maybe that was the attraction. They'd also come from different worlds. Mom grew up in Houston, the middle child of six, five girls, one boy. Her folks were originally from Louisiana, bayou country. Her father was smart, good with money. He used his modest earnings as a store worker to buy up all the houses on his block and rent them out. The rental income from his investments gave him and his family a comfortable life.

Mom was raised a strict Catholic. When she wasn't at home, she was at Mass or Bible study every other night. A nice Catholic girl, that's who my mom is. She's caring and super-sensitive, will give you the shirt off her back. Her mom, my grandma, was the same way. Pops grew up in church as well, Southern Baptist. He reads his Bible and believes in God, even to this day. That was probably why he even had a chance with Mom. They eventually tied the knot and settled in Houston. Dad's first two children, SheKera and DeCarlo, lived between Dad's house and their mom's. In 1985, my parents had my older sister Pier. Five years later my lanky ass rolled in.

Mom has two nicknames for me: Britt and Ladybug. The second clearly doesn't fit. With a wingspan of seven-four, I'm a damn giraffe, not some cute little bug. But she occasionally still calls me Ladybug. Lord Jesus, and it makes me feel like a kid. Mom is so sweet you can't get annoyed; all you can do is smile. My tender side comes from her. It's why I didn't turn on every guard in Russia. It's also why, tough and tall as I am, I sometimes still tear up. She raised me with the feeling that there are always good people in the world, and she is definitely one of them. At home, she picked up where her mother left off, always willing to give. Perfect example: Pier and I were picky eaters. I liked only meat and potatoes. Pier was iffy with her preferences, but definitely no red meat, just chicken and fish. Like me, Dad was all meat and potatoes, usually with a side of pinto beans, which I can't stand. So Mom basically made three separate meals on most nights. If everyone was eating greens (also not my thing), she'd make me beef tacos on the side. Or if Dad wanted rice with those damn pintos, she'd put on a pot. As long as we were happy, so was she.

Much as I loved Mom, I was my father's shadow. If he left a room, I was right on his tail; he couldn't even *sneak* out the house without my following. Everything he did, I wanted to do. He loved cars and the outdoors. So did I. And he never shied away from teaching me what he knew. He had me under that car hood, changing oil. Mom sure as hell didn't like me being out there. She wanted me indoors, wearing pretty dresses and socks with lace on them. I'd rip off that lace, go get some shorts, and run outdoors with Dad. With him, I never had to be some little princess. I'd be shirtless in the yard even at ten, eleven, twelve, with no tits to shake and jigglelate. Most folks mistook me for a guy anyway. That's how flat chested I've always been.

While under the car hood, Pops gave me little lectures. "These dealerships are crooks," he'd say. "They try to get one over on you, and especially on women. I don't want you to be that woman who goes in for an oil change and ends up with a big bill 'cause they say you need an alternator." He taught me how it sounds when the alternator's freaky. He taught me how to change a tire. Matter of fact, he taught me everything important about making it in this world. "I don't want you out here living some fast life, surviving from check to check," he'd say. "You've gotta pay your bills on time, keep good credit." The following day he'd be onto his next lecture. My siblings and I can recite all of them. "You can't trust anybody," he'd say. "Keep everything to yourself. You don't really have a lot of friends in life. Maybe one or two, but you still gotta watch 'em." And even when it came to cops, he kept it real. "You have some good ones," he'd say, "but you have to be careful with some of 'em. They'll shoot you just 'cause you're Black. Depending on how you act, that's how they'll act." That was why I knew to keep my head down in jail. I didn't need more trouble.

Pops and I had our own traditions. Like on summer weekends, I'd ride to Jasper with him, just the two of us. His family still owned land there, and we'd cut the grass. We'd also check on my great-aunt, a retired schoolteacher. I'll always remember a trip we took in 1998. That June, Jasper had made national headlines when James Byrd Jr., a Black man, was murdered by three white guys. For us, this wasn't just another story. It was personal. James was my father's third cousin. Our family was still reeling from the murder, shocked by how gruesome it was. James had been walking home when these dudes in a pickup offered him a ride. Instead of taking him home, they drove him to Huff Creek Road, a one-way dirt trail that cuts through the woods. They beat James bloody, spray-painted his face, and chained him by his ankles to the back of the pickup. They then dragged him for three miles down that road, severing his head along the way. His torso, legs, and arms were later found near a Black cemetery.

Two of the men were self-proclaimed white supremacists. All three were eventually convicted. One was sentenced to life in prison; the others were executed. The Texas Legislature passed the James Byrd Jr. Hate Crimes Act a few years after the murder. It was a victory, but here's what I know: you can't legislate hate out of people's hearts. I saw that for myself a few weeks after James was murdered.

When we got to Jasper that weekend, Pops pulled up at the courthouse. I saw several men in robes and white pointy hats. "What's that?" I asked my father. "That's the Ku Klux Klan," he said dryly. He'd already told me about the Klan. At eight, I knew the one thing every Black child knows: the Klan hates us. That day in front of the courthouse, they were protesting the arrest of the men who dragged James to his death. Dad's voice didn't crack when he explained that. The facts were the facts, no need to get emotional. Long ago, life built a cage around my father's heart, on that day his brother's body floated to the surface and when he lost his dear mother. The cage got reinforced when Watts went up in flames and when he watched his friends die in 'Nam. Pops didn't whine or cry. He bucked up and carried on.

That's the toughness I get from my dad, softened a bit by Mom. I also have Dad's rebellious streak, and he spotted it in me early. I didn't like school. I found it hard to focus unless I was doing something hands on. So I was a bit of a class clown, making jokes instead of finishing my work. I loved the attention. When the other kids laughed, I felt like I fit in, 'cause God knows I didn't otherwise. One day in fourth grade I got bold. The teacher told me to stop the jokes, but I kept on. "I'm gonna call home," she warned. "Okay," I snapped, "then call home." That was the worst thing I could've done, because she rang my father's cell while he was patrolling. She even told him what I'd said.

Dad was beyond pissed when he got home that evening. "You want to act like a hoodlum in school?" he shouted. "Then I'll treat you like one. You're going to jail." He stripped my bedroom bare, took out the TV, the dresser, even my clothes and stuffed animals. I literally had just my bed and sheets, with a pile of homework on top. For the next three days he picked out my clothes for me. I even had to eat dinner at a certain time. And it was just my luck that Mom made his favorite. "You're gonna eat these pintos," he ordered. He thought I'd cave, but I didn't. I inherited his hard head. So I bypassed the beans and ate a few bites of rice and then went to my room half hungry. I might've won that battle, but Dad won the war, because I straightened right up in school. It was either that or pintos and a homemade prison.

Dad's tactics might seem harsh in hindsight, but they weren't. They were his way of protecting me, of giving me better than he had, of putting me on the right path. Pops wasn't super affectionate, but I knew he loved me. I could see it in the way he provided. I could feel it when we were together, under the hood of his car or riding to Jasper. He loved me by teaching me I could survive anything. The way I acted during that bedroom lockdown, you would've thought he'd sent me to Pelican Bay. Not even close. And while neither of us could've guessed where I'd end up, Pops prepared me for my biggest nightmare.

If you have nothing else in this life, you have your good name, your rep. My father's name stands for pride. Respect. Showing up early and staying late. Dad didn't do everything perfectly. Nobody does. But he carried himself with dignity. And thanks to him, the Griner name had never been tarnished. That was why when I wrote "Hey Pops" on that paper, I couldn't continue at first. How do you explain to your hero that you've let him down? You don't. Instead, you lie there at sunrise and quietly weep, hoping the news never breaks.

5

IN THE GRAY

While I was thinking about Pops, Lindz was trying to get me home to him. My first three days in jail hit during the NBA All-Star weekend, the annual exhibition viewed by millions. Basketball's top brass—NBA commissioner Adam Silver and WNBA commissioner Cathy Engelbert—were in Cleveland for the celebration. Lindz cut that party short with the news flash: I'd been arrested.

Though the situation was terrible, they were hopeful it could be fixed. Maybe I'd get thrown out of Russia. Maybe I'd be cut from the team. Or maybe I'd have to pay a huge fine. Whatever the penalty, Lindz and everyone she talked to early on thought we'd get through this; we just had to figure out how. After all, I'd played in Russia for eight seasons. I'd paid taxes there, had no record, not even a whiff of drama. Frankly, I had the footprint of an angel. On top of that—and I don't mean this in a bigheaded way—I was a major star in the country, and the club I played for was influential. So it seemed Russia had good reason to resolve this on the hush and let me get back to hooping. Me and a bunch of other Americans had headlined their league for more than a decade. During that time, women's pro ball had become big business.

Shabtai Kalmanovich had everything to do with that. The businessman had deep pockets, a passion for basketball, and a colorful past. Shabtai grew up in Lithuania and emigrated to Israel. After amassing a fortune in trade deals with South Africa, he was outed as a KGB spy and convicted of espionage by an Israeli court. On the other side of the slammer, Shabtai reinvented himself. He relocated to Moscow in the early '90s and found success in various businesses. He fell in love with a star of the Russian women's national basketball team, married her, and subsequently poured millions into his wife's sport. He sponsored three women's clubs and also became the general manager of Russia's women's basketball team. This dude didn't just invest in women's ball. He turned his clubs into some of the world's most dominant by signing legends of the sport. Lisa Leslie was one of his first big American signees. Then came Tina Thompson, Lauren Jackson, and my friend and Phoenix Mercury teammate Diana "Dee" Taurasi, along with Sue Bird. When Dee and Sue joined his club Spartak Moscow around 2006, they'd heard whispers of his past but weren't sure what to believe. One thing, however, was certain: they'd earn a fortune. On top of offering American players several times what they could make in the WNBA, Shabtai spoiled them with hefty bonuses, personal drivers, private jets, luxury hotels, and shopping sprees. The money was one draw. Another was the notoriety. At home, WNBA players were often treated like NBA afterthoughts. In Russia, we were sports royalty.

When I started balling in Ekat in 2014, Shabtai was gone. Five years earlier he'd been gunned down in his Mercedes in a drive-by assassination. There was a lot of speculation about why he was killed, but the official reason still remains a mystery. Whatever led to his murder, the unprecedented salaries he'd put in place for stars lived on. So did the huge fan base he'd built. He'd led his Spartak team to three back-to-back Euro-League championships (and Dee led them to a fourth soon after

Shabtai's death). During his reign, Russians had gone wild for women's basketball. Oligarchs had bought up sports clubs like they were toys, as much for investment as for bragging rights. When I signed with Ekat, that spirit had taken hold. Dee and Sue eventually left Spartak but returned to Russia to play for Ekat—Spartak's rival and Shabtai's first club investment—two years before I got there. So our team was stacked and had the hardware to prove it. We won back-to-back championships my first couple of years on the squad, and icons like Maya Moore, Candace Parker, and Breanna Stewart joined along the way. We were also better paid than the Ekat men's team. That was how huge women's pro ball was there.

Crazy as it sounds now, I loved playing in Russia. Fans recognized me on the streets but still mostly left me alone. I felt safe, despite concerns at home about LGBTQ+ rights in Russia. I even had a favorite market around the corner from my apartment, and I'd duck in there to buy snacks. The country felt like a second home, but only because I'd never actually been inside that house. From my place on the porch, I couldn't see the dirty politics, the corruption, the old-school views of women. The club handled all my business and kept a bubble around the players, which kept a lot of the real Russia out of view. I'd chuckled at ladies wearing furs in the grocery store, decked out in Versace and red-bottom heels, lips pumped up, trying to catch men so they could marry early. I'd rubbed shoulders with the ultra-rich VIPs who invested in our league. I saw regular folks too, families with kids, and factory workers bused in for games. They were in the stands, cheering us on, or lined up at my locker room after. But that was Russia from the outside, not up close. Inside, I was learning, was another story.

My agent was starting to feel that, one convo at a time. If Shabtai had still been alive when I was arrested, Lindz would've called him first. That was how important he was to women's basketball, and how connected he was to Russia's ruling class. He seemed to know everyone, from the Kremlin down, and my ordeal might've gone differently if he'd intervened. Instead she rang Max Rybakov, my team's GM, and a long list of others. That list included Casey Wasserman, who owns and leads Wasserman Agency, and is also the head of the LA28 Olympics and very politically connected. Lindz also called Travis Murphy, a former foreign service officer who oversees the NBA's relationship with the State Department, as well as various experts on Russia and hostage diplomacy. My agent heard the same advice from every quarter: Keep the arrest quiet. Because if we got loud, things would escalate, which would make it harder to cut a deal to bring me home. She didn't know if Putin even knew about the incident at that point, so it was better not to draw attention to it. That was our only shot at resolving things discreetly.

How? Maybe as a sports diplomacy issue, separate from politics, a favor granted in the name of Olympic spirit. Or we could play the star Russian-baller card, remind them how much positive recognition I brought their country through my success with Ekat in the EuroLeague. There were other possible strategies as well. By then, Lindz and Relle had researched the hell out of my charges, and also Russia's criminal code. In Article 229.1, anyone caught carrying any amount of drugs could be charged. In Russia, that article was legit and led to a 99.9 percent conviction rate. That's not justice; that's tyranny. And when you're in a system with no true justice, you're also in a system with a bunch of gray areas. You can pay your way out of trouble with a million rubles, for instance. Or you can make some calls to well-placed contacts, and, voilà, those vape pens magically disappear. Enter my agent's plan: stay in the gray. We'd slide into one of these zones and try to get me home. Lindz didn't know exactly how she'd make that work, but she was optimistic that she could.

And then came February 24. Exactly one week after a dog sniffed my suitcase, Russia invaded Ukraine. Millions looked on in dismay and confusion as troops stormed across the border. Putin called it a "military operation" to "denazify" its sovereign neighbor. The West called it a declaration of war. Putin warned America, Europe, and NATO not to assist Ukraine. If they did, he threatened consequences. As the world teetered toward global crisis, I sat alone in a personal one. The invasion changed everything for me. Suddenly, my arrest wasn't just an arrest, and I wasn't just another prisoner. I was a possible chess piece in a showdown between superpowers. The timing of my episode couldn't have been worse. The stakes had just been raised.

Around that time, Lindz got news that deepened her dread. She'd connected with a basketball agent who knew the mayor of Moscow. She hoped the mayor could pull some strings, since I was in his jurisdiction, but he closed that door. "I can't help you," the mayor said. "This is past me." The answer was no, end of discussion; read between the lines. The takeaway was clear: my case was already at the Kremlin.

....

Alone in my cell, I knew little. Alex told me about the invasion and agreed it made our hill a whole lot steeper. He gave me verbal updates on the efforts being made to get me home, but, frankly, I was too depressed to absorb much. Also, with no TV or radio, I couldn't watch the war reports. And with no phone, I couldn't actually talk to Lindz or Relle. My wife had written to me, so I knew she and my agent were working around the clock. Relle's first letter was dated February 19, but it took a while to get to me. Relle emailed her letter to Alex, who printed it out. But he couldn't get in to visit me as often as he wanted, so he held it until he could. When Alex finally handed me Relle's letter, I bawled just seeing it.

"Hey, baby," Relle began. "It's me, via paper but still me. I love and miss you so much. THANK GOD for all the voice memos I had you send me over the last few months! Thanks for being the world's best spouse and having a way for me to hear you without literally speaking to you every day. We are truly working hard to get you back home. I pray your mental is good. Just know you CAN do all things through Christ, who strengthens you. Don't beat yourself up about being in this position. We all love you and are still Team BG. I am doing good, my love, so find peace in knowing I am okay. You've provided in such a way that this time away is not going to hurt me, or us. I'm only hurting because I miss you tremendously. I remember you joking and saying I'd leave you if you ever got locked up 'cause I'm not about that life. Well, you're clearly wrong lol. For you, anything. I love you, honeybun. Muah."

I read that letter over and over, tearing up every time. Relle didn't mention anything about the case or Russia, nor did she update me on all the efforts she and Lindz were making to try to bring me home. Alex had made sure she knew the letter would be monitored, that she couldn't be totally candid in writing. I'd have to read between the lines on most things, but clearly not when it came to her love. That came through in every sentence. I knew she was pulling for me, and that was all I needed to know. It was a gift to be cut off from the worst news. I wouldn't realize till much later how bleak things were becoming.

Several days after that first arrest hearing, my world had become even more depressing. During my arraignment on February 24, the judge said I'd be moved soon, to serve my month till the next hearing. Per Russian law, I could be held at county for ten days max before I had to be transferred to a women's detainment center. I'd already been locked up for several days, with no sign of transfer. In America, holding me even one minute past a deadline would be enough to have the case thrown out. God, I missed my homeland. The reason for the delay: my chest X-ray. The results showed signs of lung damage from Covid. I told them I'd gotten over it a few weeks earlier. Still, detention center officials demanded I be retested, to be sure Covid was out of my system. They couldn't risk a prison outbreak. So back to the medic I went for another X-ray, followed by days of hearing nothing.

Well, I heard something, just not what I wanted to hear. One guard was noisy as fuck, stomping through the halls during his evening shift. After dinner and tea from that rusty-ass kettle, he did our nightly cell check. You stay in your cell while a few guards and a dog sniff the place. No one had to tell me to play by the rules. Pops had warned me years ago. Then it was lights out, supposedly for sleep, but this guard never got that memo. I couldn't stand the dude. He honestly looked like he was doing meth. Sunken face, teeth missing. And I could hear him before I saw him, thanks to his loud voice. He'd be slamming our little metal peepholes all night, yakking with other guards like it was high noon. I'd be lying there thinking, *Come on, dude, I gotta try to sleep.* Then, just as I'd nod off, I'd hear his loud ass, saying to someone, "The American's in there."

I looked for ways to distract myself. On day three, I decided to go vegan. Why not? If you saw the food they brought me, you'd go vegan too. Suddenly I wanted to save the fish, the chicken, the cows, the whole damn planet. But the experiment quickly ended 'cause I had to save myself. Without meat or dairy, I was basically left with a spoonful of grits. I got so hungry I had to cave. When you've got nothing but silence, you can't ignore your stomach growls. And when you've got nothing but hours dragging by, all you can do is think of home. That's the funny thing about time. Most of us want more of it because our lives are moving so fast. But while time is a blessing, too much can feel like a burden. Minutes seem like hours, hours like days. You feel stuck, frozen, invisible. Your world is four walls, a ceiling your sky.

As I stared up at concrete, I mostly thought of Relle. *What's she doing? How's she really handling all this?* I knew what she'd written. I also knew my baby's nature, which was keeping a brave face, even when hell was breaking loose. Also, I was sure she wanted to protect my mental, make sure I stayed strong. We usually talked several times a day. So strange not to hear her voice. At that point I didn't have a picture of my baby. I just imagined her face, the jokes we swapped, how her eyes lit up on that Valentine's Day.

I also thought about my family. Pops was dealing with some health issues that I hoped weren't getting worse. As much as

I cringed at Dad hearing I was actually detained, I was just as concerned about how Mom might take the news. She was such a delicate flower, I feared this would destroy her. Both she and Dad knew I'd been stopped at the airport, but not that I'd been hauled off to jail. In my last call with Relle, she'd asked me how much to share with my mother in particular. We agreed she shouldn't give her the blow-by-blow. "Let's just see how it plays out," I said. "No need to make her worry unnecessarily." Sometimes loving a person means telling them everything. Other times it means leaving them with hope.

As the days crept by, I felt more and more miserable. The war broke out on a Thursday. *Is it Friday? Saturday? Monday? Not sure.* But I knew I'd been in jail for over a week, by the number of entries in my sudoku margins. Honestly, I just felt hopeless.

I'd dealt with suicidal thoughts back in my Baylor days. I'd grown up having faith, a reason to keep living, but then I got turned off from all that as I got older. I hated when people tried to force religion on me, and when they did bring it up, it was always something about being gay. I was like, "Nah, I'm cool." Also, I was super into science and wanted proof. *How can we be sure there's a God?* Relle, a preacher's kid, grew up strong in her faith. When we got together in college, I'd ask her questions here and there, and that was about it. But while I had my doubts, I was still curious. Curious enough to pack a Bible when I left for China in 2013. Before Russia, I played there for one season. I kept thinking, *There's gotta be something bigger than just this.* By "just this," I meant our time on earth. I didn't know if there was a heaven, or even a God, but I thought I'd find out for myself. I started in Genesis. Somewhere around Leviticus I nodded off.

The questions persisted, and so did the panic attacks. I'd struggled with them throughout my twenties. When I was tired or stressed, I'd get overwhelmed with the thought that this life was all there was. I remember the night in college when I reached out to Relle, told her I was about to end it. I was exhausted: basketball, family stuff, everything. "Yo, I can't deal with this," I said with tears in my voice. She was at my door in less than ten minutes. There I was in bed, trembling and sweating. Relle wrapped her arms around my body till I stopped shaking. She always knew how to talk me off a ledge. She also had what I was still questioning: an eternal hope to cling to.

Now, in my cell alone, a world away, I imagined her next to me the way she was on that evening at my apartment. I couldn't yet finish my letter to Pops, so I started one to her. "To my wife and only love of my life," I began. "I love you with every inch of my soul. I'm praying hard every day that I'll get to see you soon. When I do, be ready for me to pick you up off the floor and hug you so tight. You are the sole reason I'm holding on. Your faith has definitely rubbed off on this kid. Thank you for showing me the way I should love God."

It was Relle's strength I borrowed when mine ran out. I wanted to take my life more than once in those first weeks, felt like leaving here so badly. In that cell I didn't care anymore if there was an afterlife. I just wanted that one to be over. Suicide would've been easy. I could've broken off a piece of rusty metal, sliced it into my wrist. Or I could've found a loose screw. Nothing was bolted down well. But when I thought about ending it, I imagined my mom's face, the way she'd howl and double over at hearing her child was dead. I also didn't know what Russia would do; they might refuse to release my body. I couldn't put my family through that nightmare, and I especially couldn't do that to my momma. That, and Relle's faith, are what kept me here.

PART II

LOCKDOWN

Once you lose language, your isolation is absolute.

–Andrea Dworkin, *Life and Death*

February 24, 2022

Hey Pops,

I want to thank you for being such an amazing dad, always teaching me and showing me the right way. You never failed me once. I have failed you by ending up here. I will never let you down like this again. I'm so sorry for the stress I have put on that old body lol . . . but really, I'm so sorry, Pops.

You came to me in my dreams last night. We were driving and talking like when I was little. Miss those days. I also miss talking to you on the phone so much I want to cry thinking about it. When I get home I promise we will talk every day.

I want you to know that I'm being nice and following orders. They are moving me to Big Prison soon. I'm glad cuz I can shower and get yard time as well. Also I can buy things with money on my books. Downside, I will be in a cell with 6 to 8 girls! Don't worry, I will be safe.

I pray that you rest easy, Dad. Please be there for Mom. She's going to need your strong presence to make it through this. Guards about to do cell check and then lights out. Love you to the moon and back, big man. Muah.

Love,

Britt 🖤

6

PRISON PLAYBOOK

I don't know when I got moved to detention. By my count, it was a few days after war broke out. By Alex's count, it was earlier. What matters is what I saw when I got there: a big-ass knife.

Alex had given me the lowdown on Correctional Colony No. 1, or IK-1, as it was known. It was a former orphanage the Russians turned into a massive women's prison. Two kinds of prisoners ended up there: those already sentenced and serving their time, and others, like me, waiting for trial. Same property, separate buildings. The facility was about fifty miles from central Moscow. I'd spend my first eight days in quarantine with other rookies, Alex explained, to air out any Covid. The day I got transferred, a guard at county cuffed me and shoved me in a steel cage in the back of a square-box truck. The cage was so small I had to sit sideways with my knees pulled to my chest. I felt like cattle being transported. After two hours in slow traffic, we finally pulled up to tall gray walls lined with barbed wire. Inside, a monument to Vladimir Lenin sat in a courtyard. We entered a building that looked like a shack.

Two female guards, one blond, one jet-black, looked me up and down. They led me to a nearby room and motioned for me to stay in there. No idea why I had to wait. A couple of hours later, the black-haired guard finally returned, pointed to another nearby room, and said, "Go." Inside, Blondie snatched my small duffel, filled with the few things Alex had brought me, and dumped everything on a table. She rifled through the items, removing the laces in my shoes and the drawstrings in my sweats. *Possible noose or weapon.* She kept my stuff, I guess for more inspection, and sent me to another room for medical paperwork. God only knows what the prison doc wrote on that paper. She checked a bunch of boxes as I sat stone-faced but with my heart racing, wondering what was next. Soon after, I was handed a mattress and a blanket, along with an aluminum cup, a spoon, and a green plastic bowl.

With Blondie on my right side and Jet-Black on my left, I walked down a long corridor. The hall had steel doors along both sides, twenty doors give or take. Each door had a rectangular peephole at eye level, and a second, wider food-delivery door at belly button level. We stopped. Blondie unlocked the door with a skeleton key. Right behind it was a second door, a *Shawshank Redemption*-style cage with bars going across. She unlocked the cage and signaled for me to step forward.

When I entered, seven sets of eyes stared up at me. Most of the women were on bunks. Two sat at a table in the middle of the cold space, a tiny room with one dusty window. Everyone gawked like I was an exotic animal, a Bengal tiger on the loose. On the table lay this giant knife. My eyes widened. *What the fuck is that for?* A young girl stood up from the table and came over to me. "I'm Olya," she said in a thick accent. I don't know what shocked me more, seeing that knife or hearing English. "I'm BG," I mumbled. "Give me that," she said, grabbing my bedding. "I will help you."

That was my intro to lockdown, detention-center style. Rule one: Whoever's been in quarantine the longest initiates the newcomers. That meant Olya was in charge. Rule two: Do exactly what Olya tells you, including making up your bunk correctly. Rule three: Only socks or slippers in the cell, which is why I kicked off my Jordans. And rule four: Every day at lunch the guards bring a knife so you can cut your own fruits and vegetables. Similar thing on Scissor Sundays, when they dropped off nail clippers and hair trimmers for grooming. The guards were supposed to pick up the sharp items. On this day they'd forgotten. *Um, you can't have shoelaces, but you can have a knife? So ass-backward.* As I'd learn, that was how things went at IK-1. A few of the guards were men, Olya said, but most were female. Jet-Black was an MMA fighter.

With my mattress tucked under her arm, Olya led me around the room and introduced me to the women, told me a bit about each. A few were older, maybe fifties. Several were around my age. Olya, with her straight brown hair and pale face, was the youngest at twenty-one. All of us were first-timers in prison. The room was crowded, with three sets of bunks against one wall. Two extra twin beds sat along another wall. Off in a corner, out of the view of the camera, was a rinky-dink plastic toilet, the kind you sit on. There was also a sink. Olya put my stuff on a top bunk and rolled out the mattress.

"Make your bed as soon as you get up," she said. "It has to be like this." She placed a top sheet on the mattress and tucked it on all sides. Next, she took my wool blanket, the granny kind that itches, and spread it across. She then folded the blanket the long way on each side, hot-dog style, so that it looked like a stripe going down the middle.

In my socked feet, I slid over to the table and sat. A few others pulled up chairs. We all talked, well, really, just me and Olya, and also this other girl, Tanya. She spoke a tiny bit of English and laughed a lot, seemed like a bit of a cutup. I clicked with her right away. She was built like a softball player, short and stubby, with a buzz cut and dancing eyes.

"What are you in here for?" Tanya asked through Olya. Tanya's English wasn't good enough to ask me herself.

"Drugs," I said. Everyone was in for drugs, Olya told me.

"What happened?" Olya asked.

I sighed. "I just forgot some fucking vape pens in my luggage," I said.

Olya nodded. "You know they can't shoot you if you escape," she said.

I studied her face in search of what she meant.

"The guards," she said. "If you try to escape, they can't shoot you because you haven't been sentenced yet. You have to have a verdict to get shot."

I laughed. Whether that was true or total BS, where was I going? Fucking nowhere. I had no phone, no fam close, no getaway car. At six foot nine with tats and dreads, I don't exactly blend in. Soon as I'd ask to use anyone's cell, they'd be like, "Wait, aren't you that big-ass American hooper?" They'd then haul my butt to the basement of the Krem and lock me away forever. "Olya, I ain't trying to escape, so they're good," I said. I had to squash that rumor before it even got started.

Olya talked me through the rest of the prison playbook. Two cell searches a day, 6:00 a.m. before showers, 9:00 p.m. before lights out at 10:00. You got an hour a day "outdoors," in a caged space called the Yard. The other twenty-three hours were spent in your cell, bored as hell on that bed. No napping, though. I guess they wanted you awake for your suffering, or worn out enough to sleep at night. Every room had a small TV, which guards controlled. It mostly stayed on the Russian propaganda channel, except on the weekends, when we could watch whatever. You got three meals a day, prepared by the convicts in the many buildings near ours. For food, the same gravelly grits as at county, but this place had a perk: Your family could drop off food, a limited amount of kilos, though the staff never weighed it, said Olya. Our mini fridge in the room was stuffed with chicken, salami, fruit. Once a month you got a single roll of toilet paper, and good luck if you ran out. Soon as you wiped yourself, it ripped. You could buy more TP at what was known as the Market (think jailhouse truck, not Kroger).

Oh, and you wore you own clothes. No uniforms till you were convicted.

Blondie cut our convo short when she brought me my stuff, minus the shoestrings. She also gave me my TP and a tiny tube of toothpaste. I pulled the tube close to my face and read the words on the back: "Best if used by September 2007." *Holy fuck.* If I didn't die of heartache first, I'd be killed by mildewed white paste. A short time later Blondie returned and said something to Olya. "She will take you to the bathroom now," Olya translated. New inmates got to shower on arrival. I'd keep on my dirty clothes for now, she instructed, and carry my clean ones to change into. Um, nothing in my bag qualified as clean. I still had on the hoodie I was arrested in, musty as hell, like me. In a letter to Relle I'd written, "I can't believe I haven't showered in over a week. All I've had is a hoe bath in a sink." That was way back at county. By this point I could smell my funk. I fished out a tee and some underwear, threw them in a plastic bag, and followed Blondie.

We walked down a long hall and stopped at a door. She nodded for me to enter and—*click*—locked me in there. I looked around. In the WNBA, my teammates and I joked about our so-called prison showers, a big space with spouts spread around. This was the real thing, and it was nasty: exposed pipes on every wall. Long hair strands all over the tile floor and gathered in the drains. A bloody tampon tucked between two pipes. As disgusted as I was by the scene, I was just as repulsed by my stench. I undressed, found the cleanest part of the floor, and turned on a faucet. Rusty brown water came spouting out. I jumped back at first but then leaned into the flow, 'cause the alternative was staying ripe. Honestly, once I ignored the color, the hot water felt so good on my skin. I closed my eyes tight, trying to forget where I was, thought of Relle and home and all I'd left behind. Down the water slid from my dreads onto the floor, splashing away the hell I'd endured. I stayed in there a good thirty minutes, until I banged on the door for the guard to let me out. That was the nastiest shower I've ever taken. It was also the best.

At county I'd been up around the clock, listing ways I could end my misery. But that night, boy, I knocked out. I didn't care that my legs dangled off the mattress. I didn't care that the bed-springs dug into my back. I didn't care that it was freezing, even under that itchy-ass blanket. I was a legit zombie. Still, I kept one eye open, as Pops had taught me, 'cause you can't ever really trust nobody. Especially when you're new. Especially when there's a knife still on the table. Especially when you're the only one in that room you can be sure isn't a murderer. Anytime I heard noise, my eyes flipped open.

The lights blared on the next morning, ahead of roll call and room search. That was also when the guards handed out meds. We filed out of our cell and lined up facing the wall until our names were called. "Griner!" the guard yelled. "Brittney Yevette!" I replied, as Olya had told me to. Yevette is my middle name, not my last, but the guards insisted I use it. That was because Russians sorta have two surnames, their fathers' first and last names put together. So there, I'd be Brittney Yevette Raymondovna Griner, with *ovna* added to my Pops's first name. But during roll call I had to yell out both my names because they didn't understand the whole middle name thing. "Brittney Yevette!" I shouted again, to be sure the guard heard me. "No medicine!" I added, and Olya translated. The guard then moved on to the other girls.

After roll call we showered, one group at a time. You didn't shower daily, just twice a week, and only with your cellmates. The guards took one group to the shower, they went back to roll call, they took another group, and so on. Shower order was up for grabs. The night before, the girls in various cells asked to be taken first, since the earlier you got in there the longer you could stay, up to a half hour. Plus, the shower room was dirtiest at the end. If you were last on roll call *and* shower, your guard was like, "You've got ten minutes. Make it work."

That morning I didn't even need ten minutes. I got in and out of the filth in five minutes flat. My ass was clean enough. I'd made sure the day before. Plus, I caught a couple of girls staring at my chest, searching for tits I'd never had.

....

Near the end of quarantine I begged to be put in a room with Olya. Same with Tanya. I was teaching Tanya a little English, and in exchange she was teaching me how to cuss. *Pizdets* was the most versatile Russian curse word. It means *fucked up*, but you can also use it just to say "Fuck!" if someone is on your nerves. When Tanya explained that, I thought to myself, *That'll come in handy*.

I needed Olya in particular to be in my room since she spoke the best English. Prison ain't about finding your BFF. It's about surviving to get home to your real one. The guards kept me with Olya, but not Tanya. In fact, they made sure Tanya and I were nowhere near each other. They cut her quarantine short by a couple of days and moved her into another cell. They'd spotted trouble.

Tanya raised hell in quarantine. If the guards told her to go left, she went right. Tanya did whatever Tanya wanted to do, including eating at midnight. Even after lights out, a dim light stayed on so the guards could observe us from their camera station. Well, in the middle of the night, that girl pulled out a chicken leg, unwrapped the loud foil, and started grubbing. Next thing I knew the guard was pounding on the door, yelling "Go to sleep!" in Russian. The commotion, of course, woke my vigilant ass up. Tanya kept right on chewing. I somehow nodded back to sleep, but the next morning I heard how things got settled. Tanya offered the guard a piece of chicken if he'd let her stay up and eat. The dude actually agreed. He came in, took a couple of pieces through the cage bars, went back to his station, and left her alone. That was life in the gray zone. Most everything was negotiable; you just had to find the right price.

So the guards split us up real quick, because they didn't want drama even in my orbit. Tanya was the hellion, not so much me, but they could see I thought her stunts were funny. That chicken episode still cracks me up. Real talk: Together, Tanya and I would've set that detention center on fire. Had they put us in the same cell, my laughter might've stoked the flames. I would've separated us too if I had been those guards. So they moved me and Olya to a small room built for three, with this Russian girl named Alena. That was the best thing that could've happened to me.

First, the good news: Alena was beyond cool. Not only did she speak English, but she spoke it even better than Olya. Years earlier she'd been an exchange student in London. Alena was tall, at least six feet. She'd played volleyball once upon a time. She was younger than me, twenty-seven, with bone-straight brown hair down to her ass. She'd been in detention for a year when I got there, which meant she knew the lay of the land. She was waiting for her trial to start. She and her husband got busted selling drugs. He was an MMA fighter, teaching kids at a gym, and she drove trucks for a living. Covid hit and their money got tight, so she started selling methadone, a real-life *Breaking Bad*. Now, methadone ain't meth. You can't cook it up in a kitchen. It's a synthetic powder, made in a lab, and it's common in Russia. They love synthetics over there. Alena sold it first, and then her husband began helping. They both took the rap. He was awaiting trial at a men's detention center.

"Do you like *Transformers*?" Alena asked me on our first evening together.

"Hell yeah," I said, while thinking, *This is my kind of girl.*

I still can't believe what Alena did next. That night, *Transformers* was airing and our guard had put it on. Line by line for two hours, that girl translated the movie for me. That was just the beginning. Alena provided subtitles for my entire life, from revealing what the guards were whispering to ordering from the Market. She helped me out tremendously, and to this day,

I'm grateful. From jump she replaced Olya, who was getting on my nerves. Why? Not tidy enough.

Anyone who's ever had roommates can tell you the first commandment of sharing: You've got to keep shit neat. I'm neat to the nth degree. Mr. Clean ain't got nothing on me. Alena and I were in sync on that too, which is why we agreed on a cleaning schedule. Our room was smaller than where I'd been in quarantine but set up similarly, with me on a top bunk initially, right underneath the camera. Olya was below, Alena in a twin. On Sundays we each had a chore. Alena cleaned the toilet and little bathroom area, which had a privacy wall in front of it. I started out as the mopper, which involved getting on my knees and wiping the floor clean with a towel. "Stop, BG," Alena said when she saw me hunched over, clutching my back. "You're too big for that." So she mopped, I swept. Our "broom" was this raggedy set of tree limbs we'd found in the Yard and tied together. I also cleaned everything up high, like the bars over our one window. Then I'd pick up the fridge so she could mop under it. Olya couldn't clean worth shit. We'd give her a small job, like scrubbing the sink, and we'd still have to go behind her. Me and Alena wanted our cell spotless. Olya was the odd girl out.

That was also true with the Market, which is really just a jailhouse hustle. Somebody got in good with the detention center and made a deal to earn money from prisoners. So once a month, give or take, a dude rolled in with a truck packed with basics: dishwashing soap, cleaning supplies, toiletries, bottled water, snacks, even electric kettles. Your family and friends could add money to your account. Whatever you ordered got debited, and I'm thankful Relle kept mine full by arranging payment through Alex. He was my only liaison to home and how I kept in touch with everyone. My first order revealed my priorities: TP, lemon dish soap, and six liters of water. The items, all Russian brands, rotated constantly. You ordered only what was available. That was where the so-called application came in. Every day when the guard yelled, "Market!" the girls started screaming, "This room, we need the list!" The guards brought a list of what was available. Those lists were often printed on the backs of old case files, with inmates' names and charges clear as day. I guess scrap paper mattered more than privacy in Russia's prisons. You'd then rip out a sheet of your own paper, write out which items you wanted, and give your order to the guards. Everything was in Russian, so Alena wrote my list. When our items arrived a couple of days later, she and I shared everything we'd bought.

Olya was a different story. "I'll give you some salami if you give me a bottle of water," she'd say. That was cool, until it wasn't, because her trading scales got tilted. She already couldn't clean worth a damn, and then she started dipping into my water stash. Alena and I didn't operate that way. If she was short on food, I'd offer her a big piece of salami. Smoked meat was popular in prison because it lasted when the fridge blew out, plus cold-ass Russia itself was an icebox. "I'll just take a tiny piece," Alena would say. "Just take the damn salami," I'd insist, laughing. "You gave me three packs of noodles just the other week."

Not true with Olya. She'd seemed cool in quarantine, and I'm glad she helped me. But more and more she got on my nerves, to the point where I tried to avoid her. No chance I could, since you did everything with your cellmates. You rarely saw the girls in other rooms, only if you happened to spot someone the guards were moving. Detention had two floors, and I was on the first, hadn't seen the second at that point. Alena had, and she said it had just as many cells as the first, at least twenty. Most rooms had five or six girls, she said, and a few big ones housed as many as thirty. I don't know how many were there during my time, but it had to be a few hundred.

My small world was just us three. We showered together every Wednesday and Sunday, our designated days. Three times a day the guards came through with gumbo-size pots of grits, noodles, and that funky fish. The guards stood by as the convicts from the other buildings scooped food into our bowls, one at a time. They then slid it back through that little grungy door, which had old dried food on it from years of sloppy deliveries. We ate together, watched TV together, even pissed in the same shitty toilet. Much as I wanted to drop Olya, I honestly didn't mind having cellmates. When you get thrown in prison, your world suddenly shrinks, but mine had also expanded. At county it was me, alone with my morbid thoughts. At least here I had chatter to distract myself. With twenty-three hours a day indoors, company becomes your sanity.

The Yard was a joke. I don't even know why it was called the Yard. There was no grass, just a big box split up by three concrete dividers, each section roughly ten by ten. The dividers were supposed to keep inmates from mingling. A lot of times two or three groups were out in the Yard at once, but in different sections. You couldn't see the other girls, but you could hear them. We shouted things over the divider all the time. It was like our social media, a prison-style Facebook without the faces. In each section, three walls were concrete, one was steel bars, and the ceiling was raggedy rebar. The steel-bar side faced a building. On one wall there was a rim, five feet up, but I had zero interest in basketball. It made me think of what I'd lost and where I was. Also, I was already out of shape.

I spent my time in the Yard looking up. I lived for seeing the sky, even if it was through rebar. It was my only window to the outside world, a reminder to hang on. The guards took us to the Yard whenever they felt like it, which on some days was not at all. And in the winter our one hour was more like five minutes since temps were usually freezing. Plus the guards were lazy and wanted to stay indoors. Can't blame them. Russian cold is bone-chilling, so brutal it bites you in the ass. Still, I looked forward to the Yard for the change of scene, and most of all for that sky. Plus, I smoked like crazy in the Yard. Alena did too. Every chance we got we bought cigs at the Market.

Technically, we could smoke only in the Yard, not indoors. Our cell was a nonsmoking cell, since it had normally been where the prison's visitors stayed: inspectors, ex-cops, government officials. But the guards put us in there knowing we were legit chain-smokers, and they never complained when we lit up. Hell, they even gave us matches since lighters weren't allowed. Like everything else in Russia, rules were mostly suggestions. That whole facility was one big smokehouse. Smoke even floated through our vents, from the women puffing upstairs. Olya didn't smoke, so she complained when we did. "You're young," I told her while pulling out my next cig. "Your lungs can take it." I secretly wanted to smoke her ass right out of there.

I'd rarely smoked cigs back at home, but over there I lit up constantly. I'd wake up, have a cig. Eat breakfast, have a cig. And if me and Alena were bored, which was always, we'd pull out another pack. I probably went through twelve, thirteen cigs a day. How much I smoked depended on my stress, how badly I missed my old life. I loved Philip Morris, Kent, Marlboro Reds, and I went hard on Camel, which the Market carried a lot of. Alena told me what the guards were saying about me: "Wow, she smokes men's cigarettes." *Yeah, so what?* I'm sure, like everyone, they thought I was a man. Might as well smoke like one. I smoked so much the smell came through my pores.

The whole time we smoked, we gossiped. Alena had been in detention so long she knew a lot. She'd been moved from cell to cell. Typical prison. The guards didn't want inmates getting too cozy. Might mean trouble. The only reason I wasn't moved was 'cause they needed Alena and Olya to translate for me. "Don't touch any toilet seats if you get put in another cell," Alena warned me. The place was crawling with diseases. With all her moving, she'd figured out who had what diseases, from herpes and chlamydia to HIV and AIDS. In Russia, HIV is called spid, pronounced like *speed*; God only knows why. But according to Alena, there was a lot of spidding going down in detention. Same with herpes. Super common. At roll call, when meds were handed out, you could see who was getting syringes, pills, whatever. Her advice: keep to yourself, clean constantly, and always wear gloves.

Alena had also figured out laundry. Our laundry day was one of our shower days, Sundays. We were supposed to hand-wash our clothes in the sink and dry them on top of the tiny radiator in our cell. Hanging shit up was against the rules. But nothing ever got fully dry on that radiator, plus you could lay out only a couple of items at a time. Alena had a work-around. She'd befriended a redhead, one of the inmates serving time in another part of the complex. We didn't really mix with the convicts, all second offenders, but we occasionally saw them. They ran the place: sewing uniforms, washing the lumpy mattresses we slept on, dropping off items we ordered from the Market.

So Alena made a deal with this redhead to pick up our laundry bag on Sundays. At morning roll call we brought it into the hallway and left it there. The redhead would later pick up the bag, wash our clothes in a machine in her part of the complex, and return everything a day later, give or take. Me and Alena paid her in cigarettes, one pack from each of us tucked between the clothes. Olya sent no cigs, which was probably why her laundry came back tumbled. Ours was neatly folded. This arrangement was of course against the rules, but the guards didn't care. When the redhead came through, they just looked the other way.

Alena was the best thing that ever happened to me in detention. If we'd met in the real world, we still would've clicked. On the inside, our friendship moved fast out of necessity. She knew people. She knew the system. And above all, she knew English. We gossiped our way from one roll call to the next, never sure what day it was or whether we'd make it out of prison. My life became a blur of sweeping and dusting, cleaning and praying, hoping I could somehow get home. That hope got dimmer one morning in March when our TV flickered on.

7

PUTIN'S PAWN

After roll call, the guard turned on our TV, same damn channel as always. Didn't matter. I couldn't understand it anyhow, just the bits and pieces Alena translated. That was how I knew it was 24/7 propaganda. Honestly, when I hear the word *propaganda*, I think of a past era, with Nazis spreading lies about the Jewish people. Well, the past is very present on Russian TV, where Putin claimed the Nazis controlled the USA. One time I spotted a clip with President Joe Biden, on a podium at the White House with two American flags behind him. Next thing I knew, those flags had been turned into Nazi flags by some shady production trick. Biden's voice was even distorted to make him sound like Hitler. I was like, *What the fuck.*

On this particular day, I did a double take. *Is that me?* Yup. There I was in a grainy image, going through the security checkpoint where my hell began. Alena saw my jaw drop and started translating. "They're saying an American has been detained on drug smuggling charges," she said. My name wasn't used but didn't need to be. It wasn't like I was hard to recognize. I stared at the footage of that dog sniffing my roller, of me rifling through my bag as the customs dude looked on. Sometimes it takes a while to realize you're fucked. I knew it in that moment.

I flopped down on my bed and stared at the ceiling as a major *whoosh* surged through me. I now know that on that Saturday, Alex flew into action. As soon as he saw the report, he texted Relle and Lindz with a heads-up that Russia had released the story. "The news just broke here," he wrote with the clip attached. A few hours later, that clip was everywhere, of course with my identity outed. *The New York Times* summed it up this way: "Russia said on Saturday that it had detained an American basketball player—quickly identified as Phoenix Mercury center Brittney Griner—on drug charges, entangling a U.S. citizen's fate in the dangerous confrontation between Russia and the West over Ukraine." When Russia released its footage, my first thought was, *This is it for me.* My second thought was, *Oh God—my family.*

By this point Relle had told Pops I'd been detained for at least thirty days. She had to. It was the only way to explain that out-of-nowhere text I'd sent from the airport and why I'd gone silent after. You can't pull one over on Raymond Griner, an ex-cop trained to spot trouble. Pops was dealing with health issues on the day of my arrest, so Relle didn't share much at first. She feared it might make him worse. Well, the opposite turned out to be true, 'cause that old man is the Terminator. When Relle gave him the news, he was, of course, worried, but he perked right up soon after. "This ain't the time for me to be sick," he said. In true Pops fashion, he was determined to be strong for me.

But Pops didn't yet know the full nitty-gritty. And we'd continued guarding my mother from even more of the story. For Mom, it wouldn't have been strange that I'd gone quiet. My family was used to me going overseas and off the grid. As I'd be flying out, I'd say, "I'll call you when I get there." Weeks later, I'd call like, "Hi," with no memory that I'd said I'd reach out. "What happened to the call?" Mom would say, laughing. *My bad.* In this case, she obviously knew I was in some kind of trouble. My airport text made that clear. But Relle did as I asked and minimized the ordeal. The rest of the fam did the same. The less Mom knew, the more at peace she could stay.

I was also worried about my nephew E.J., my sister Pier's son, who was fourteen then. That's my boy. He and all my nieces and nephews, they call me Nene (pronounced *knee-knee*). E.J. started calling me that when he was a toddler, probably because all he saw were two knees when I stood. I'm close with E.J., the way me and my brother, DeCarlo, were when I was young. My brother and I are far apart in age (he's seventeen years older), but that guy is my best friend. We text five, six times a week. He lives in Houston and works as a mechanic. As a kid, I'd hear his motorcycle pulling up in our driveway and run out screaming, "Carlo here! Carlo here! Carlo here!" I am E.J.'s Carlo. My nephew and I have been inseparable since the moment I first held him, since the years when we kicked it with PlayStation. I feared the news would break him. And now, before I could even talk to E.J., the Russian media had slandered his auntie with three ugly descriptions: Smuggler. Criminal. Prisoner.

Also in play was a fourth description—Black. My face in that footage revived a centuries-old narrative, that Blacks are lawbreakers. Blacks are thugs. Blacks are savages who should be locked away. Putin didn't need to say those words because history had already spoken. We know the stories of Blacks beaten down, both with slave masters' whips and the knees of cops. We've seen footage from *Birth of a Nation*, a film that portrays us as apes and the Klan as heroes. Back in the day, President Woodrow Wilson actually screened that crap in the White House. We've been hosed, lynched, and dragged to our graves, the way James Byrd was on that dirt road in Jasper. We know all the names, from Emmett to Breonna, cringe when we hear of the senseless murders. It's clear how the world sees the average Black person, and mostly that it doesn't. When others do look our way, it's often to confirm a stereotype, that we're ignorant, uncivilized, aggressive. Putin didn't create that stereotype. He was just gearing up to exploit it.

Blackness doesn't make you less, but it does frame your life. When you walk into a room, so does race. Frankly, it shows up before you do. It colors every conversation, shapes how you're viewed, determines whether you're even heard. From the day you get here, Blackness hangs over everything, from comments about your hair ("Can I touch it?") to mentions that certain Black people are "smart" ('cause it's assumed we're idiots). The message comes through loud and clear: You're not one of us, you're less. Black lives matter. We hear that in the streets, but what is a Black life really worth? Judging by our history, it seems not much, and even less if you're gay. For Putin, my worth was as a pawn. My arrest gave him leverage in his clash with the West. He was well aware of America's long history of racial tensions, and he knew how to use that to his benefit.

As the news sank in that morning, I cried because I'd let down my father. The Griner name was now stained around the globe: dopehead, drug dealer, dumb. I hurt because I knew I'd handed the world a weapon. When you're Black, your behavior is never just about you. It's about your entire community. You live with this responsibility to represent the best of us, to prove the haters wrong. Doesn't matter if you actually want that job; how you act will be seen through that lens. If someone white messes up, most folks just shake their heads. But if a Black person makes the same mistake, it's like, "See, I told you they were worthless." I wear my Blackness with pride, just as my parents do. I cried not just because I'd failed Mom and Pops, but also because I felt I'd shamed my people.

....

Alex visited soon after the news broke. Once I got to detention, we began meeting every Tuesday and Thursday in a room with plexiglass dividers. The dividers were rinky-dink, like those flimsy plastic ones used in restaurants during Covid. I once stumbled into one and the whole thing crashed down. Alex sat on one side, me on the other, with guards roaming around the ten stations. Not much security, though. It was against the rules to touch, but Alex could reach around the divider and hand me stuff, like the letters I lived for. They were my only connection to the outside world, since I had no access to a computer or email. The chairs were a joke, especially for someone my size. They were mini stools, so small and shaky I almost fell off mine on the first afternoon I met Alex.

"Well, it happened," I said. "I saw myself."

"You've seen the clip?" he asked.

"Yup," I said, sighing. "Saw my name smeared all over the world."

"At least it was short," he said. The footage Russia had released was less than a minute, with no audio.

"True," I said, staring down at the floor.

Alex wasn't surprised the clip had been released. After Russia invaded Ukraine, that seemed inevitable. But the newsbreak came sooner than he'd expected. When you've got a powerful chess piece, it can pay to hold off on playing it. But the quick release made sense to me, like a throwdown at the start of a match. In this case the match was U.S. midterms that November, so the timing wasn't a coincidence. The FSB has been manipulating U.S. racial politics forever, meddling in our elections to get its way. As I saw it, the clip release was Putin's way of saying, "Game on, Biden. Your move." It was also a sign that the Russians intended to control the story, to tell it their way. Lindz had hoped we could resolve this quietly. The Krem clearly intended to be loud.

"This could be good in some ways," Alex said.

"How?" I asked.

"Because it gets the two countries negotiating," he said. Whatever Putin wanted, we were now that much closer to a compromise. The early release of the video might mean I'd get home sooner.

"But we can't get our hopes up," he said. "This is Russia."

This is Russia. Alex said that a lot in those first weeks, I think to lower my expectations. He knew his country inside out, understood that things rarely went the way you thought they would. You could be on the verge of going home, he said, and then, *Oops*, end up rotting in jail. Nothing was ever certain in the gray zone. Nothing was done until it was actually done.

Alex gave me an update from Lindz and Relle on what was happening in the world. When war broke out on February 24, flights between Russia and the USA began drying up. FedEx, UPS, and other corporations suspended services into and out of the country. Then, on the same day Russia released the clip of me, the State Department urged Americans to leave the country immediately. My Ekat teammates, the American ones, had already gotten out. Lindz represented players in Ekat and other Russian cities and rushed to get them home. She was so worried that she got Alex to escort her players right up to Customs, to be sure they made it out. Because once I got snatched at the airport, she didn't know if my arrest was part of a coordinated strategy. When Alex showed up to walk players through security, they had no idea he was my attorney. They also didn't know that my ass was in jail, with no phone to return their missed calls. The real story had to remain quiet. Now they and the whole world knew.

Meanwhile, Lindz was still working the phones, desperately trying to get me home. She met with various people connected to Russian sports. When she asked for their help, they either didn't have the sway or seemingly didn't want to risk involvement. The best that most could do was connect her with others who maybe could give her some intel. That, and supply me with toiletries in jail, which I'm grateful some of her contacts delivered to me. With FedEx shut down, Lindz and Relle couldn't send me care packages, or for that matter anything but letters. Frankly, that's what I wanted most.

Alex brought me stacks of letters. Near the top was one from my agent's son, Drew, then five. He'd drawn a dinosaur shooting a basketball, with four words next to his creation: "Stay strong, say nothing." It brought me a needed smile. I slid it into the front pouch of my letters folder as a daily reminder and some joy. I also received a printed-out email from my baby, dated March 8. For once I got a note close to real time. Relle had sent the letter that day, just before Alex's visit.

"Hey baby," she wrote. "Ohh, my freakin' gosh! I have so much to tell you about my last 48 hours. A lot has changed in two days. I've cried a lot, and I mean the ugly tears I hate. It feels like the devil is sitting on my shoulder, like, 'What's good, sis?' If you can, please write me back on this same visit, something to help my mental. I need a BG speech right now. I'm not well, if we are being honest. This situation hit American media on Saturday, March 5, around 8 a.m. I'd had an appointment that morning, and by the time I got home it was everywhere. My phone was ringing nonstop with everyone who knew us trying to reach me. Also, my inbox was full of news outlets asking me to do interviews with them, as well as everyone else in the family.

"Here's that vulnerability moment," Relle continued. "I hate having everyone in the world looking at me while I'm at my weakest moment in life—because I am so weak without you, my love. You truly are my best friend and heartbeat. Who knew a girl like me could even cry like this! But I know I don't break. The way God loves me, I just know He works it all out for my good. Good news is, I'm still standing and I'm still managing to get what's necessary done, school-wise. So don't wonder if I'll make it, that's never to be questioned. The way my God is set up, and the way my faith in Him is set up—this too shall pass. Rest assured that you are GOOD! You are not one circumstance. Your character is defined by your heart, and you have one of the most genuine souls on this earth. I see you and I love what I see."

My whole body ached when I read Relle's letter—not because she'd said anything wrong. I hurt because I knew my actions had hurt *her*; burst the bubble she found her peace in. She'd been dealing with this crisis mostly alone. She actually preferred it that way. As much as Relle and I love each other, we're nothing alike. In our two-person crew, I'm the face of the ship. She's the one steering in the background. She's extremely private, so this newsbreak was her worst nightmare. She's built a small but mighty group of trusted friends, but even with them, she's the strong one. I'm her anchor, the one place where she can be a mess. And there I sat thousands of miles away in prison, unable to hold my baby through the shitstorm I'd created. "Babe, your superpower is not caring about the noise," she'd often told me. Her superpower was escaping to her closet, which was exactly what she did when that headline hit. My baby crawled into our closet, got down on her knees, and asked God to intervene. Putin might've made me his pawn, but he'd met his match with a prayer warrior.

There was also a letter from my brother. I teared up as I read it. "I know this wasn't intentional," Carlo wrote. "We all fuck up. I just want you home, baby girl. Stay strong, keep ya head up, and stay on ya toes. I luv ya and miss ya, and I'll be here as soon as you get home."

I'd messed up. I was locked up. And back at county, I'd almost given up. And yet my ride-or-dies were still with me, carrying me with their love.

....

Prison doesn't care if you're having a rough week. The humiliations continue. I experienced one soon after the news broke, during a Sunday-morning shower.

The guard with jet-black hair, the MMA fighter, was on duty that day. Some of the girls thought she was a hard-ass, but I'd never had any problem with her. But I could tell that she was curious about my body, always looking me up and down. She took my cellmates and me down to the shower room and waited at the door. "Damn, Alena, I ain't got my shirt," I said after we'd showered. I'd forgotten it in the room. "Just put a towel around your neck," she suggested. So I draped it around so that it covered my pecs.

Back at the room the guard did her usual search. Ain't no cameras in the shower room, so she had to be sure we were clean. We faced the wall, she patted us down, and then we turned around for a bag search. Well, after she'd poked through my bag with her little baton, she used it to move away my towel. She looked at the left side of my chest, then the right, before saying something in Russian to Alena. My cellmate just stared at her.

In the room I said to Alena, "Damn, she was checking me out. What did she say to you?"

Alena seemed reluctant to tell me. "They've never seen anybody like you," she said. "They're just curious." *Welcome to my hell.*

"Yo, what'd she say?" I kept pestering Alena. "Come on, just tell me."

She finally caved just before lights out, probably to shut me up. "She asked me if you had the surgery," she said.

"What surgery?" I asked.

"Like to change from a man to a woman," she said. "That's why she moved your towel. She wanted to see if you had scars."

Alena was pissed. I was hurt but not shocked. I'm used to that shit. That's been the story my whole life, questions about my identity. Sometimes I'm like, *Whatever, doesn't bother me.* But then, later, it ticks me off. People try to insert themselves in others' lives. Then they'll turn around and say, "Oh, you're intruding on me," or claim that we're weirdos. I'm like, *It's you who's in* my *business. I'm just minding my own.* If I went on my Instagram right now, probably fifteen people would be on there saying something about my being a man. Stay out of my underwear. Stay out of my tits. Stay out of my private life.

Later that evening another guard posed an even more disturbing question. "Does she have a dick?" she asked Alena about me. "All the guards are wondering." Alena rolled her eyes and walked off, again refusing to tell me what was asked. This time, she didn't reveal it till much later, and even then, I had to pull it out of her. She knew it would be too upsetting in a week when life had already gone left. That newsbreak almost broke me. Like a true friend, she spared my heart.

8

JUSTICE DELAYED

My thirty days were up. I went to court on March 16, almost two weeks after the story broke. I'd finally get to hear whether my case would be dropped or if I'd be granted house arrest in Russia. Hope is a funny thing. It can be comforting. It can also be a mindfuck. In this case, it was both.

By this time I had two attorneys. In early March, soon after the news of my detainment hit the headlines, Maria Blagovolina began co-representing me. We'd connected with her through Mike Pickles, my agency's chief legal officer. Mike anticipated that my case would get a lot of international attention and wanted a woman lawyer with extensive criminal experience who could also be a media spokesperson. I loved the idea of having Maria on the team, in case issues arose that I'd feel most comfortable discussing with a woman. I first met her in detention. One look at her next to Alex, and I immediately knew they were night and day—him with his hippie hair, his locks pulled back in a pony; her with her pearls and heels and a perfectly trimmed bob. Basically, Alex is me if I was a lawyer, and Maria is Relle. Their stylistic differences made them the perfect pair. So did the most important thing they had in common: the immense skill, experience, and passion to advocate for my release.

At this hearing, Alex was there with me, while Maria spent long hours determining our best legal strategies. I remember feeling hopeful that I'd at least be given house arrest. You are, of course, optimistic when you think that your attorneys will be allowed to do their jobs. In a country with a 99.9 percent conviction rate, a defense attorney is more like a friend, advisor, and legal guide, which was what Alex had become for me. He and Maria's hands were completely tied in a rigged system where the house always won. What was the point of arguing a set of facts in a case that had already been decided? For a defense attorney in Russia, winning means something different than it does in America. In part, this hearing was about following the rules and pretending to be in a just court, my lawyers said. The worst thing we could do was make a mockery of Putin. Then I might never get home. Some part of me hoped I'd be the exception, that 0.1 percent of people who got off. A bigger part of me knew I had zero shot. Still, I was nervous with so much at stake.

I was transported from IK-1 back to county a day ahead of court, which was close to the jail. That was the way it went with all inmates whose cases were in Moscow's jurisdiction: you rolled in the night before and stayed till the day after. Two guards loaded me onto a square-box truck, the same kind I'd squeezed into on the previous trip, only smaller. This one had four tiny cages. A guard shoved me into a cage, but I was legit too big for the door to close. So she chained my wrist to the ceiling and just left the cage open. The door swung back and forth for the entire ride, with my right arm stretched over my head and my heart in my throat.

The ride to county was long and bumpy. There was no window in my cage, but I could feel the driver braking every other minute. Moscow has notoriously bad traffic, made worse by constant construction. The ride can be shorter if the driver puts on the siren, which should be used only in an emergency. As far as my knees were concerned, this was a 9-1-1. No lie: it took three hours to pull up to county. By then my arm was numb and my knees and back were on fire. When the guard uncuffed me, my arm fell limp to my side.

I did my best to clean my cell, and then I went straight to bed. No napping allowed in detention, but at county, boy, you could sleep all day. The guards didn't care. In fact, they liked it when inmates were knocked out because it meant less work for them. They could just sit on their rusty behinds at the guard station and watch you toss and turn on camera while not having to deal with you bothering them. The two times I had to be up were at morning check and night check. Even when they brought me food in between, they didn't wake me. I just missed eating, which was frankly a gift. More food for other inmates, less indigestion for me.

At 9:00 the next morning, the guards loaded several of us into the square-box truck. My hearing wasn't until the afternoon, but the guards took all the inmates at once. Too lazy to go back and forth all day, even though court was close by. The ride to county is the only kind of democracy you'll ever find in Russia. Doesn't matter if you're a first-timer who forgot some vape pens (me) or a big-time dope dealer (the woman next to me in the truck). Everyone's thrown in together, first-time offenders and hardened criminals, hauled like animals to slaughter. In that truck, men were in one cage, women in the other, three or four per cage. I recognized the girl next to me from IK-1. She wasn't as tall as me but still tall, with an athletic build and a buzz cut, probably thirty. She'd been accused of selling major synthetics and would be sentenced that day. I'd heard that rumor in the Yard.

The guards uncuffed us and led us indoors, one after another down to the Dungeon. Alena had warned me about the Dungeon, a filthy space beneath the courthouse with zero ventilation. It was basically a prison-style waiting room, where inmates hung out before and after their hearings. I glanced around the dark space, lit by one dim, blinking bulb. Cigarette butts littered the ground, along with candy wrappers, trash, Popsicle sticks. The walls were covered in black soot and piss, or whatever bodily fluid I smelled.

"Everyone writes their crime on the walls," Alèna had told me. I spotted dozens of markings, all in soot from cigs, smeared in black. Every last name was followed by an accusation. If my name had been up there, I'd have been Griner, 229.1, part 2. On one side of the room were three cells, two for men, one for women. On the other side, several guards sat playing cards, laughing, smoking, drinking vodka. The courthouse was supposedly nonsmoking. Good luck enforcing that in Russia. The smoke was so thick down there that even I, Camel Queen, coughed as I entered. The guard locked me and the other women into our cell to wait, in my case for hours. My hearing wasn't till 1:00 p.m. I swear I smoked a full pack. *Can't breathe in here anyway*, I thought. *Might as well light up.*

Also, my stress was off the charts. So much was on the line: Would I stay locked up, or would I leave for home? And if I remained under arrest, would this judge do the humane thing and let me serve my time in the apartment my team had rented for me, literally steps away from the courthouse? On the one hand, this could be the day I walked free, boarded a flight back to Phoenix. But this could also be the beginning of the end, if the judge ruled to lock me up indefinitely. That was what happened to Alena and many others at IK-1. Alena had been in and out of hearings for more than a year, with no sign of a trial date. The judges just kept kicking her case down the road, giving her more time and weak excuses for why a trial date couldn't be set. I feared the same thing might happen to me.

Around 10:00 a.m., the girl who'd been chained near me during the truck ride got escorted up to her hearing. An hour later, she came back hysterical, wailing and moaning. I didn't know why in that moment. All I knew was that I'd never seen anyone so distraught. Later, back in detention, Alena told me she got twenty years. *Whoa.* I didn't know this girl, but I felt sorry for her, imagined what it must have felt like to have your next two decades go up in smoke. All morning in the Dungeon, prisoners returned boo-hooing, the life drained out of their eyes. The trash and cigarette butts on the floor made sense now, signs of inmates facing grief square in the face.

Around 12:30, a guard led me up the rickety stairs and down a hall. Alex was at the end of it. He walked alongside me as we entered the courtroom, before the guard locked me in my cage. The hearing was over almost before it started. Alex said a few words, and then the investigator stood and addressed the court—I guessed about my charges. A court-appointed translator sat near my cage, relaying what was said, but his English was so bad I didn't understand a word. The judge, a cold Russian lady who never once looked at me, glanced down at her notebook. A moment later she spoke briefly. She then slammed shut that notebook and—*bam*—hit her gavel. *Did she even hear my case?* I thought. Yes and no. Alex again made the arguments he'd made in my first hearing: I should be freed immediately given my spotless record and the low-level nature of the offense. And if the judge was determined to keep me locked up, house arrest was warranted.

Denied and denied, all for the same stupid reasons. First, the judge insisted I was a flight risk. Second, she sided with the investigator, who claimed she needed more time to complete her "investigation." I thought, *Are you kidding?* This investigator already had the footage of me going through security. She had the vape pens they'd confiscated. She had my signature on a document I'd been pressured to sign, after a duty-free Russian cashier—um, "translator"—couldn't tell me what I'd signed. So why did she need more time to "investigate"? She didn't. The judge's biggest reason for overruling us was the one she couldn't state: she'd been ordered to keep me detained, likely as leverage for Putin. Alex and Maria said that was obvious, since in similar cases at least house arrest often would've been granted. And I knew by how quickly the judge closed her notebook that my verdict had been decided in advance. My detainment would be extended, she ruled. Not one month this time, but two. As Alex gave me that news, my world went as dark as the Dungeon.

Maria texted Relle the news before it hit the headlines. She was deeply frustrated and disappointed. "You're not a threat to society," Relle wrote in her next letter to me. "You're also not a flight risk. First, our resources aren't that long. And second, at 6 foot 9, how are you escaping? With house arrest, we'd at least be able to see each other on FaceTime." But the judge didn't bother contradicting those arguments. She just hit that gavel and sent me back to jail.

Alex promised to appeal at the next hearing, which was when the extension would need to be reviewed. Even in Russia, you can't hold a prisoner indefinitely. A judge has to decide whether there are grounds to continue detaining you. Much as Relle and I appreciated Alex's and Maria's support and expertise, this ruling knocked the hope out of both of us. They were doing all they could in a corrupt system. The same was true for the judge, the lawyers explained. This ruling came from higher up. If that judge had dared to go against Putin, she might've lost her job or even her life. I understood that. It made me no less pissed.

We'd held our breath while awaiting that hearing, all so we could get the middle finger. As I left the Dungeon, I put out a cig and smeared my deets on the wall. Later, as the guard locked me in the square-box truck, I said to myself, *Game on.*

Back in detention it was Scissor Sunday, when guards dropped off hair trimmers, nail files and clippers, and tweezers, plus needles and thread for sewing up holes. "You trim hair?" Alena asked after our shower. "Sure," I said. "I don't know how, but tell me what to do." As I carefully clipped her ends, I told her about the verdict. She just stared ahead blankly the way inmates did, with a look that asked, "Will I be next?" A guard cut our convo short when he came in and spoke to Alena in Russian.

"Your bed," she translated. "They're going to make you a longer one today."

Up to then I'd been on the top bunk, with Olya below and Alena in the single. That made no sense to me. If my legs had to be dangling off the edge, at least they should be resting near the floor, not in midair. But when the three of us first got assigned to our room, Alena steered me toward the top bunk. She later told me why. The guards had pulled her aside and insisted that she take the single and that I be the one up top. They wanted to keep a close eye on me, Putin's newest pawn and prize. The top bunk was right under the camera, where the guards could monitor every twitch of my eye. There was also a mic on that camera, so they could hear *and* see me. But I'd told Alex that my legs were cramping, and he'd passed my complaint along to the warden. I'd injured them badly in 2017. In a game against the Minnesota Lynx, I jumped up while defending Sylvia Fowles and landed awkwardly, like Bambi on skates. It was some of the worst pain I'd been in. I blew out my right ankle and the weight-bearing bone in my left leg and spent a month in a wheelchair. I never fully recovered, so my legs stayed on fire. I guessed Alex's complaint to the warden had gotten through. Either that or the guards wanted to shut me up. Alena would now be up top, while I'd be on a longer single bed, the guard said.

Now our beds: Picture the kind you'd see in a 1920s orphanage, in one of those old black-and-white films. In place of a box spring there were solid metal bars. My mattress was constantly falling through those bars, just like it had at county. I'd wake up in the middle of the night, reposition the mat. Never worked. Because two minutes later my shoulder would be sliding through again, with my back protesting the whole time. So the guards dragged the single bed into the hall as Alena spread her mattress on the top bunk where I'd been. Two hours later the guards returned with hell 2.0. They'd cut off the footboard railing, laid it flat to extend the end, and welded that piece on with an L bracket. They then painted over their hack job with a brand of gray spray paint illegal in America—totally hazardous.

The bed was still wet when the guard threw my mattress onto the rails, staining the mat permanently. My bed was longer for sure. But now none of us could breathe, thanks to layers and layers of that paint. The smell was so strong I almost passed out. Same with Olya and Alena. For the first time since being arrested, I was able to stretch out fully. What was crazy was that I still got no sleep because I was up all night coughing.

A few days later, Alex came for his visit. Even after Maria joined the team, we decided Alex would keep doing most of the visiting while she handled other aspects of the case. She visited too, just not nearly as often. That's because UMMC Ekat was paying for Alex's services, while I was covering Maria's fees. And anyway, Alex had become my homie. That plastic divider couldn't keep us from connecting. There was no limit on how long a visitor could stay. We'd sit there for hours talking about rock and roll, Keith Richards, the Rolling Stones, his favorites. He was in a band called Poppa's Pipe, played guitar. And Alex *knew* music, from rock to deep-South blues. Me, I've got super eclectic taste. I love everything, and I do mean everything: rock, heavy metal, EDM, house, hip-hop, country. If Maria had been at every visit, we probably would've put her to sleep with the hours we spent on the topic.

For this visit, Alex arrived with another stack of mail. There were two types of letters. The first was the kind I'd keep, like those from Relle, the fam, and other friends and supporters, mostly WNBA players. The second was what we called "take-back letters," meaning he'd bring them, I'd read them, and then I'd give them back to Alex. Any letter from Lindz was usually in that category. She'd send articles and regularly update me on what was happening behind the scenes, but still leave a lot unwritten. She had to. She would ensure Alex or Maria quietly filled me in or gave color around the bullet points, but she couldn't take the chance that Putin and his cronies would know all our business. We needed to stay vague. Both kinds of letters were vetted before I received them. By "vetting," I mean that Alex handed the letters to the (non–English speaking) guard on duty and he or she scanned them (I'm talking five, ten seconds) before handing the letters back to Alex. My lawyer then leaned around the plexiglass and gave the stacks to me. Those guards didn't know what was in those letters. Still, we had to stay vague in all correspondence.

Alex also shared news from the U.S. State Department during that visit. They'd issued a statement on March 18, demanding that they be allowed to see me. "We are closely engaged on this case and in frequent contact with Brittney Griner's legal team," the statement read. "We insist the Russian government provide consular access to all U.S. citizen detainees in Russia, including those in pretrial detention, as Brittney Griner is." *U.S. citizen detainees in Russia.* That list included Paul Whelan, serving a sixteen-year sentence on (bogus) espionage charges. And then there was Trevor Reed, the marine veteran slapped with nine years after supposedly assaulting a Moscow cop. I'd seen enough in Russia to raise a brow at any charge, because the Kremlin didn't need a reason to hold Americans. All they needed was their word against ours.

When I heard the State Department's Bureau of Consular Affairs was pushing to send an officer to check on me, I hoped he or she would be allowed in. But Consular Affairs wasn't my ticket home. Its leaders couldn't negotiate for my freedom, Lindz told me. Not their role. For a bargain to be possible, I'd have to be designated "wrongfully detained," based on criteria in the Levinson Hostage-Recovery and Hostage-Taking Accountability Act, which had been signed into law in 2020. By declaring an American "wrongfully detained," the U.S. government asserted that one of its citizens was being unlawfully held as a political prisoner, as a way for a foreign country to meddle in U.S. policy. The secretary of state—in 2022, that was Antony Blinken—made the determination. Only with that designation could my case be kicked over to the Office of the Special Presidential Envoy for Hostage Affairs (SPEHA). SPEHA's leader, Roger Carstens, has the power to negotiate for the release of U.S. citizens. While the Bureau provides valuable services to Americans at home and abroad, it couldn't pressure the Kremlin to send me home. Still, I looked forward to possibly connecting with an American. The last few I'd seen had been on my flight to hell.

Alex left me with letters from my family. I saved them to read on my new bed. Later that evening, after lights out, I pulled out the stack of notes. I felt nervous as I started the first one, from Pier. A couple of weeks earlier, I'd finally given her the go-ahead to tell Mom the full story. "Hey sister," she wrote. "Lordy, I miss yo' tall lanky self, and I hope everyone's treating my baby sis good. Mom and E.J. both now know, and they're doing okay. Mom has obviously done some crying, but she's okay. I'm watching her and taking care of her. When I told E.J., his eyes got watery, but he held it in. He did ask a lot of questions. I felt like I was talking to an adult. But he is really trying to be strong. He gets that that from his Nene."

Mom knows. I'd find out later from Relle that our timing had been perfect: when I gave Pier the go-ahead to tell Mom, she sat her down that same day. The next morning, no lie, the news broke, and my dear Momma handled it well. I'd underestimated her strength and should've known better. Because like millions of Black women before her, she did not flinch in the face of pure hell. "Rest assured, Sis, I'm taking good care of Mom," Pier continued. "I took her with me to Starbucks, and guess what, I got her hooked on my favorite drink, the White Chocolate Peppermint with Mocha. E.J.'s good too. The other day he got dressed for school and came out of his room in your Team USA stuff, looking just like his Nene, tall and skinny. I miss you so much, Sis. I can't wait till you get home. It's gonna be the hug that never ends."

I tried not to wake the other girls with my sniffles, but I'm sure they heard me since they stirred. I read my mom's letter last, mostly because I felt it might undo me. Her note was a short paragraph dated March 7, two days after the story broke. "Hey Ladybug," she wrote. "I love you. I'm crocheting a blanket, a purple one this time. Gonna put a puzzle together soon.

Saying my prayers every day you will be home soon, and we'll make Honey Bun Cake and cookies. I miss you." She signed it simply "Love, Momma."

My mother's note didn't mention my case or even that I was in prison. That told me a lot. First, Momma was still digesting the news, with her feelings stuck in her throat. I knew she'd say more when she could. Also, like Relle and Lindz, she was protecting me, didn't want to write anything that might jeopardize my freedom. The last message came through loud and clear, in spite of her brevity. Momma missed me. Momma mourned for me. Momma forgave me.

9

I PLEAD SANE

W hen did you decide you were gay?" asked the psych doctor, a skinny blonde.

I stared at her, and then at the translator who'd just relayed her question.

"I never *decided*," I snapped. "This is just how I am."

She frowned and gripped her clipboard. "How often do you have sick thoughts?"

"I don't have sick thoughts," I shot back. "There's no *often*."

This was how the "investigation" in my case began in late March—determining if I'd been insane when I left those pens in my luggage or if I'd knowingly broken the law. The process also clearly included having this blond woman shine a light up my butt. What did my being gay have to do with being sane? To her, it seemed plenty.

Me and Blondie sat across from each other in a small room in a hospital psych ward. I'd been driven there that morning. The translator was on my right. Alex and Maria sat nearby. Lawyers weren't usually allowed in these interrogations, Alex told me, but he and Maria had insisted they be present in my case. The investigator-appointed translators I'd been assigned up to then had such poor English that I often couldn't understand what they were saying. Too much was at stake for my answers to get lost in translation. My attorneys won that argument.

The doctor sat forward and crossed her legs. Her whole vibe made her contempt for Americans clear. She glanced down at her clipboard at the next question in a long list.

"When did your drug problem begin?" she asked.

I glanced at Alex. He nodded for me to continue.

I sighed. "I don't have a drug problem," I said.

"Then why were you using cannabis?" she asked.

"Because it helps with my pain," I said. Though cannabis was illegal in Russia, I told her, the United States and many European countries—including Spain, Italy, France, and Germany—acknowledged medical marijuana as a safe, effective, and legal medication for pain relief. She glared at me like I'd just told her the earth was flat.

Two things I'd figured out about Russian officials: First, cannabis was the devil in their eyes. They saw all forms of cannabis—marijuana, hashish, hash oil, edibles, sprays—like they saw crack cocaine. And in their view, cannabis was definitely more criminal than the synthetic drugs popular there. As far as this psych doctor and others were concerned, the vape pens in my bag didn't simply mean I was forgetful. They meant I was a crackhead. In the court of public opinion, those pens made me guilty before a trial date could even be set. And when you factored in my Blackness? Case closed. I'd seen the bias starting with the airport security guards grilling me about my "addiction." The same happened when I arrived at that clinic on the way to county. Even before I could pee in a cup, the doctor was like, "You addict?"

The second thing I know about Russia: being gay is frowned upon. That disapproval often isn't voiced. It's understood. There were lots of lesbians on my Ekat team and in the Euro-League. Most of us were out in our home countries, but we knew to stay quiet about our sexual orientation while balling in Russia. We could feel it. So could the oligarchs who were funding our teams. They realized most of us were gay, but it was never openly discussed. When you were filling seats and earning millions, everyone shut up. I never felt unsafe on the streets, but that was because I didn't advertise my gayness. I knew better. In Russia, you never saw gay people hugging and kissing. Homosexuality was officially legal, but unofficially, it was scorned. And there were no antidiscrimination laws protecting gay people. In detention, rumors swirled about girls messing around with each other in the shower room, the no-camera zone. They weren't sneaking just because intimacy was forbidden. They also knew their relationships would draw disgust.

Not every Russian despises gays and cannabis users. Like America, Russia is a nation of individuals, each with his or her own beliefs. But I encountered these attitudes enough to sense they were widespread. You smoked cannabis, you were a junkie. And if you liked girls, you were a person of low morals headed straight to hell. That was the feeling I got during my psych eval.

When the doctor couldn't get me to admit I was an addict, she moved on to what she really wanted: a confession.

"So are you guilty?" she asked. My eyes widened.

"Are you guilty of your crime?" she repeated loudly and slowly, as if my crazed look meant I was deaf. Alex, realizing I was about to burst, interrupted. "That's it," he said. "My client cannot discuss her guilt or innocence. It goes beyond the scope of this evaluation." I hadn't even entered an official plea in court, and here this woman was trying to trip me into incriminating myself.

The doctor countered with a threat. "If she won't answer," she barked, "I'll have her committed to the psychiatric hospital." She continued pressing, and I gave one-word answers, just enough to show I was cooperating. When the doctor realized she'd gotten as far as she was going to get, the guards escorted me to the square-box truck.

The ordeal wasn't over. Back in detention, Alex and Maria warned me I'd have to return to the hospital to complete the evaluation. "They'll probably try to question you without us there," Alex said. They weren't supposed to interrogate me alone, just like they weren't supposed to ask me if I was guilty. But this was Russia, so all bets were off. When the guards came for me, Alex instructed, I should contact him. "Ask Alena to tell her dad you've been taken, so he can tell me," he said. Alena was allowed one or two calls to her father each week, approved by a judge. Alex had asked if I could have calls home, but we didn't yet have an answer. I wasn't holding my breath. Thankfully, Alena and her dad agreed to help us.

"And what should I do if you and Maria aren't there, and the doctor asks me something I can't answer?" I said to Alex.

"Do your best to get around the question," he said. He paused. "But if you feel like you're in danger," he continued, "just answer. We don't want you in the psych ward."

The psych ward. This psych doctor couldn't herself declare me insane, he said, but she could come up with reasons I should be sent to a Russian mental hospital for a more thorough examination. In detention, I was an inmate awaiting a trial date. In a psych ward, I'd be a prisoner strapped to a table. I'd also be doped up with meds much more potent than cannabis and branded with three labels some Russians found interchangeable: Addict. Crazy. Gay.

....

I've always known I was gay. Long before I'd heard the word *lesbian*, I sensed I was one. My first clue came in kindergarten. I had a huge crush on my teacher, Miss Wagner. The crush itself didn't make me gay. Many people, regardless of sexual orientation, fall in love with their teachers. But my crush was more than admiration. Even at age five I felt drawn to her figure. She was mixed race, maybe Black and Latina, with a nice shape, hips and all.

The clues continued as I grew, and boy, did I grow—everywhere except in the boobs department. When other girls were getting interested in boys, I didn't want no boyfriend. I wanted to *be* a girl's boyfriend. In hindsight, I realize I was a young stud. That plus my height made me an easy target for bullies. Honestly, even as I clapped back at the bullies, I believed something truly was wrong with me. *I can't wait to hit puberty*, I'd think. *Finally, my chest will come in. Finally, my voice won't be so deep. Finally, I'll be normal.* Finally never came.

I didn't talk to my parents about my attraction to girls. I could've spoken to Mom, who has always been cool, but it was just so awkward. If I brought up my feelings, she and my father would want to do a deep dive, which was what I was avoiding. I sensed Pops in particular wouldn't approve, because whenever he'd mentioned gay people, it was in a negative light. And Mom, while she's understanding, comes from a devout Catholic family. Even if she understood, what would my grandparents, aunts, and uncles think? I was worried I'd be shunned.

When I was in fifth grade, Pops and I were in our driveway with his police buddy. Along came a woman, a real estate agent they'd met. She was dressed like a man: baggy pants, big tee, buzz cut. After she passed, Pops said something about her being a dyke. He also frowned. I'd never heard the word *dyke*. This was in the early 2000s, before the Internet blew up. In that moment, I thought, *Well, I'm trying to be like her, so I guess I'm a dyke.* Dad also said she had a "partner." *In business?* I thought. I figured out what he meant when I later spotted that woman kissing another woman. I also concluded I was right: I couldn't talk to Pops about being gay.

Then again, I felt he already knew. When I was near the end of middle school, Pops started making weird statements. "You're always with these girls," he'd say. "I don't know what's going on, but if I find out anything, there's gonna be hell to pay." By "anything," I guess he meant he'd better not discover I was a lesbian, but he never used the word. Still, I understood him. I also understood that Pops was just repeating what he knew, the beliefs he'd been raised with in his small Baptist church in deep-woods Jasper. I didn't have a girlfriend in middle school, but I did once mess around with a girl during that time, nothing serious for either of us. But by eighth grade, and probably before, Dad had caught my vibe. Same with Mom and my siblings. I remember standing in the yard with Carlo when this fine girl walked by. He looked at her. I looked longer. Then in silence we stared at each other. "Uh-huh," he said, laughing. "I see you."

Instead of talking to my family, I lashed out at classmates, got into fistfights constantly. If I saw a bully picking on someone, I was ready to rumble. Later, at home, Pops would whup my tail and then grill me. "Why are you fighting all the time?" he'd ask. I'd sit on the couch with my arms folded and stare at the floor. "What's going on with you?" he'd press. My silence looked like stubbornness, but it was actually pain. I was hurting. Deeply. More than I could make him or anyone else realize, and for reasons that only outcasts understand. When you're born in a body like mine, a part of you dies every day, with every mean comment and lingering stare. You're the biggest person in the room, but you're also the loneliest. That was what it felt like to be me in middle school. That is sometimes what it feels like now.

At night, in the shadows of my bedroom, I'd write short stories. I'd create a random character, usually a kid being picked on, always crying and depressed. The character was me, of course. I was so afraid my parents would find my stories that I'd rip them up into tiny pieces so they couldn't be taped back together. I'd also burn them. I was a legit pyro back then. When my parents weren't around, I'd gather the shreds of paper, take them into the backyard, and light a match to them. I'd then dig a hole and bury my truth, evidence I was a freak.

I came out to Mom first. In ninth grade I decided to talk to her, mostly because I was tired of keeping a secret that really wasn't one. Also, by then many of my classmates knew—or at least had guessed—that I was gay. So were half the girls on my basketball team, and I felt ready to bring the truth home. Mom was lying on her bed when I sidled up to her.

"Ma, I gotta tell you something," I said.

She sat up. "What is it, Britt?" she asked with worry in her voice. "Did you get in another fight?" I didn't answer right away. "Are the cops gonna call?" she asked. "What's going on?"

I laughed. "Nah, it's nothing like that," I said. I cleared my throat. "You know what my basketball team is known for?" I asked.

"I think so," she said. I knew she'd heard the rumors, but I clarified.

"Do you know what the *girls* on the team are known for?" I asked.

She nodded.

"I'm one of them," I said.

Silence.

"Did you hear me?" I finally asked.

"I heard you," she said.

"I'm telling you I like girls," I spelled out.

She smiled. "Okay, and . . . ?"

I studied her face to be sure she'd understood me. "You cool with that?" I asked.

"I love you regardless, Ladybug," she said, hugging me. "I'm always gonna love you." That was all she said then. Years later she told me she'd already known. Her intuition told her.

And just like that I stepped toward freedom, from holding my breath to exhaling. The conversation went so smoothly that I wished I'd told my mother sooner. Mom and I didn't specifically talk about my being gay. It's not like I could ask her or Pops, "Hey, how do I pick up a girl?" But the fact that she knew was a burden lifted, and my shoulders relaxed afterward. I now had a confidante. I was convinced Dad already knew too but had chosen to live in denial. With him I'd have to wait on my freedom, possibly forever. That was how long I thought it might take me to work up the nerve.

Meanwhile, on campus and away from Pops, I leaned into my identity. In eighth grade I'd worn semi-girl clothes like capris and had always dressed like a tomboy. From ninth grade on I went all the way masculine: saggy pants, oversize tees, Evisu, Red Monkey, Girbaud jeans. By then we had a computer. I logged onto Yahoo! and figured out there were lesbians everywhere, and also what they wore. I thought I was cool as hell in my Dickies suit, and I rolled around my 'hood like I owned it. When I was in tenth grade, Pops got me my first car, a Dodge Magnum, silver with a hint of blue, chrome rims. It was *fire*. Dad claimed he bought it for Mom, but that was his way of asserting his manhood. I knew it was for me, and I drove it everywhere, decked out in my Dickies suit. When I pulled onto my street, neighbors could hear me before they saw me, blasting Lil Jon and the East Side Boyz, Limp Bizkit, Papa Roach, Linkin Park. I was Houston to the core. And I loved that Magnum because I could actually fit in it. Finally, I fit someplace.

My first real kiss came around that time, with a classmate who lived near me. I was fifteen or sixteen. She was a couple of years older and also out around campus. I knew she braided hair and asked her to braid mine. At my house one evening when my family was away, she cornrowed my frizz into Iverson braids, fishbone style, named after the ball player Allen Iverson. The whole time I sat on the floor between her legs, I flirted with little dabs: brushing against her legs, touching her toes, giggling the whole time. "You ain't nothing but a little kid," she said, laughing. Next thing I knew we were rolling around on the couch. She led. I learned.

The fun screeched to a halt during my senior year. One afternoon while I was at basketball practice, Mom called. "Your dad knows," she said. A teammate's mother had discovered that her daughter was gay, along with half the team. She was pissed and called my father. "He's furious," Mom told me. "Just be prepared."

A minute later Pops called. I picked up on the first ring. "What are you doing?" he asked, as if he didn't know. "I'm at practice," I said with a quiver in my voice. "When you get done," he said, "you bring your ass straight home." He hung up before I could respond.

I drove home in silence, my heart beating as loudly as the music I usually blared. I thought about driving out of town, escaping. I was on my way to college anyway, had already been accepted at Baylor. In two months I'd be out from under my father's roof. I didn't want to hear whatever he had to say, because I knew it wouldn't be good. Still, I felt I had to face him.

I parked out front and walked up the driveway. Dad was working in the garage. "Something you want to tell me?" he asked.

"Nah," I replied. "Ain't nothing I want to say."

He scowled. "Your teammate's mom called to tell me you're a fucking lesbian," he said.

I stood there like he wasn't talking, totally still but boiling inside.

"I ain't raising no gay bitch!" he shouted. "And ain't no gay bitch coming to this house," he went on. "I'm taking your keys, your phone, everything. Now go upstairs."

I stormed through the front door, slammed it shut, and stomped up to my room. I crashed onto my bed and wept hot tears, with rage coursing through my body. Moments later Dad came in, yelling, cursing, tripping. "Raymond, stop!" Mom pleaded as she tried to back him away. "Go in the other room!" But he kept at me, and we shouted our way downstairs, with me bucking up to Pops for the first time in my life. I love my father. I always will. But in that moment I felt wounded by my hero, deeply hurt by his insults. In the living room we clashed chest to chest, or as close as our chests could get given my height. Dad finally piped down, but the fight wasn't over. In a way, it was just starting.

That night I decided it was time for me to leave. Dad hadn't yet taken my phone, so I called my favorite teacher, Mr. King.

We'd always been cool. He knew I'd been having problems with Pops. He was also friends with Coach King (no relation), the junior varsity coach. She'd taken in a girl on her team who was having similar issues at home. Mr. King told her about my situation, and moments later, she was on the phone. "Come on over," she said. "You don't need to deal with that. You've got enough on your plate with college coming."

The next morning, after Pops left for work, I quietly gathered my things. Mom saw me packing and started crying but didn't try to stop me. She knew I needed to go. I called Carlo, who came by and slipped me some money. Same with my sister SheKera. Pops hadn't yet taken my car, probably because he didn't want to chauffeur me. So I drove myself to school as usual, but that evening I didn't go home. Instead, I parked the Magnum a couple of streets away and left the keys and my phone in the car. Mr. King, who'd followed me, drove me to the coach's place. Late that evening I texted Pops on Mr. King's phone. "You can go get your car," I wrote, telling him where it was parked. "I don't need none of your stuff. Bye."

Pops was livid. Carlo told me so the next day. My dad had assumed that when I moved out, I'd also given up on college. He also thought I'd moved in with a lover. "She's throwing her whole career away for some bitch," Carlo told me he said. Mind you, I never mentioned I was quitting college, nor did I say I'd be boo'd up with a girl. And I definitely had no intention of throwing away my future. I was like, *I'm gay, not a crackhead.* But in Pops's mind back then, and in the minds of so many to this day, being gay somehow makes you emotionally unstable.

After I left home, Pops and I didn't talk for a few weeks. He finally called me on my new phone just before my high school graduation. I missed my hero, which is why I picked up. He didn't say, "I'm sorry." That's not my father's way. The call itself was his apology, and on my end, it was accepted. It wasn't like he could snap his fingers and magically accept me as gay, just like I couldn't immediately brush off his hurtful statements. But the call created an opening for both shifts to happen gradually.

I left home in spring 2009. That June, President Barack Obama signed a memorandum allowing same-sex partners of federal employees to receive some benefits. The next year, the Senate overturned the military's "Don't Ask, Don't Tell" policy. Pops increasingly saw successful gay people on the national stage being celebrated rather than condemned. He went from not acknowledging I was gay to occasionally joking about it. On a trip to Tulsa after I'd signed with the Mercury, Pops and I were at Twin Peaks, a sports bar similar to Hooters. One of my coaches was with us. The waitress started flirting hard with Dad. When she left the table, Pops turned to my coach. "Yeah, she's gonna go for my daughter," he said, laughing. "She ain't going for me."

I'll probably never have a kumbaya moment with Ray Griner, with us hugging it out over my identity. But that old man has come a long way, especially in light of his Baptist upbringing.

Things aren't perfect. He'll sometimes say, "Please don't be out there trying to be the face of this movement. It's for a great cause, baby, but I'm worried about you. You're already Black. You're a target." I don't get offended, because I know he's trying to protect me. That has always been his intention, even when he's being hard-core. I'm proud of Pops, he's proud of me, and we're finally at peace. It took a long time for us to get there, but we're there. And as America has continued changing its attitude toward gay people, so has Pops. Russia is still catching up.

....

My attorneys were right that I'd be dragged back to the psych hospital. When the guards tried to take me, I threw a fit. "*Advocat!*" I shouted, demanding in Russian that they go get my lawyer. I'd just ended a visit with Alex and knew he was still on the premises. When the guards refused to find him, I refused to be cuffed. I paced all over that cell, dodging their attempts to restrain me.

I made such a scene that the guards finally took me to Alex in the visitation area. "I can't go with you this time," he told me. Though the investigator had allowed him and Maria to accompany me on the first visit, the psych hospital administrators pushed back on that for the second one. They insisted I be interviewed on my own, with a translator they claimed spoke better English. That was what they said, but here was what I heard: they could best pressure me into a guilty plea if they questioned me alone. "Just do what you have to do to get out of there safely," Alex reiterated.

The guards escorted me from the square-box truck and into the hospital at Moscow's center. The place was massive, a general hospital with a psych ward attached. As I shuffled down a long hall in cuffs, I spotted a pregnant woman waddling by, an elderly man inching forward on a walker, folks dashing to their appointments while shooting glances at me. At the end of the hall we stopped at the psych ward. Even before the door creaked open, I heard moaning, shouting, spitting, yelping. It was awful.

Inside, the blond woman went back into battle mode. Same questions, just louder. She shouted something in Russian. We both looked at the translator, a short man with thick, black-framed glasses. He paused long enough for me to realize his English was likely *not* better than the last translator's. "She wants to know what day did you get gay," he said choppily.

"I didn't 'get gay,'" I said, using air quotes. "I was born the way I am."

"Are your teammates drug addicts?" she asked.

"No, they're not addicts," I said with an eye roll in my tone. "They're basketball players."

On and on the outrageous questions went, with her interrogating and me sidestepping. During this dance, she slid in the question she'd asked during our first visit. This time, she came on stronger. "Do you understand that you are guilty?" she said, in a statement masquerading as a question. I stared at her blankly. When she posed the question for the second and third times, I honestly wanted to go off on her. But I remembered Alex's warning about the psych ward and heard the moaning around me. The awareness put a clamp on my tongue.

"I understand that I had something I wasn't supposed to have in your country, and I understand that breaks the law," I said matter-of-factly. "But I'm not telling you if I plead guilty or not. That's for me and my lawyers to talk about. Also, if I say I'm guilty, that's gonna help you and the prosecutor, not me." By the look on Blondie's face, the translator had relayed my message cleanly. She stared at me like, *You have a point.*

The interrogation lasted two hours. Later, in detention, I gave Alena the details while she cut me several slices of salami. Olya listened intently but said nothing, probably pissed we weren't offering her food. Partway through our convo, Olya pulled out her diary and started scribbling notes. Alena shot me a look like, *What's she doing?* I had the same question.

As for Alena, she'd been holding her breath all day, fearing I'd be thrown in the psych ward. "So what happens now?" she asked. I told her I'd have to wait for the doctor's conclusion: sane or insane, guilty or not guilty, gay by choice or by birth. I didn't care anymore about Russia's labels. Only one designation mattered.

Around the time of my psych eval, a Consular Affairs officer came through. What a relief to talk to someone on my side. The friendly officer asked how I was doing (*Terrible, but thanks*) and looked around my cell (*Excuse the tobacco smell*). I was grateful for the check-in and also that he promised to stay in touch. Later, at the White House, Ned Price from the U.S. State Department told the world I was doing "as well as can be expected under these very difficult circumstances." True. While the visit did raise my spirits, it did nothing to lift my hopes. I'd been praying I'd be declared wrongfully detained. By late March, I'd heard nothing.

10

SPRING

A lot changed in April, starting with the weather. When I was arrested in February, it was freezing. As winter melted into spring, daytime temps rose from the twenties to the fifties—not warm, but warm enough for me to take off my shirt in the Yard. I didn't care anymore if the guards stared. I'd been humiliated into numbness. It was still gray—Moscow always is—but occasionally the sun peeked through. If you stood in the right spot, you could catch a tan through the bars.

Spring also brought my first ray of hope. On April 27, Trevor Reed walked free. Trevor, a U.S. citizen and marine vet, had been arrested in Moscow in August 2019 while on a trip with his Russian girlfriend. One night he got drunk, the cops were called, and things went sideways. The police arrested Trevor, drove him to jail, and later claimed he'd grabbed the cop's arm while in transit, causing the police to swerve. Never mind that Trevor's girlfriend, Lina—a lawyer who'd been with Trevor that evening and followed the cop car—testified that the vehicle did not swerve. And never mind that the Russian authorities claimed all footage of the incident had somehow been erased. Despite Russia's lack of evidence during the shoddy trial, Trevor was given nine years of the possible ten. The U.S. government declared him wrongfully detained and bargained for his release. Meanwhile, in a forced labor camp, Trevor endured solitary confinement and such horrid conditions that he went on a hunger strike. Nearly three years after his arrest, he was traded for Russian cocaine smuggler Konstantin Yaroshenko. Frail yet elated, Trevor flew home for an emotional reunion with his family.

When Alex gave me the news, I teared up for two reasons. First, I felt happy and relieved for Trevor and his family. Though I didn't personally know Trevor then, I felt like I did. We'd walked a similar path. Only someone who has lived, prayed, cried, and slept in a Russian prison can truly comprehend the daily indignities, the deep isolation that weighs on your spirit. Hearing that Trevor had been freed gave me strength to continue. And second, Trevor's release signaled that a trade was even possible. When Putin invaded Ukraine, the chances of that seemed zero. Russia and America have a long history of prisoner swaps stretching back to the Cold War, but before Trevor's trade, the last exchange had been in 2010. That, plus the war, is why Alex and others doubted a trade would happen. But Trevor's release gave us hope. If the U.S. government designated me wrongfully detained like they had Trevor—and that was still an *if*—a trade could happen. Even with a war raging.

More sunlight followed. When Putin released the footage of me, he also broadcast his plan to manipulate the story. That was when Lindz and Relle, who'd been privately working the back channels, began publicly advocating for my release. That hadn't been the plan. They'd still been searching for a gray zone they could use to quietly get me home. But once Putin picked up his megaphone, they had to respond openly. When the video aired, Lindz scrambled to coordinate statements from the WNBA, NBA, USA Basketball, and Phoenix Mercury. "We are aware of the situation with Brittney Griner in Russia and are in close contact with her, her legal representation in Russia, her family, her teams and the WNBA, and NBA," read Lindsay's statement. Her point: Yes, we know Britt is detained, and we're on it. And PS: Team BG is in lockstep.

That same day, sports journalist Tamryn Spruill posted on change.org. She appealed to the White House for my release. The Women's National Basketball Players Association (WNBPA) would later join that appeal. "We ask that you take action today—doing whatever is necessary—to bring Brittney Griner home swiftly and safely," read the plea. I didn't know it, as I sat cut off from the world in my cell, but that petition went viral, with more than four hundred thousand signatures. As Lindz and Relle stood with these supporters, they also huddled behind the scenes. What was the smartest way to get the attention of the White House and the world? In a word, strategically. Lindsay's statement, along with the petition, marked the start of her and Relle's deliberate noisemaking. From then on, she and the team would slowly and methodically turn up the volume in their efforts to bring me home.

For Relle, being forced to go public was particularly wrenching given how private she is. Relle had been locked in her prayer closet and wanted to stay there. She'd gotten off all social media and tuned out the trolls. But Putin's video release, and her fierce determination to help me, pulled Relle into the public square. While dodging the paparazzi at our Phoenix home, Relle released her first statement on Instagram. "Thank you to everyone who has reached out to me regarding my wife's safe return from Russia," she wrote. "Your prayers and support are greatly appreciated. I love my wife wholeheartedly, so this message comes during one of the weakest moments of my life. I understand that many of you have grown to love BG over the years and have concerns and want details. Please honor our privacy as we continue to work on getting my wife home safely. Thank you!"

All this was happening as Relle was within weeks of graduating from law school. She couldn't sleep. She couldn't eat. She couldn't focus. At a time when she should've been sprinting toward the finish line of a major achievement, she was limping and aching. But my wife held it together because failure wasn't an option. She'd come too far to quit. Two days after that first post, Relle demonstrated her tenacity by getting back on Instagram. "People say 'stay busy,'" she wrote beneath a throwback picture of me with our family and friends. "Yet, there's not a task in this world that could keep any of us from worrying about you. My heart, our hearts, are all skipping beats every day that goes by. I miss your voice. I miss your presence. You're our person! There are no words to express this pain. I'm hurting, we're hurting. We await the day to love on you as a family."

Even with the bright news of the campaign gearing up, doubts lingered. What would be the results of my psych evaluation? The Russians had locked Trevor away in a psychiatric treatment facility for a more thorough psychiatric evaluation. After his return to America, he shared his nightmare with CNN's Jake Tapper. "I was in there with seven other prisoners in a cell," he said. "They all had severe, serious psychological health issues, most of 'em. Over fifty percent of them in that cell were in there for murder, or, like, multiple murders, sexual assault . . . just really disturbed individuals . . . There was blood all over the walls there where prisoners had killed themselves, or killed other prisoners, or attempted to do that. The toilet's just a hole in the floor. And there's crap everywhere, all over the floor, on the walls. There's people in there also that walk around that look like zombies." "You thought they might kill you?" Jake asked him. "Yeah," Trevor said. "I thought that was a possibility." He'd tried to appeal his conviction. He said he believed he was thrown in the psych ward as punishment for pushing back. If I did as he had and bucked the system, I was terrified I'd face the same.

....

When I get scared, I get prayerful. That is Relle's influence. Before I left for Russia, my wife had prayed I'd embrace my faith. That started my shift. Prison took it from there.

Back at county, I'd asked Alex to bring me my Bible. It was at the Ekat apartment my team had leased for me. Alex got it from my team and gave it to the guards for inspection. Two months later, around when Trevor was released, I finally held it. There was a stamp on the blue cover, certifying inspection by the Russian Orthodox Church. Alex told me it had been sent to a priest for review. The second stamp was from the prison warden. Above the gold-embossed words *Holy Bible* sat a tagline: New International Version.

After my little experiment in China, I'd moved on from the King James Version. Too many *thees* and *thous*. This NIV Study Bible was in plain English. There were notes throughout, breaking down how Scripture applies in our times. Also, you could read on one of the three tracks offered. Track 1: Get your feet wet with two weeks of basic passages. Track 2: Spend six months studying the Bible's high points. Track 3: Read every word, alternating daily between the Old and New Testaments, three years total. I chose the third track, a sign of how long I thought I could be locked up.

I didn't do much Bible reading as a kid. Faith was my mother's thing, not mine. In her bedroom I'd see her reading her Bible and praying, grabbing her cross. She taught me to pray the bedtime kiddie prayer "Now I lay me down to sleep, I pray the Lord my soul to keep." I only prayed it if she was standing over me. Pops definitely had faith but didn't seem to pray much. Now, if we were at a funeral or anything official, boy, he could pull out a prayer. But Mom had God on speed dial. She took me to Mass when she could drag me, but mostly I got out of it. I'd stay with Pops doing our usual weekend yardwork. Nothing against church, but I wasn't feeling it. All that kneeling, standing, and bell chiming wasn't for me. Some of my friends were Baptist like Pops. In church they sang old hymns, but sometimes I'd hear them playing Kirk Franklin, the gospel R&B singer. I'd be like, "That's lit." When I heard Kirk's music, I felt something. I know now that was the Spirit.

Before I'd left for Russia, I'd gotten curious again about

faith. I'd see Relle reading her Bible and say, "Yo, so you really believe?" She did with all her heart. Or I'd read a verse and ask, "What does that mean?" I still had my doubts—"How can you just believe without proof?" I'd ask Relle—and her answers made me want to learn more. Also, we'd planned to start a family as soon as that last season in Russia was over. Little did we know. If we were blessed with children, we wanted them to grow up with faith. So a few months before my flight to hell, I'd moved from occasionally questioning Relle about her beliefs to asking her to help me go deeper. She was the one who'd given me the NIV Study Bible. She also introduced me to Maverick City Music, an Atlanta-based group of contemporary gospel singers. The first time I heard "Mercy" on their album *Old Church Basement,* I lost it. Mercy—that was what I now craved.

Once my Bible arrived in detention, I devoured it. On Track 3, you had to read only a chapter a day. I read two or three. I'd start in I Kings and end up in Acts, amazed at Saul becoming Paul on the road to Damascus. Reading the Bible in prison, everything was different. One, I had nothing but time, ticking by more slowly than it ever had. Two, my stakes couldn't have been higher. Freedom gives you the luxury of asking, "Does God exist?" For years I'd been on the fence, but prison knocked me off the ledge. The moment you realize you may never walk free, doubt disappears. Some call that Jailhouse Jesus. I call it sense. And it's the same good sense my foremothers had, navigating swamps in the pitch-black, escaping bondage and heading for the North. They weren't asking God for proof of His existence. Our survival as a people was evidence enough.

In the mornings after cell search and showers, I did my own Bible study. At one point I attended a service led by a priest the warden allowed in who came on random Sundays. Like with everything else in Russia, the rules were subject to change. But we could count on the priest showing up on Easter, which was the first time I went. Now, Easter over there is on a different day than it is in America. That's because the Russian Orthodox

Church follows the old Julian calendar, while Catholics and Protestants go by the Gregorian one. Families typically gather for meals. In detention, we gathered upstairs.

That year Russian Easter fell on April 24, around the time Trevor was traded. Once the guards led me up the stairs, I finally got a look at the second floor. Same layout, same filth. I entered the church room. When I'd heard there was a service, I'd imagined a space big enough for us to sit, read our Bibles, pray. I should've known better. This was a tiny room the size of my cell, with a good twenty inmates standing shoulder to shoulder. Pictures of saints lined the walls, with lighted candles beneath each. The girls were coughing, sneezing, blowing their noses. My first thought was, *Lord, please protect me.* My second was, *Lord, get me up outta here.* The priest was frail and skinny in a dark cloak, standing in the far corner. His sermon was in Russian, and Alena wasn't there to translate. I begged the guards to take me back to my cell. They wouldn't, but they did take me downstairs first when service was over an hour later. Bible study I could handle. A virus, not so much.

After reading several passages each morning, I moved on to other books. I hadn't ever been much of a reader. As a kid I struggled with ADHD and couldn't concentrate long enough to finish a novel. That short attention span followed me into adulthood. I preferred fast media, clips and summaries digestible in under a minute. In detention, however, I fell in love with reading. Prison slowed me down long enough to reflect, jot notes, get lost in other worlds for hours. Alex gave me rocker Keith Richards's memoir, *Life.* I loved every word, so raw. His voice leapt off the page. I also read the *Shadow and Bone* trilogy by Leigh Bardugo. I'd seen the Netflix series and asked Maria to find me the books. Totally riveting. The prison had a library, but almost all the books were in Russian. I pored over the only two available in English: James Patterson's *1st Case,* about an FBI agent on the run, and the thriller *In the Water* by Paula Hawkins. Both were page-turners. I had no appointments to cancel, but if I had, I would've cleared the calendar.

I ended every day the way I began it, by pulling my NIV off the shelf in our shared cabinet. "Whatchya doing?" Alena asked the first time she saw me reach for it. "About to get in the Word," I told her. Alena, who'd grown up Orthodox Russian, nodded her approval as she lit a cig. Regardless of a day's designated reading, I usually started with Psalms. It was so relatable. One of my favorites was Psalms 56:3–4: "When I am afraid, I put my trust in you. In God, whose word I praise—in God I trust and am not afraid. What can mere mortals do to me?"

All through the Bible I read stories of people questioning God even as they pleaded for His help. Being faithful wasn't about having blind faith, I started realizing. It was about bringing your doubts to God, the way a father in Scripture once did. The man's son was sick, so he took him to Jesus for healing. "Everything is possible for one who believes," Jesus told him. The father exclaimed, "I do believe; help me overcome my unbelief!" (Mark 9:23–24, NIV) That statement summed up my journey toward faith. It also became my prayer: *Lord, I believe. Help my unbelief.*

In prison you seemingly had more time than you'd ever had, which made it easy to lose track of it. My Bible and sudoku diary became my calendars, my way of marking time. Even after lights out, I'd often open my Bible and read another passage. For each one I completed, I checked a box. I loved checking those boxes. Before long, my NIV was filled with highlighted passages and notes. After reading I'd pray—silently, so I wouldn't wake the others. You don't have to pray loud for your prayers to be heard. You can *feel* a prayer, mouth it, whisper it. I'd never seen God, but in the dark I sensed His presence.

As I got to know my heavenly Father, I received a letter from my earthly one. Pops wrote soon after I got arrested, and while the notes were loving, they were short. He'd read my tearful February letter, apologizing for failing him. He responded with a full-length letter, his first, dated March 28. I got it in April.

"Hey Britt," he wrote. "I've been wanting to send you a longer letter. Please excuse my writing because I'm talking this to

you so I won't have to type so much. I read your letter and I
don't want you to feel the way you do. You still have a daddy
and always will. I've always been there for you, and I will be
there for you when no one else is. You are still my baby no matter how old you are or how tall you get.

"I pray for you every day, for your health and return home.
Everything will work out. Being you are there, it'll take time.
This war going on don't help. When I see it all over the news
I switch over to a western so I won't lose my mind looking at
it. But I really feel you'll be home soon, I'm looking for it to
be before May. When you get home I have a place we can go
fishing. A friend has a two-story cabin in the woods. It's close
to a creek with plenty of fish. We can fish, talk, and sleep. E.J.
can also go.

"This really hurts that they are holding you over there. The
Lord has His hands on you so don't worry. I ask Him every
day to take care of my baby. Just take care of yourself and do
what they ask of you. I'm glad you got another bed. I hope
you're getting some sleep now. I know you probably get tired
of answering so many letters, but just let me know if you get
this one, even if all you write is, 'I got it.' Remember, I love you
and always will, no matter where you are. Nothing and nobody
can change that. Your dad and mom are with you for life. Please
don't ever forget that. Love you, Dad."

Mom's note had made me cry. With Pops's letter, I bawled.
I know my dad. He wasn't just hurting because of where I
was. He was also hurting because he couldn't do anything about
it. Dads fix things. That's especially true of my Pops, who spent
his career cleaning up messes. If my father had been in better
health, he would've tried to show up in Moscow. Even with no
U.S. flights going in or out, Ray Griner would've found a way.
Big as I am, I'm still his kid, and for once he couldn't save me.
That killed him. And his pain, in turn, hurt me.

I read my father's letter two or three times before tucking it
in my Bible. You can withstand just about any shame so long as
your tribe stands with you.

PART III
·····················

SHOW TRIAL

*The problem with Russia is not corruption per se, or
even Putin per se. Russian government is not corrupt because Vladimir Putin has absolute power.
Russian government has been corrupt, and will
always be as long as* anyone *has absolute power.*

–Robert Zubrin, American aerospace engineer

May 3, 2022

Hey Babe,

Hope you're doing okay! Not good though, because you'd better not ever be good without me lol . . . just kidding, hope you smiled. I miss you badly, especially not hearing your voice for a while. Not going to lie: I found myself wondering whether you still love me and want to be with me. I quickly realized that victimizing myself was unhealthy, so I started a morning meditation routine to help me establish peace in this situation. I first center myself with calming tunes and then worship with gospel music. It helps me find peace throughout the day because I am not whole without you, Babe. You are my person, and this situation has confirmed that for me. I love you so dang much.

Update: Your case was deemed a wrongful detention by the U.S. Department of State. As a result, your case was moved to SPEHA. This is great news because SPEHA focuses on negotiating to bring Americans home. I had a good call with the team assigned to your case. I hope you find peace in hearing that. They asked to visit our house in Phoenix. I felt it would be better if they flew to Houston because the majority of the family lives there and could benefit from their support. I think this visit will be good for your dad. He needs to feel a sense of purpose and value when it comes to helping you. He was very happy when I asked him if the meeting could take place at his house. He was like, "Just tell me when so I can cut the grass." You always say that man doesn't play about that grass, ha ha. Also, your dad, mom, and siblings will feel good knowing they have an open line with State.

One last thing: Our grades were posted today and I made all A's this semester. My GPA is now in the honor category. Thank you for supporting me! I couldn't have gotten through the last few years without you. I love you very much, and send me a smoke signal to let me know you received this letter.

Muah,

Relle

11

WRONGFULLY DETAINED

In late April I started a countdown in my sudoku diary. Two weeks till my third hearing. Alex, Maria, and I were busy preparing for that showdown when the chessboard suddenly shifted. "High level," Lindz wrote. "You've been reclassified as 'wrongfully detained.'" It was stunning. It was game-changing. It was May.

I don't know all the reasons I was tagged "wrongfully detained." One seems obvious: Russia had already held me for nearly eighty days, longer than someone with a pristine record typically would've been held. The miracle isn't *why* I was tagged, but that I was. The designation swung open a door. Like Trevor, I could be traded.

That tag also changed our approach to my third hearing, on May 13. My attorneys were already doing the best job they could in Putin's kangaroo court. After my designation, they decided to majorly push the pace. Why? Because my *only* way home was now through a trade—and a trade would be possible only following a conviction, said Alex and Maria. No way would Putin swap me before one of the judges in his pocket slapped me with a guilty verdict. He needed to show the world he was a political strongman. My job was to smile and nod, hoping that would get me home soonest.

My third hearing went like the previous two—short and pre-determined. After those first hearings I'd been super deflated. I'd hoped there was a slim chance I'd walk free, or at least be granted house arrest. But with this hearing, I honestly didn't even want to show up. I knew I needed to, but I also already knew the outcome. Still, I dragged myself into court wearing my orange hoodie, my head hung low, but not because I felt ashamed. I was legit exhausted, hadn't slept the night before. Alex and Maria presented their arguments passionately. Their intensity changed nothing. "Your next hearing is in mid June," Alex told me. Another extension, another heartbreak. After the hearing, Alex called the judge directly. He asked again if I could get a phone call home. I'd gone eighty-five days without hearing my loved ones' voices. The disconnection was killing me. She'd consider it, she said. We'd have to wait to find out.

Around the time of my hearing, Relle graduated (cum laude, baby!) from North Carolina Central University School of Law, one of six historically Black law schools. For three years I watched my wife work her tail off, admired her smarts and per-severance. I was crushed I couldn't be there. "Missing my wife's graduation sucks so much," I wrote in my sudoku diary. "I let her down." Relle reassured me I hadn't failed her. I wanted to believe her but didn't fully. I had this nagging sense she was pro-tecting my heart, didn't want me to feel worse than she knew I did. That's Relle—emotionally generous. Later, when I read her letter about the day, it made me wish even more I'd been there. "It was a beautiful ceremony and so many loved ones came," Relle wrote. "Dawn Staley [the head coach of South Carolina women's basketball team and our longtime friend] was going to come but one of her players graduated that weekend so she couldn't make it. However, she posted my graduation brochure on her page and made a nice post about you: '#BrittneyGriner has missed a huge milestone in her wife Cherelle's life . . . law school graduation. 79 days is way too long to be wrongfully detained. We won't stop until BG is home! Keep the pressure on!' That was really sweet of her!"

Even while finishing her JD, Relle had thrown herself into Russian law. That was why she knew these hearings were as pointless as my attorneys were powerless in Putin's corrupt courts. Also, Relle was pissed when she read letters from me about the psych eval, how I'd been badgered to admit I was guilty. She did not hide her annoyance. "Why am I reading that BG is being interrogated?" she asked my lawyers on FaceTime. All defendants endured that kind of grilling, they said. It made the trial go "more smoothly." Relle lost it. "More smoothly?" she snapped. "I'd never allow my client to be pressured into a guilty plea. It's *insane!*"

It's ludicrous in America, but those evals are mandatory in Russia. My lawyers didn't even *expect* they could defend me using the same tactics a defense attorney in the United States can employ. The best they could do was minimize my sentence. Up to then, Relle had ridden the wave of hope that I'd be released, but that hope ran dry after this rejection. "Stop wasting time appealing these extensions," she told my attorneys. "They're not letting BG go; they're not giving her house arrest. What my wife needs is a conviction. It's the only way she's coming home." Alex and Maria got her point but still pushed back in court.

When my sister SheKera heard I'd been denied yet again, she sent comfort through the mail. "Have you ever heard that God gives His toughest battles to His strongest soldiers?" she wrote. "Well apparently, you are a tough one. I'm sure it's easier said than done, but you gotta keep ya head up, kiddo. You have a great team working for you, and above all, prayer works. God has a way of putting the right people in our paths just when we need them most. Remember, this process will unfold in HIS timing." God's timing clearly wasn't May.

After the hearing I returned to my cell. Olya met me at the door.

"So what happened?" she asked. "Are you going to be traded?"

"No idea," I said, shrugging. I glanced at Alena, who raised her eyebrows like *What?!*

"Who do you think they'll trade you for?" Olya pressed.

"I don't know," I snapped. "Everything's still up in the air."

The one thing that *was* settled: Olya's nosiness. It was so obvious that me and Alena had talked about it when Olya was away in the visitation area. "What's up with her constant questions?" Alena said. "I *knooow*," I whispered in case she rolled back in. We'd also noticed how interested she seemed whenever Alena and I talked one-on-one, which was pretty much all day. We'd strike up a convo while Olya was supposedly asleep on her bottom bunk. Bottom bunkers got away with daytime napping because the guards couldn't fully see them on camera. Soon as we'd start talking, Olya would sit up and tune in. I'd say something, she'd stare. Alena would reply, and she'd then swivel her neck and gaze at her. Sometimes she'd pull out her diary and start writing as we talked, as she had when I'd returned from my psych eval. *Is this girl taking notes on our conversations?* Alena had the same question, but neither of us knew. I got so suspicious that I said to the room, "I better not ever find my name in nobody's diary." Alena knew I wasn't talking to her. Olya said nothing.

Alena and I debated whether to look through Olya's diary the next time she was out of the cell. We didn't because that was against jail etiquette: you didn't go through people's stuff.

A couple of weeks after my hearing, my left eye started twitching. "What's wrong with your *eye*?" Alena said early one morning. I'd felt it twitching all night but hadn't looked at it. Our cell had one tiny mirror embedded in the wall above the sink. It was so small I could never see my full face. But it was big enough for me to spot the yellow gunk stuck in the corner of my left eye. I gasped when I saw it.

First came the spasms, and then the aching. My eyeball throbbed so badly I developed a migraine. When I gently pulled down my lower lid, the yellow pus didn't roll out. Too thick. But the gunk seemed to be multiplying. By the next day there was double the amount. I complained to a guard. "It's just stress," she said. I thought, *Are you a guard* and *a medical doctor?* I talked to another guard. She also dismissed me. Now, granted, prisoners lied all the time about being sick. It was a way to get out of your cell, and also to possibly get some drugs. But you could look at my inflamed eye and tell I was being truthful. The guards didn't care.

I figured I'd caught a virus, and who wouldn't? That place was teeming with germs. "Could it be pinkeye?" Alena asked. Maybe, except my eye wasn't pink. She also wondered if it was pollen. From May through the end of summer, big pieces of white pollen called Betula fill the air in Russia. It looks like someone has blown a million dandelions. There were heaps of this pollen in the corners of the Yard, piled up like snow. The other girls, who called it *plouf* as slang, were used to it. My eyes weren't.

"I need to see the medic," I said.

"You really don't want to go to the infirmary," Alena warned. While our detention center had just a medical office, some facilities had a full hospital ward. "They'll put you in a bed right next to someone with active TB," she said.

I knew she was right. That was why I'd declined the medical checkups the prison offered. A few weeks after I arrived in detention, for instance, the guards urged me to see the gynecologist. *Nope.* I wasn't about to catch spit, nor was anyone cranking a dirty tool up my privates. Next the guards insisted I go see the dentist, even though they'd been saying how great my smile was. "You see these good teeth?" I said, grinning. "Well, they're fake. They were the first thing I bought as soon as I got money." Before then, my front teeth were crip-walking. That's why I hate my draft-night photo from 2013. When I look at it, all I can see is my crooked smile. I don't even have that picture hanging in my house. It reminds me of how insecure I felt. But now? Sparkly whites. And no way was I letting Russia mess that up. And also: diseases.

"They just need to look," the guards said. They could do that from a distance, I insisted. They agreed and took me for a check, no poking or prodding. Olya went so she could translate. While I was in the dentist's chair, I looked at his utensils. Rusty. Bloodstained. Filthy. If that dentist had tried to reach his hand in my mouth, I would've bitten off his finger. "Your teeth look good," he said as he shined in a light from his old-school headlamp. *I know. I paid for them.*

So when Alena warned me to avoid the medic's office, I nodded. But as my eye got worse and the migraines intensified, I felt I had no choice. To see the doctor I had to write an "application," a short note (in Russian) explaining my condition. Alena wrote mine and gave it to the guard, who then gave it to the warden for review. That process took a week. By the time my visit was approved, my eye was on fire. The guard escorted me down to the doctor's office in the basement. Alena came too.

The medic's "office" looked like an old bunker. I took a spot near ten or so women crammed in there, all standing. One woman, stoic and elderly, had a bandaged leg with blood soaked through her dressing. She told Alena she'd broken it after slipping in the shower. The doctors had inserted metal rods in her bones, but one had come loose and punctured her skin. She'd returned to get it reset. Another woman wiped snot from her nose with her hand, while several more sneezed in unison. "What the hell," I whispered to Alena, whose look said, *I told you so.* The whole scene was disgusting. I hovered in a far corner, praying I wouldn't catch TB. The guard locked us in there and went to fetch more sick inmates. We waited for an hour before the doctor finally showed up.

The medic, a petite woman with short silver hair, yanked down my eyelid and stared at it. "It looks bad" is all she said. She offered no diagnosis, nor did she ask about the progression of my symptoms. She just scribbled a note on her prescription pad, tore it off, and handed it to me. "You need drops," she said. To get them, I'd have to fill out another "application," she told Alena. If the warden approved my request, I could then ask Alex and Maria to fill the prescription at a local pharmacy. No American-brand meds were allowed. The guards had to be able to read all labels to keep out contraband. Several agonizing days later, I finally got drops. That week in the Yard, I found out the "doctor" who'd seen me was actually a veterinarian.

My eye was mercifully on the mend when I got a note from Tanya. Our shower room was also our mailroom. You'd write a note, fold it, and jot the recipient's name on the front. You'd then slide it beneath this Chernobyl-type metal door on the far side of the shower room. We never used that door. But Alena and I peeked in there once, so I knew it led to a drafty area where guards hung items to dry. Under the door was a crack, just big enough for us to slide messages. On shower day, you'd look through the notes to see if you had one. That was how we secretly stayed in touch with girls from other cells.

In the shower that morning I found mine. "How are you?" Tanya wrote. In the Yard, she'd heard about the extension. She'd also heard I'd finally been tagged "wrongfully detained." The whole prison had gotten that news. Even the guards followed my case like it was theirs. "I'm all right," I wrote back. I wasn't, but A) Not enough room to explain why on the four-by-four paper I had with me, and B) I'm not stupid. I knew my note was discoverable, even if the guards hadn't busted our little letter-writing ring. The couple times I left a note for Tanya I didn't use my name or initials. I signed it "42," my jersey number. Tanya knew that was me. The next time I checked, she'd written back: "Keep standing." I was. Barely. On the one hand, I was elated SPEHA was now handling my case. On the other, SPEHA was also overseeing Trevor's and Paul Whelan's cases. Trevor served 985 days. Paul Whelan was arrested in 2018 and was still locked in hell. I feared I'd never make it out.

Back in the States, Relle and Lindz were fine-tuning my campaign. They needed a slogan, a hashtag to inspire millions. "How about #LoveBG?" Lindsay suggested. "It's good, but we need something more," Relle said. "We don't just want people to love BG. We also need them to understand her, to identify with her." Lindz agreed. Soon after, they brainstormed their way to #WeAreBG—a slogan and a rallying cry all in one.

A slogan isn't just a slogan. It frames your story, just like race does mine. "We need to humanize BG," Relle insisted. "A lot of Americans don't really know her." True. I might've been the female LeBron in Russia, but many in my homeland hadn't heard of me until Putin released that footage. And at a moment when Americans were deeply divided over race, some who discovered me for the first time used my case to disparage Black people. Only 4 percent of U.S. sports coverage is devoted to women's sports. Black female athletes get even less airtime. And then there's the issue of how I'm perceived. When most folks look at me, they don't think *vulnerable*. When you're six nine and covered in tats, you're seen as menacing, not in need of protection. That's true of Black people in general. We're viewed as thick-skinned, immune to the aches others feel. It's why a little blond girl is often regarded as soft and innocent, all over the news if there's a kidnapping. Meanwhile, Black children are roughhoused by racist cops.

So my campaign slogan had a couple of big jobs. First, it had to make me visible in a world where Black women are often ignored or demeaned. Second, it had to make me relatable. Yes, I'm Black, gay, a female baller. But when people saw my face and heard my story, we needed them to say, "Hey, she's me"—American first and foremost, and someone with feelings. Humanizing me involved widening the frame to reveal more of my face. I wasn't just an athlete imprisoned overseas. I was also a sister, a daughter, an Aunt Nene, a friend, a person with a heart much bigger than my screwups.

My team made sure that messaging carried over into all

parts of the campaign. When folks protested as a way to keep the spotlight on my case, Lindz encouraged them to use photos of me in my USA uniform, rather than those of me frowning or holding up a fist. Imagery is powerful, often more so than words. Folks won't always read or listen, but they will stop and look. I've represented my country on the world stage, earned two Olympic golds. At every turn, we wanted to remind Americans how I'd made us proud. This wasn't about pretending to be someone I wasn't. It was about ensuring I'd be seen fully.

A freedom campaign has a question at its heart: Who deserves our sympathy? That's what Dr. Danielle Gilbert, a political science professor who has advised the U.S. government on hostage recovery, calls hostage "deservingness." In the view of Americans, not all hostages are created equal. Some easily earn public sympathy, while others are scorned. Dr. Gilbert's research has shown one reason why: When deciding whether a hostage deserves our compassion, we consider that person's characteristics and whether he or she seems to blame for being captured. Those viewed as the most blameless garner the greatest support. But if there's even a hint of culpability, good luck with getting pity. Also, in the eyes of some, my Blackness alone made me guilty.

Thanks to smart positioning by my team, the WNBPA, Vince Kozar, and the Mercury, the #WeAreBG movement caught fire early. On May 6, days after I was tagged wrongfully detained, WNBA players began their season wearing "We Are BG" shirts and then wore them during warm-ups and player introductions for every game. The league put "BG 42" decals on all its courts. When teammates and supporters gave interviews and posted messages, Lindz encouraged them to incorporate a countdown—as in "BG has been detained for eighty days." That message came with a drumbeat: "We urge the White House to do whatever it takes to bring BG home." In media, from CNN and NBC's *Today* to ESPN and CBS, my people raised their voices.

While my friends turned up the volume over the airwaves, Lindz made noise in Washington by pressing Congress to call for my release. She worked with Representative Greg Stanton from Arizona, as well as Representative Sheila Jackson Lee and the Congressional Black Caucus. Both asked President Biden and Vice President Kamala Harris to meet with Relle. A face-to-face would make my case as personal as it was political. Also, the connection might move Biden to quickly cut a deal for my freedom. That was our prayer. Meanwhile, Lindz and Relle kept my name in the administration's view. At a Team USA event held at the White House, my agent distributed orange "We Are BG" pins to high-profile Olympians. She also shipped pins to every WNBA and NBA team. My Phoenix Mercury teammates wore the pins while taking part in the Heart and Sole Shoe Drive—an initiative I launched in 2015. When driving home from practice, I'd pass homeless people without shoes. It broke my heart. In my trunk, I began collecting sneakers I could hand out. That effort grew into distributing collection bins at retailers all over Phoenix. While I was in prison, my teammates continued the kindness.

As the campaign took off, my family met with Ambassador Roger Carstens, the head of SPEHA. In Houston, Relle gathered with my tribe in Pops's living room and leaned in as Roger spoke. He was hopeful he could bring me home but hesitated to put any definitive timeline on it. He was optimistic that our noisemaking would improve my chances. How? Staying visible and rallying support would help the president make a hard decision in a trade.

All of this was one big maybe, for my family and especially for me. With hostage bargaining there are no guarantees, just lumps in the throat and tears. While I sat in prison that spring, so did dozens of U.S. hostages all over the world, from China, Cuba, and Cambodia to Iran, Afghanistan, and Mozambique. In take-back letters, I read the bullet points of my team's amazing efforts, perked up when I heard of Roger's optimism. But

I cried myself to sleep in that cell most nights, with a giant *if* hanging over me. "Relle, I'm looking at the picture you sent 'cause you're heavy on my mind," I wrote one evening. "I'm rubbing your cheeks and wishing I could hold you, even just for a moment. I miss you so much, Baby. Please keep praying I get out. I'm scared I'll never make it home."

12

RUMOR HAS IT

When you've got nothing but time, you talk. And when you talk in prison, you hear frightening stories. There was the one about the detention center where the power went out for three days in deep winter. No light or heat, no generator. No cameras, no one watching, no one to come for help. And because the cameras were off, the inmates could've attacked each other in their cold, dark cells. I don't know if they tried, but the thought scared me. Then there were the forced labor camps, like the one Trevor was sent to. Since everyone in detention was awaiting a sentence, the camps were a big topic.

Even before my detainment, I'd heard about the penal colonies. They're basically leftover gulags, the vast, brutal system of Soviet labor camps started in 1919 that peaked under Joseph Stalin's dictatorship. The conditions were so grueling that more than a million inmates died. Some literally starved to death as they slaved in mines and built railroads in the bitter cold. Others were executed. Those who survived were physically and psychologically tortured. After Stalin's death in 1953, the gulags were disbanded but lived on by another name: the penal colonies. Trevor served his time in one of the more than eight hundred camps scattered across Russia. I was terrified I'd be next.

Alena had heard about two camps in particular and speculated I'd end up in the one closest to Moscow. "They have a lot of foreigners there," she said, "especially ones with money"— not rich, but wealthier than the average Russian. The upside of this camp: Western-style toilets had been installed, replacing the pee-and-squats of the gulag era. The downside: it was strict, which I could've predicted. The closer a prison was to the capital, the more frequently high-up prison officials, lawyers, and human rights organizations showed up to do checks. That was why there'd been so much foot traffic at county. Camps far from Moscow were monitored much less often, which meant anything went.

The second colony Alena said I could be thrown in was one with men *and* women, although in separate buildings. This camp, a couple of hundred miles outside Moscow, was also filled with foreigners. The rules were super lax. "Have you heard about 'The Roads'?" Alena asked. I hadn't. "The inmates rip their bedsheets into long strips, tie one end to their window bars, and swing items to other cells," she said. Using these handmade freeways, the prisoners traded all kinds of contraband: liquor, drugs, cell phones, cig lighters, anything they could tether to a sheet and hurl. The guards didn't care. They probably pulled up a chair and had shots of vodka right along with the prisoners. The drawback of this place: major squalor. The crumbling walls had huge holes. Rats scurried around in broad daylight. Cells were crammed with sometimes ten, fifteen prisoners. That was the rumor.

I didn't know where I'd end up, in a gulag near or far. I prayed I'd be sent home, and if not, then to house arrest. All the talk of labor camps terrified me. It reminded me I was powerless. I had no say in a country where Putin controlled everything.

As my next hearing approached, Relle and Lindz were on the hustle. I know that now. Alex gave me some verbal updates, but my team's letters were *verrry slooow* to get to me, even slower than they'd been at county. The mail had always been censored, but the guards started arbitrarily holding letters longer. Alex would bring in a stack, hand them to the guards, and sometimes they'd hold them a week or more before allowing me to read them. It was torture. It felt like dying of thirst near a creek you could see but not reach.

My outgoing letters got slower too. In the beginning Alex could scan and email my notes to family within a day of receiving them. That changed. I now had to (1) drop my letters in the metal mailbox that all inmates used; (2) await the warden's review, which usually took at least a week; and (3) pray my letters were picked up by local carriers and shipped to Alex, who would then scan and email them to my family. I'll never complain about the pace of the U.S. Postal Service. Some of my letters got lost, or they might've been trashed by the warden. Others arrived a week or two after I wrote them. Even once this new way of sending mail began, it changed constantly. The main guard would give one set of directions. A lower guard would contradict her. Alena would be back and forth between the two, just trying to get our messages out. Finally, there'd be a pistol match between the top wardens about the best rule, at least for that day. There was supposedly a chain of command in detention, but it often wasn't honored. Like Putin's courts, his prisons are chaotic.

So the team's May updates took forever to reach me. My mood was sliding downhill with talk of the trial and the gulag rumors. Also, some on my team thought I'd be freed by summer, and that made me even more antsy to get home. I felt like I was stuck in the fourth quarter, with the game clock permanently on pause. To deal with my nerves I'd been smoking twice as much. I felt so down late one night that I wrote to Relle in the dark, knowing my letter might never reach her. "Hey there, my moon and sun," I wrote. "So today was a rough one. I went to the toilet to smoke a cig and just broke down. I read some old articles of people locked up and getting home two, three, five years later. Ugh. I'm just not in good spirits. I hit the ninety-day mark and feel like I've been here a year." Heaven must've realized I was depressed 'cause a couple of weeks later a stack of letters arrived. I started with Relle's.

My baby was preparing for two big television interviews. The first was an exclusive with Robin Roberts on *Good Morning America*. "Lindz is having Robin come to our home in Phoenix for the interview," she wrote. "I'm nervous, but for you, I'll do anything. TV is your strong suit. My lil' Arkansas behind has never been front and center on anyone's TV! I'm trying to tap into you because you make it look so easy." Lindsay's letter, which I read next, gave me the happy ending. "Relle crushed it on *GMA*," she wrote. The same was true during Relle's heartfelt conversation with ESPN's Angela Rye. Ahead of the taping, Relle and Angela had a moment. She told Relle, 'People need to know you. Your presence, your passion—that's what's going to save BG.'" Relle took those words to heart. "There is one person who can go get [BG], and that's our president," Relle said during the interview. "He has that power . . . We're expecting him to use his power to get it done." That language was intentional. In the weeks since I'd been tagged wrongfully detained, my team had moved from simply asking the White House to act to urging President Biden to call my family. A conversation would not only mean the world to them. It might also keep my case at the center of the president's desk.

Relle gave me other news in list form, from the personal to the OMG. She'd started her bar prep, ten hours a day till the exam in late July. *Go, baby.* She and Lindz had the State Department on speed dial and had started a press strategy text chain. *Amazing.* They'd been in touch with Governor Bill Richardson and Mickey Bergman, the VP of the Richardson Center for Global Engagement—an organization dedicated to the release of U.S. hostages. Relle also caught me up on basketball. "The girl outta Baylor is killing it for Indiana," she wrote of NaLyssa

Smith. "You'll give her the business when you come back!" And PS: My Phoenix Mercury teammates Skylar "Sky" Diggins-Smith and Diana "Dee" Taurasi got heated with each other in a game against Vegas. Breezy (Brianna Turner) and Soph (Sophie Cunningham) thankfully stepped between them.

Vanessa Nygaard, the coach, addressed the dustup. "We're not the first team to have any arguments or disagreements on the bench," she said. "We've seen it throughout the NBA this season and other leagues. The players, they play hard, they play with passion and this is their lives . . . and there's a lot going on. Our team has even more going on with the BG situation, too. That isn't something that goes away for us." My detainment wasn't just killing me. It was also affecting the people I loved. WNBA players united on the hundredth day of my detention, through the WNBPA, the WNBA players' union. "Brittney Griner is our teammate, our friend, and our sister," the statement read in part. "She is a record-breaker, a gold medalist, a wife, a daughter, a champion, a role model, an all-star and so much more. Right now, BG is an American citizen who has been wrongfully detained in Russia for 100 days. That's 144,000 minutes. Anyone who has followed us knows the power of The 144 [the number of players across the WNBA's twelve teams]. We know that speaking up together, as a collective, is game, life, and world-changing . . . Let's show the world the power of our collective voices, and get BG home."

My league. It's crazy how you can devote your life to something and then, just like that, it vanishes. I still cared deeply about basketball. My lungs begged to differ. I knew my smoking was doing big damage, but relaxing my nerves felt like the priority. Also, I was majorly out of shape by that point. I'd gotten thick through the middle, a combo of more weight (hello, salami) and a helluva lot less muscle (no iron-pumping). That spring, my Russian team, UMMC Ekat, donated a basketball to the detention center as a way to get it to me. Some of the girls dribbled while out in the Yard, which was where the guards kept the ball. Every now and then Alena and I would play horse out there, using that five-foot rim with no net. After a few rounds I was out of breath. It occurred to me that I might not ever play again professionally. Before prison, I'd spent hours a day pounding up and down a court, during the season and off. In detention I was too depressed to even do sit-ups in my cell, much less stick to a workout routine.

June began on a good note. First, my next hearing date was finalized for the fourteenth. My paperwork had finally been signed off on. Alex took the paperwork straight to the warden for inspection.

The U.S. Embassy would also arrange to receive a call from me at their offices, Lindz told Alex. It would be my first conversation with Relle in more than one hundred days. We. Could. Not. Wait. "The rule here is that you get five minutes, but we might get fifteen," I wrote to Relle. "It's a win however it goes 'cause I get to hear your voice. When it's set up, please turn on your ringer and *test* it! The call could be early or super late. Let's be ready for anything." I was—or so I thought.

13

ON THE LINE

My call with Relle was a while in the making. First, a date was set. I then had to wait for the next Market so I could buy a phone card. Prisoners paid for their calls. You could make calls only while your group was in the Yard, at whatever time that was. At the start of the break, the guard would yell, "Who needs the phone?" One morning in June, my arm shot up.

I pulled out the required paperwork: the judge's signed consent for the call; the warden's approval of that consent; and my "application"—a handwritten note saying who I was calling and that the U.S. Embassy would patch me through to Relle. I'd have five minutes, maybe fifteen, depending on the mood of the guards. These two glanced at my papers and led me and Olya down a hall. Alena was away at an appointment, so Olya would help me use the phone card.

We walked to a row of phones. Wall-mounted. Black. Side by side with long coil cords. Of the four push buttons, three worked. The guards usually hovered during calls, Alena had told me. This day they left, not sure why. "Give me your stuff," Olya said, snatching my card and the number. She pulled the card close to her face, studied the tiny Russian print on the back, and began dialing. "I don't know if this is right," she said, "but let's see." She pressed the receiver to her ear and wrinkled her face. "It's saying 'This call cannot be connected,'" she said. My heart sank.

Olya dialed again, the second time more slowly, to be sure she had the numbers right. Same error message. I begged her to try again. No luck. Just as Olya was making a fourth attempt, the guards returned. One shouted in Russian. I gripped the phone and looked over at Olya, who translated what I feared she might. "We have to go," she said. "Time's up." I stood there for a moment, staring at the card like *Whaaat?*, confused and crushed. At the guards' insistence I clicked down the receiver, and they escorted us back to our cells. Honestly, I don't recall that walk. My only memory is holding back tears, which poured down my face as I crashed on my bed.

Alex visited a day later. I was still devastated. "What happened?" he asked. Relle had waited around the clock, but her cell never rang, she'd told him. When she reached out to the embassy, she heard I hadn't called. "Bad connection, I guess," I mumbled. Alex promised he'd get the call rescheduled, which he did a week or so later. When the day finally rolled around, I was ready with a new card. This time, Alena came with me.

She dialed as I read off the digits. A moment later her face lit up. "It's going through!" she said, handing me the phone. I pressed the receiver to my ear. *Ring. Ring. Ring.* "What's happening?" Alena asked. More rings. No answer. "Let me try it again," said Alena, who was sacrificing her own call time. She pressed each digit hard and held it. Once she'd dialed the numbers, she gave me the receiver and dashed over to another phone to call her father.

Ring. Ring. Ring . . . click.

When I heard the three rings and then a click, my heart skipped a beat. "Hello?" I said. *Silence.* "Hello, hello, hello?" *Nothing.* "Is that you, Relle?" I repeated but still got no response. Alena glanced over and saw my lips trembling and cut her call short to help me. I hung up and redialed—same thing. With the previous call I'd made four attempts. This time I made eleven. It'd just ring and ring, followed by that click, and then the line would go dead. The guards motioned for us to wrap up as hot tears flooded my face. I never wanted the guards to see me break down. But I couldn't control it. I'd been counting the minutes till I'd hear my baby's voice for the first time in over a hundred days.

Later, Alex gave me the backstory. After my first call didn't go through, the team at the U.S. Embassy had rescheduled for a date when the most direct line was available. That way, I wouldn't lose two or three minutes of a five-minute call waiting to be transferred. But the phone line they'd given me for the call wasn't manned on weekends. My call had been on a Saturday, which the scheduler clearly hadn't realized. In private, the team apologized profusely. In public, they did the same. "We deeply regret that Brittney Griner was unable to speak with her wife because of a logistical error," a State Department spokesperson told ABC News. Their intentions were good. Still, that didn't take away the sting, the disappointment. I'd waited nearly four months to talk to my person, and Relle was understandably angry. This was now twice she'd stayed up 24/7, praying for her cell to ring. "I was distraught. I was hurt. I was done, fed up," she told the Associated Press. "I'm pretty sure I texted [Brittney's] agent and was like: 'I don't want to talk to anybody. It's going to take me a minute to get my emotions together, and just tell everybody I'm unavailable right now.' Because it just knocked me out. I wasn't well, I'm still not well."

While Relle blew off steam in the press, I vented in my sudoku diary. "Worst day ever," I wrote. "I'm away from my wife on our anniversary, and the embassy didn't pick up my call. I'm pissed I let my baby down." It wasn't my fault, but it felt like it was. "Stop blaming yourself for everything," Relle wrote. She knew me well. That was how my folks raised me: take ownership of your choices, the good and bad. Relle understood that, but she also felt my constant apologies in my letters might be used against me—give Russia a way to twist my natural remorse into an advantage for themselves. The punishment I'd already endured was wildly disproportionate with the small mistake I'd made. I saw her point and pulled back on apologizing in my notes to her. But in my heart, I couldn't help but blame myself.

....

My detention was extended until July 2. Same song, third verse: No house arrest. No charges dropped. And by this time, a second major charge had been added.

In the redbrick building on the night of my arrest, Alex had warned me of this. I'd already been charged with violating Article 229.1, part 2 of Russia's criminal code—smuggling a "significant amount" of contraband. The punishment was five to ten years. This second charge involved the illegal possession of drugs. Didn't matter where you got the drugs, how long you'd had them, or if they were just for personal use. The fact that they were in your possession meant you'd broken Russian law. In most cases, it was a two-for-one deal: If you were charged with smuggling narcotics, that meant you were in possession. If I was convicted of this second charge, three years could be tacked onto my sentence (though if they were added, they'd run concurrently with the five to ten). As Alex talked, I stared at him blankly. *The investigators knew I was in possession from day one, so why didn't they just charge me then? Stupid.* The authorities had to come up with something during their "investigation," Alex said. The extra charge made me look more guilty.

Moments later, Alex gave me the best news I'd heard since arriving in hell. "Your trial is likely coming soon," he said. "How do you know?" I asked. You don't know anything for sure in Russia's courts, Alex said. Still, he thought the short extension (one month rather than two, as the last extension had been) signaled we'd soon have a date. I was elated. Because once we had a date, even if it shifted, the fact would remain: Finally, I'd take the stand. Finally, I'd inch closer to a verdict, and then, please God, a trade. A verdict didn't guarantee a swap. Paul Whelan's family had been desperate to bring him home for four years. But once a trial date was set, a trade would move from *hell no* to *perhaps*. Alex and Maria were so sure my trial was close—maybe July—that they began prepping me like it was. The hearing brought a second bright spot: the psych doctor's findings showed me to be sane.

With the strong likelihood that I'd soon stand trial, the campaign cranked up its volume to 10 out of 10. If there was ever a time to make noise, it was in the lead-up to a trial that would change everything for me. In late June, Lindz got loud on X, then known as Twitter. "The fact remains that the U.S. Government has determined that Brittney Griner is wrongfully detained and being used as a political pawn," she wrote. "The negotiation for her immediate release regardless of the legal proceedings should remain a top priority and we expect [President Joe Biden] and [Vice President Kamala Harris] to do everything in their power, right now, to get a deal done to bring her home." Notice the name-checking—an example of more escalation. Also notice the urgency—not *tomorrow*, not *next year*, when my case would have fallen out of the headlines, but *right now*, while I had the world's attention with this trial. Whatever my team could do to stay on the president's radar, they did it in lockstep with SPEHA. Roger Carstens, Fletcher Schoen, and Ken Kosakowski—all SPEHA—talked and texted around the clock with Lindz. During that time, the U.S. House of Representatives raised a unified shout by passing a bipartisan resolution for my immediate release. Representative Greg Stanton of Arizona sponsored the resolution. "Not a day goes by that we aren't thinking of Brittney and working to get her home," he said. "We will continue to push for her release and make sure that she is not forgotten."

That was just the beginning. My team arranged major press interviews, called on anyone who could keep my case in the headlines. When Alex handed me Lindsay's June take-back letter, it was so heavy with bullet points I almost dropped it. "I know from where you are it probably feels like nothing is happening," she wrote. "But I'm in convos every day and there is so much energy pushing toward you. Big focus last week, as we dialed up the volume, was to organize a group of some of the most influential, legacy, civil, and human rights orgs to sign onto a letter (think NAACP, GLAAD, Human Rights Campaign, Al Sharpton's National Action Network, and Jesse Jackson's Rainbow PUSH Coalition). Big lift, big impact. It's one thing to have individual activists talking. It's another level to have powerful organizations advocating for you directly to the White House. My goal is to bring together the LGBTQ, women-focused, and racial justice orgs under one tent to represent your intersectionality."

Goal accomplished. Lindz teamed up with Democratic strategist Karen Finney and others to rally forty-four powerful organizations to sign the letter. Their message: Negotiate for BG's release *now*. Message received, apparently, because when White House officials saw the *New York Times* June 22 article titled "Brittney Griner's Supporters Call on Biden to Strike a Deal to Free Her," they commented. "President Biden has been clear about the need to see all U.S. nationals who are held hostage or wrongfully detained abroad released, including Brittney Griner," a White House official told *The New York Times*. "The U.S. government continues to work aggressively—using every available means—to bring her home."

Relle wasn't so sure that was true. After our fumbled call, and with still no word directly from the president, she'd lost faith in our government. I tried not to do the same. Our distrust wasn't just about this incident. The roots of Black skepticism go back generations in a country that hasn't always had our backs; it was too busy breaking them. Also, if U.S. government officials couldn't even make one call happen, how could we trust them to do all the T-crossing involved in getting me home to America? In hindsight, I understand why the phone call was flubbed. It's a mistake anyone could've made. But in the moment, Relle and I had no clarity. Instead, we had anger, heartache, fear, and regret—and so many troubling question marks.

....

How do you prepare for the most terrifying turning point of your life? With the trial likely coming soon, Alex and Maria began the prep while consulting with Relle, Lindz, and my family. Together, we decided how I'd plead: guilty.

That might surprise some, given that I'd adamantly refused to admit I was guilty during the psych eval. But that resistance was about keeping my next move quiet. My choice to plead guilty was about answering the most important question: What would get me home the quickest? If I pleaded not guilty, I'd basically be calling the Russians liars. So rather than spitting in Putin's face, it seemed smarter to allow him to *save* face. By pleading guilty, I'd be saying, "You're right, Putin—I did it. I didn't intend to break the law, but I did." Putin would then appear to be the strongman, the almighty savior. I believed it was my only chance to get my sentence reduced. In a system with a 99 percent conviction rate, it was virtually certain I'd serve time. How much depended on our trial strategy. Trevor Reed knew that. "I understand in this country that pleading guilty may lead to you having a shorter sentence," he said in a Russian court. "But I think it would be unethical and immoral to plead guilty to a crime that I truly did not commit, and if I'm going to be given a prison sentence, I would rather stay in prison an honest man than walk away tomorrow a liar and a coward." I respect Trevor's choice. I made a different one.

The U.S. government recommended that I plead as Trevor and Paul Whelan did: not guilty. I understood the administration's reasoning. A not-guilty plea would make officials' jobs easier. From their perspective, it'd be simpler to explain why they'd designated me wrongfully detained, because *wrongfully detained* and *not guilty* seem to go hand in hand. From our perspective, not necessarily. You could admit that you were guilty but still argue that your crime was incommensurate with the penalty given, and that the reasons for imposing that punishment were politically motivated. The wrongfully detained tag had to do with the *why* of my imprisonment. SPEHA concluded that Russia purposely used my arrest and severe treatment as a bargaining chip, a way to score political points. Whether I pleaded guilty or not guilty wouldn't change that motivation. But it would somewhat complicate things for U.S. government officials. It'd be more straightforward for them to say, "She's wrongfully detained, in part, because she did not commit the crime she's accused of."

We were grateful for the administration's partnership and advice, but in the end, we went our own way. Especially when your life is on the line, you've gotta think for yourself. "BG doesn't win in Russia's system," Relle told the team. "This system eats her alive because anybody who gets a charge there is guilty. That's why I'm like, 'Okay, she's guilty—now how do we get her back?'" The not-guilty strategy might've turned out to be successful. Though Trevor pleaded not guilty, he still made it home. Hostage negotiation was a game of likelihoods, with more than one route to checkmate. The administration's strategy wasn't right or wrong, certain or uncertain. It was simply a calculation based on the factors in play. And as we evaluated my game board, my team felt that kissing the king's ring was my fastest way to freedom. I'd do anything to get home.

Once we settled on a plea, my attorneys helped me write the statement I'd give during the trial. Not only would Putin and the Kremlin be watching, but millions would tune in to hear what I had to say. For the first time, they'd draw their own conclusions about me based on my words, rather than relying solely on the media's portrayal. For those few minutes, I'd have their full attention to plead my case. To appeal to their compassion. To represent my family, teammates, and community after letting them all down. This was my chance to restore honor, to remove the tarnish on the Griner name. So much was riding on this statement, which was why I spent hours working on it in the dim light of my cell. My attorneys didn't draft any part of the statement for me. They just gave me guidelines for writing it. "Be remorseful," Alex said, "but make sure you're clear that you had no intent to commit a crime." That was super clear to me. Now I just had to make it clear to the world.

As June drew to a close, I'd written and rewritten my statement a dozen times. It's easy to tell the truth. It's tough to do it eloquently. I was working on it one evening when I heard the guards yell the usual "Cell check!" For our searches, the guards always appointed a room captain, one inmate who stayed in the cell during inspection. I guess that was to make sure our items weren't taken or damaged, not that we could've done anything if they had been. I was never chosen as captain. Couldn't speak Russian. On this night, the guards picked Olya, which happened a lot. Five, six nights in a row, they'd skip Alena and choose Olya.

Alena and I filed out to face the wall and put our hands behind our backs while Olya and the guards chatted about God knew what. At one point I heard a snicker. After the inspection, Alena and I returned. Just as I walked in the cell, I spotted Olya slipping one of the guards a folded piece of paper. I stared for a second in disbelief but then quickly looked away so they wouldn't know I'd seen the exchange. Alena noticed it too, but neither of us said anything right then. I just filed it away in my head, in a case folder that now bulged.

I kept the statement I was writing and my anxiety about the trial away from Olya. Everything about her said *spy:* her ears perking up when Alena and I talked, her nose in that diary afterward, the note she slipped to the guard. Clearly she was in cahoots with the staff. I had no clue what she was sharing, and that was what scared me: not knowing what she was whispering about me, and to whom. That was why I said less and less to her. Until the day, weeks later, when I could no longer bite my tongue.

14

HEARING DISORDER

My trial began on July 1—my wife's birthday. That cruel coincidence was yet another reminder of how much my mistake had cost us both. Relle didn't celebrate her milestone. How could she? While she was turning thirty, her person's life was turning upside down. If I'd been with Relle, I would've whisked her off to her favorite cabin in Colorado. Instead of celebrating, we were dreading what came next: seven days of testimony, through July and into August. The proceedings took place at the Khimki courthouse near county.

My world had gone nearly silent by the start of the trial. Most letters from home paused, except for a few short notes from Relle and take-back letters from Lindz. I wanted to give my wife time for intense bar prep. The exam was just weeks away. Also, my attorneys felt it was safest to temporarily halt letters from my family because they didn't want to risk an innocent line pissing off the Russians. We were *this close* to maybe having a trade on the chessboard. Why give the Russians a stupid reason to prolong the process? Strategically, shutting up was smart. Emotionally, it was tough. At the moment when I so needed my family's encouragement, I felt most alone. I was grateful to have my lawyers at my side, and especially Alex, my homie. He and Maria had been with me a few days earlier, on June 27. During a quick court appearance, my charges were read and I was booked for July 1—day 135 of my wrongful detention.

July is Moscow's hottest month, plus it rains a lot. Temps in the eighties don't sound too bad, until you factor in the average humidity—around 75 percent. I grew up in Texas and live in Phoenix, so I'm no crybaby when it comes to sweat. But the first day of the trial was muggy as hell, air so soupy you could swim in it. No A/C in Russia's prisons. None in its courthouses either. When I dressed that morning at county, I pulled on a short-sleeve cotton shirt with guitarist Jimi Hendrix plastered on the front. I chose the tee to keep myself cool and also to shout a prayer. In 1969, Jimi was arrested for drug possession in Toronto. A jury found him not guilty. I felt doomed in Putin's courts, but I still hoped I'd get off.

I waited in the Dungeon. I heard heavy footsteps and stood, felt my shirt stick to my damp back. Two cops appeared, one in blue camo and a beret, another in a navy uniform. Neither spoke. One held up handcuffs and motioned for me to raise my hands. As she tightened the cuffs, I winced as the metal dug into my skin. She then pulled out another set of cuffs, clicked the left side around her own wrist, and locked the right side to the center of my restraint. I'd been cuffed at every hearing up to then, but never like this. As if I was her leashed dog, the guard pulled me up the creaky steps, up another staircase, and down a short flight into the awaiting scene.

Dozens of cameras flashed, blinding me as I entered. In the small lobby, a hundred or more journalists were crowded behind a rope, elbowing, filming, shouting questions. "Are you guilty, Brittney?" one yelled. Other shouts followed, as rapid-fire as the *click-click-click*s of the cameras. "Are you a drug dealer? Why did you smuggle narcotics into Russia? Do you want to say anything to Cherelle?" The scene was so startling, my eyes bugged out. I felt like I'd arrived at the NBA Finals, only this was no celebration. I was in a real-life final, with stakes that couldn't have been higher. I cringed when Relle's name was screamed. *Invasive.* I knew she'd been caught in a media whirlwind, her privacy violently upended. This made the hurricane real. As the taunting continued, I shuffled along with my head down, no choice but to go where I was led.

Alex and Maria met me in the courtroom. "Are you ready?" Alex whispered. *Never.* Maria didn't say much. She just gently placed her palm on my arm. I ducked my way into the courtroom cage, and the guard locked me in. According to the Russian Constitution, defendants were innocent until proven guilty. Those bars told another tale. I already felt like a convict. I realized I also looked like one before I'd ever said a word. I sat on the bench and put down the snack I'd brought, a Russian tea bread called *sushki.* I'd also brought a bottle of water, to help me cope with the heat. The prosecution would present its case in the first two or three hearings, my lawyers had told me. We'd get our say after that.

Through the bars, I glanced around the tiny room, crammed with twenty or so people. Near my cage were boxes of old case files, so close I could've pulled out another prisoner's charges. Alex and Maria sat on a bench by my cage, next to a court-appointed translator. The prosecutor, Nikolay Vlasenko, was on one side of the room, near other officials. On the other side was Elizabeth Rood, then deputy chief of mission at the U.S. Embassy in Moscow. Crowded at the back, on their own bench, was a row of journalists. In an earlier hearing, the judge had said she didn't want any video recording of the proceedings. Maybe Russia was trying to keep its shitshow out of view. My team went along with that. We knew some kind of footage would find its way onto the airwaves regardless of what the judge preferred; the case was too big. We were right. When throngs of reporters arrived only to hear they couldn't enter, they were pissed. So the judge let in four or five. Even those few couldn't film, though a couple of local reporters secretly recorded footage on their phones. The rest sat with digital recorders on their laps.

Judge Anna Sotnikova sat on a platform at the front. She seemed young for a judge, maybe early thirties, with a short black bob and glasses. With the pound of her gavel, she called the proceedings to order. All stood. When I rose, my dreads nearly grazed the cage ceiling. I had to hunch and drop my head just to see the judge. She noticed my posture.

"Defendant Griner, do you have difficulties standing up?" she asked in Russian.

"So I can see you, I have to bend my neck," I replied through the translator. "I promise I won't move. I'll be still." I wanted even my smallest gestures to signal respect.

The prosecutor read off my charges: smuggling in two cartridges containing cannabis oil, with a total of 0.7 grams—considered a "significant amount" in Russian law. "Ms. Griner, do you understand the charges against you?" the judge asked through the translator. "Yes, Your Honor," I said. "Are you ready to plead?" she asked. I wasn't. I'd wait to reveal my plea, which a defendant can do at any point during Russian proceedings. We wanted to keep the prosecutor guessing.

Through the bars, I leaned toward the translator, a man with salt-and-pepper hair and glasses. He gripped a small spiral notebook and nervously tapped his pencil on it. Someone would speak, he'd jot some Russian chicken scratch, and then he'd whisper his translation. I tried to understand him. I mostly couldn't. His English was super broken, even worse than that of the translators I'd survived during the "investigation." Sometimes the judge would say a few words, pause so he could spit out his choppy interpretation, and then continue. But most of the time, she and others rattled on in Russian, with the interpreter relaying sentences that sounded just as foreign. At one point after the judge spoke for ten minutes straight, the translator said, "She's talking about your case"—with no explanation of the details. Alex and Maria couldn't help. Russian law prohibited an attorney from serving as his or her client's translator.

I did catch what the translator said a few minutes into the trial: "First witness here," he said. A guard escorted in a woman. She handed her passport to the clerk, who gave it to the judge.

The prosecutor asked the woman to confirm the name and address in her passport. She did so. She also stated she was a customs screener, the one seated behind the camera the day my bag was loaded on the conveyor belt. "Do you know Defendant Griner, or do have any connection with her that would impact your testimony?" the judge asked. That should've been a simple no. But this woman studied my face as if she was trying to recall if we'd run into each other at a barbecue or someplace. "I do not know her," she finally said.

The prosecutor questioned her about screening my bags. She reiterated what was in her written statement: She'd spotted what looked like two cartridges on her screen and flagged that for the bag searcher. I may not have understood all this woman said, but I definitely recall what she did during my screening. Before my bags rolled all the way through the X-ray, she got up and leaned into the machine. Nothing in her testimony revealed why. The screener was led out, and the second witness entered. It was the airport security officer who'd searched my luggage.

"May I confirm your name and address for the court?" the judge asked. He refused. He couldn't release that information with media in the room, he claimed. His job was "classified," he said, as if he worked at the Kremlin, not customs. "Does the defense have any objections?" the judge asked my team. "Nothing is more important than state secrets," Alex said with an eye roll in his voice. "At your discretion, Your Honor." The judge asked the reporters to file out.

Between February 17 and the day he took the stand, this man had developed amnesia. Regardless of the question, he either said he couldn't recall or referenced his statement.

"When you arrested my client, did you explain her rights?" Alex asked him. "Please see my written statement," the man said over and over. His statement, however, did not answer that question. Alex pointed out that from the moment he and the other customs agent confiscated my passport and ticket and insisted that I wait—and then escorted me to the redbrick building and held me there with the guards at the door—they'd officially detained me. Under Russian law, I should have been told what I was suspected of, informed of my rights, and given access to an attorney within *three hours* of arrest. And then there was the issue of how this agent mishandled my search. I shouldn't have been able to touch my belongings, much less unzip compartments and shake out clothing. "Please refer to my statement" was the only explanation Alex got when he cross-examined him.

Because I understood so little of what the translator was saying, I paid close attention to body language. This customs officer didn't change his tone or expression. He was claiming he couldn't recall much, but his vibe said, "I don't *want* to remember." As he dodged even the simplest questions, some laughed and shook their heads. Even the judge seemed to raise an eyebrow. The main investigator who'd interrogated me and confiscated the cartridges wasn't even in court. He and others had submitted written statements but didn't show. In fact, so many witnesses were absent that court was adjourned early. The no-shows could've been subpoenaed, but that process would take months, Alex said, and that would only prolong my agony.

"Do you have any questions for the witnesses?" the judge asked me. In Russia, defendants are given the right to interview their accusers, but my attorneys had counseled me against it. That might appear defiant when all we wanted was this trial *done*. "No, Your Honor," I said. I'd have my chance to speak later.

The session closed the way it began, with me ducking to clear the top cage bar. "You got through it," Alex said. Elizabeth Rood, the U.S. Embassy diplomat, spoke with me briefly before I was escorted out. "How are you?" she asked. "I'm good," I assured her, but honestly, I was a wreck. Before the hearing, I'd been scared of what I'd experience and frightened about what it would mean for me. After, my fear and anxiety had only intensified.

After the proceedings, Elizabeth Rood gave a statement to the waiting press. "[Brittney] asked me to convey that she is in good spirits and is keeping up the faith," Elizabeth said. I had told her that because I was acting brave, the way Pops taught me to. In truth, I felt weak and afraid. Back in the Dungeon, I smoked five cigs. I used the soot from the last one to smear my reality onto the wall. Day one. Two charges. Full despair.

....

After a long, bumpy ride in the square-box truck the following day, I returned to detention. My next hearing would be July 7. That gave me a lot of time to get more scared, as well as to avoid Olya. "My mom saw you on television," she announced as soon as I walked through the door. She'd just returned from one of her allotted phone calls. I shrugged, pretending not to care, but her comment bothered me as much as her nosiness did. I was already stressed. I didn't need a reminder that my face and accusations were all over the world. One reporter had been so determined to record the proceedings, Alex said, he'd climbed a tree near the courthouse window and begun filming. A guard ordered him down. If there was any upside to the exposure, it was that Relle got to see me for the first time in over four months. She'd later tell me how worried she was when she saw my bugged eyes. I looked as half dead as I felt.

Alena was eager to hear every detail of the day, and I couldn't wait to share. We tried to whisper, but I'm sure Olya heard. "So what happened when you first arrived?" Alena asked. I told her about the media circus. I also mentioned the way I got leashed. "That rarely happens," she said. "You only see that kind of treatment if someone commits a heinous crime."

Alex visited soon after the first hearing, but we didn't really get to debrief. With the trial now the talk of Russia, we knew we'd be more closely monitored. In code, he assured me we'd have our chance to rebut the foolishness we witnessed on day one. "We just need to continue respecting the judge and proceedings," he said. This was how things went in Russia, my attorneys said repeatedly. The name of the game was enduring the charade as a way to minimize the sentence. Alex gave me a take-back letter from Lindz.

On the eve of the trial, the #WeAreBG campaign had continued its intensity. My family and friends gathered for a prayer vigil outside the Russian Consulate in New York. Janell Roy, a childhood friend who had been like family to me since our days growing up in Houston, teared up while speaking to the crowd. "February seventeenth was the last time I talked to my sister," she said with a quiver in her voice. "It hurts."

Relle was at the vigil, even as she supported crusades elsewhere. In Harlem, dozens gathered holding "Free Brittney Griner" posters while shouting, "Say her name," the chant used to raise awareness of Black women brutalized and killed by police. Relle called the organizer, who held her cell to the mic. "I just want to say thank you from the bottom of my heart for saying my wife's name," she told the crowd. "No justice for any of us if there's no justice for BG." And also no sleep for Relle. Throughout July she'd juggle long study days with marches and interviews and the press push planned for WNBA All-Star weekend.

I was grateful for all the energy around #WeAreBG but couldn't help wondering: *How many people are really hearing us?* Stories come and go fast in our TikTok world. I feared I'd be glanced at but forgotten. "If it was LeBron, he'd be home, right?" said then Phoenix Mercury coach Vanessa Nygaard, about the attention my case wasn't getting. "It's a statement about the value of women. It's a statement about the value of a Black person. It's a statement about the value of a gay person. All of those things. We know it, and so that's what hurts a little more."

After day one of my hearing, I decided to write a letter to President Biden, to be sent on the Fourth of July. While America celebrated its independence, I'd plead for mine. White House officials kept saying how much of a priority my case was, but in my humid cell on the other side of the world, it didn't feel that way. How do you address the leader of the free world, the one person with the power to bargain for your freedom? I jotted notes, tried to sound official. In the end I just poured out my heart:

Dear President Biden,

I wish we could have met when Team USA visited the White House recently. One hundred thirty-seven days later, as I sit here in a Russian prison alone with my thoughts and without the protection of my wife, family, and friends, I'm terrified I might be here forever. I had no idea that February 17 would be the last day I would be able to hear the voices of the people I love most. I spend a lot of time trying to remember what their voices sound like. The limited letters I am able to receive allow me to hold onto hope. But truthfully, I fear I'll never see my family again.

On the Fourth of July, our family normally honors the service of those who fought for our freedom, including my father, who is a Vietnam War veteran. While my service looks different from my dad's, I'm proud of what I've been able to do with my freedom, for the people in our country and globally through the game of basketball. Freedom this year would mean simply being able to say hi to my loved ones. Freedom this year would be playing the sport I love. Freedom this year would be delivering food I cooked with my wife to people in Phoenix who need a little help. I have to believe in that freedom, especially the freedom to see the faces and hear the voices of my family again or I'll be nothing inside.

I realize you are dealing with so much, but please don't forget about me and the other American detainees. Please do all you can to bring us home. I still have so much good to do with my freedom that you can help restore. I miss my wife. I miss my family. I miss my teammates. It kills me to know they are suffering so much right now. I am grateful for whatever you can do at this moment to get me home.

Sincerely,

Brittney "BG" Griner

The ink on my draft was still wet when Alex rushed to pick it up from me on July 4. He sent it to Lindz, who emailed it to Ron Klain, then chief of staff to President Biden. Ron confirmed he'd received the letter and would get it to the president. Excerpts of my letter were then released to the press. The next day, Relle did an emotional interview with Gayle King on *CBS Mornings.* Gayle asked her about the most vulnerable line in my letter: "I fear I'll never see my family again."

"[BG] is probably the strongest person that I know, so she doesn't say words like that lightly," my wife told Gayle. "That means she truly is terrified that she may never see us again. I share those same sentiments."

"Have you heard from the White House since the letter was delivered to President Biden?" Gayle asked.

"I still have not heard from him," she said, "and honestly, it's very disheartening."

From Relle's lips to God's ears, and also to the president's. At 4:00 a.m. Phoenix time on July 6, my wife awakened to a string of missed calls from a blocked number. The commander in chief was urgently trying to reach her, Lindz texted her. Relle was still in bed when the president called again soon after.

"This is President Joe Biden," he said. "It's good to finally talk with you." He expressed sincere regret about my situation and assured Relle that getting me and other American hostages home was his priority. He also understood her grief, he said. He'd lost his son Beau to brain cancer and his first wife and daughter in a car crash years earlier. He finally got to what Relle was listening for: trade talks with Russia. "I'll be honest with you," he said. "We're attempting to negotiate with the Russians, but they're not responding." If he could've had me back yesterday, he told Relle, he would've. "How do we get them talking?" Relle asked. She wanted to work in conjunction with the president, rather than using her platform to pressure him. "You're a great advocate for BG," he said. "I'm never going to tell you not to make noise for your person. You're doing amazing, kiddo. Just be mindful that I'm not the only one who hears what you're saying in the press." Pressuring President Biden in public would play into Russia's hands, he explained. Putin, who thrived on conflict, could then use anti-Biden rhetoric to his advantage. Understood.

That same day President Biden wrote me back. Elizabeth Rood, the U.S. Embassy diplomat, delivered a copy of the letter, which had a White House seal up top. "Dear Brittney," the president wrote.

> *I was deeply moved by your letter, and I want to personally assure you that you are not forgotten by your country, not by your government, and not by me. You are courageous, a role model for so many Americans, and deeply missed. I am going to continue to do everything that I can to get you home as soon as possible.*
>
> *I cannot imagine how challenging the last five months have been for you and your loved ones. You are being wrongfully detained under intolerable circumstances, and my heart goes out to you and to the other Americans who are wrongfully detained or held hostage around the world.*
>
> *As President, I have directed my Administration to pursue every avenue to bring you home safely to your wife, your friends and loved ones, and your teammates as soon as possible. Getting you home is top of mind for all of us, and I receive daily updates about the status of our efforts to bring you home.*
>
> *We have been conducting, and remain engaged in, serious discussions with the Russian government. In June, we put a significant offer in front of the Russian government in an effort to bring you home. I will be candid: the talks are challenging, as our relations with Russia are at a low point due to the war in Ukraine and other tensions.*
>
> *I spoke with your wife, Cherelle, today. My National Security Advisor has been keeping her updated on the status of the talks. As he told her, we are pursuing your release through multiple channels, including directly with the Kremlin. My Secretary of State has also spoken with Cherelle multiple times, as have*

other senior officials, including the Special Presidential Envoy for
Hostage Affairs, to communicate to Cherelle the most up-to-date
information we have. We will continue to stay in close contact
with her in the days ahead.

I know all this may feel like cold comfort while you continue to
be held unjustly, losing months of your life and precious time with
your loved ones. But know my Administration will not rest—I will
not rest—until we bring you home safely, along with Paul Whelan,
and the others held hostage or wrongfully detained in Russia and
elsewhere abroad.

Sincerely,

Joe Biden

That letter gave me hope. For the first time there was mention of a trade.

15

TESTED

Day two of the trial went like the first. It ended with my finally speaking.

The prosecutor called to the stand the woman who'd urged me to sign a document I couldn't read. This lady had never served as an interpreter in any legal proceedings, she said, yet she claimed she'd translated the paper she pressed me to sign. Her English was so bad she referred to me as "citizen Greener." Just as laughable was the testimony of another witness that day, an airport employee who'd been directed by the customs agents to find this "translator."

"Do you remember asking an interpreter to translate the rights of a person subject to inspection?" the prosecutor asked her.

"Yes," she said.

"Do you remember if U.S. citizen Griner asked if she was accused of something?"

"I do not understand English," she said.

"There was a translator," he said. "You must have heard the Russian version."

"I don't know English," she repeated, "so I can't tell you." She admitted that she and the "translator" did not even witness the seizure of the cartridges and were told by the customs agents that they were found on me.

Near the close of the session I stood and gripped the cage bars. Several people craned their necks to stare back at me. "I would like to plead guilty on the charges against me, Your Honor," I said. The judge raised her eyebrows slightly. The reporters fidgeted while adjusting their recorders.

"But I had no intention of breaking any Russian law," I said with a shaky voice. "I was in a rush packing, and the cartridges accidentally ended up in my bags."

I'd known going into that hearing that I'd officially submit my plea. My attorneys had debated when I should plead and decided that early in the trial was best. I agreed. If we saved the plea until the end, Russia would likely assume I'd plead *not* guilty, as many wrongfully detained Americans did. That assumption might piss off Putin and ultimately lengthen my sentence.

Moments after I gave my plea, I was escorted from the courtroom, past the rabid press, this time with *Crenshaw* on my red tee. It was a nod to rapper Nipsey Hussle and the South L.A. 'hood his logo celebrated. When Rodney King was savagely beaten by Los Angeles cops in 1992, rioters stormed Crenshaw Boulevard in protest. If I had to endure the press invasion, I might as well tell a story, hint at the larger one I was part of. Same thing with the photos I showed from my cage. At each hearing, I held up pictures Alex had printed out for me. One was of Relle in my 42 jersey. Others were of friends and teammates.

Afterward, my attorneys spoke to the press about my choice to plead guilty. Maria said she hoped the judge would consider the nature of the case, "the insignificant amount of the substance," and my "personality and history of positive contributions to global and Russian sport." Following those comments, my attorneys released a statement. "Brittney sets an example of being brave," Alex and Maria wrote. "She decided to take full responsibility for her actions as she knows that she is a role model for many people . . . The defense hopes that the plea will be considered by the court as a mitigating factor and there will be no severe sentence."

Back in detention, Alex visited with news. On the day of the second hearing, Russian deputy foreign minister Sergei Ryabkov commented about the U.S. government's push for a prisoner swap. "The American side's attempts to foment hype and make noise in the public environment are understandable, but they don't help to practically resolve issues," Ryabkov said. "Clearly the necessary judicial procedures have not been completed. Until then, there is no nominal, formal, procedural basis for any further steps at all." He called our noisemaking "hype." I called it hope. Yes, the foreign minister had appeared to slam the door on America's efforts, but in reality he had left it open a crack. He suggested the Russians might be willing to talk after a verdict, since "we have a long-established form for discussing these matters." The longer this trial dragged on, the greater the delay in bargaining.

Also negotiating for my release behind the scenes: Bill Richardson. "Governor Richardson is pushing the U.S. government," Lindz wrote in a take-back letter, "and it's a competition on who can get you home first. That's good for you. We will keep stoking the flame. We are getting a lot of back-channel information from inside the White House that the pressure is working." My team decided early we'd accept all help, however it came. From the White House. From Bill Richardson. From heaven. "I'll say this because you know I can't say more: There is progress," Lindz reassured me. "We are getting closer. Hang in there."

....

My Ekat teammates took the stand during the July 14 hearing. Max Ryabkov, our team's GM, spoke first. He told the court he'd recruited me and called me "unique." "There was no one close to her level," he said, "and thanks to Brittney, we won." Those wins fueled Russia's rise in the EuroLeague and expanded the sport in the country, he said. Evegeniya "Jenya" Belyakova, a former WNBA player and then our team's captain, heaped on more praise. "She's the heart of our team," Jenya said. "The fans adored her. Everywhere we'd go, kids would surround her, and Brittney enjoyed it." Anatoly Kalabin, our team doctor, noted that an athlete of my caliber was drug tested repeatedly. "In all the years I've worked with her," he said, "she never failed a test."

Up to then I'd sat expressionless. I never wanted to make a scene. But when Max and the others spoke, I cried my ass off. That team was my family. We trained together, won and lost together, shared meals and memories on and off the court. Their testimonies were super emotional for me. The whole thing was surreal, like attending your own memorial service and hearing your loved ones say all that you've meant to them.

My teammates attested to my character. The next day, my attorneys made the case for my cannabis use. "The attending physician gave Brittney recommendations for the use of medical cannabis," Maria told the court. She submitted the doctor's letter authorizing cannabis to treat the severe chronic pain caused by my sports injuries. She told the court I'd once been in a wheelchair. "The permission was issued on behalf of the Arizona Department of Health." My team also submitted the results of my drug tests. In both Russia and America, I'd passed every test ever given. "We are not arguing that Brittney took [cannabis] here as a medicine," Alex said. "We are still saying that she involuntarily brought it here because she was in a rush. The Russian public has to know, and the Russian court in the first place has to know, that it was not used for recreational purposes in the United States. It was prescribed by a doctor."

I wasn't the only one in the hot seat. The crammed courtroom was so sweltering on July 26 that everyone seemed uncomfortable. The humidity was a steamy 93 percent. Alex wiped sweat from his face with his handkerchief. Maria's blouse was stuck to her back. Several minutes into the proceedings I heard a thud. A U.S. Embassy official had collapsed a few feet from my cage. I honestly thought he'd been poisoned. I knew it was hot, but it seemed suspicious that in a room mostly filled with Russians, an American passed out. I later learned that as the man was leaving the courtroom to get water, he fainted from heat exhaustion. The judge called for medical assistance. After a break, a narcologist testified that medical cannabis is a popular treatment among athletes in some countries, including America. That concluded the fifth hearing.

On July 27, I finally took the stand. Alex was so concerned about my words being relayed accurately that he insisted that he bring in his own translator. The judge agreed. The translator, a friend of Alex's, was this fit, young guy in a suit. His English was worlds better than the last translator's. In court, my team also asked if I could leave my cage to testify. The optics of me already behind bars favored the prosecution, we argued. The judge said no, explaining that it was too dangerous. *Dangerous?* I've spent my life sensing others tense up in my presence. My height, my wingspan, and my color have always been seen as a threat. It didn't matter that I had no record.

I was more nervous than I thought I'd be, and when I get scared, I get stone-faced. Maria questioned me gently, guiding me through the events leading up to February 17.

"So why did you decide to return to Russia?" she asked about my Covid recovery. "Was it impossible to take at least another week to rest?"

"It's the most important part of the season after the break," I said. "It's playoffs. The whole season my team has worked hard to get to a good position. There was nothing that was gonna change that for me. I'm coming back."

"Which team are you talking about?"

"Ekaterinburg UMMC," I said. "Best team in Russia."

I recounted all I'd experienced after entering security: The dog that sniffed my luggage. How I'd been singled out in a line of passengers, despite the fact that the dog didn't indicate anything suspicious in my bags. The agent who stood by as I searched my roller, and the other agent who seized my passport and presented me with that document I couldn't read.

"I tried to use Google Translate," I said. "There was a lady there they said was an interpreter. But it was more just her telling me, 'Surname, sign.' She didn't explain the contents of the paper. I didn't know exactly what I was signing."

"Did this woman translate your rights to you, if they were voiced by a customs officer?" Maria asked.

"My rights were never read to me," I said. "No one explained any of it to me."

The same was true of an interpreter assigned to my case during the "investigation." While I was in detention, this interpreter showed up with the investigator, there to question me before trial. "I remember one time there was a stack of papers that [the translator] needed to translate for me," I told the court. "He took a brief look and then said the exact words were, 'Basically, you're guilty.'"

When Maria finished questioning me, the prosecutor took his turn. He stood, wiped his forehead, and met my eyes.

"Defendant Griner, do you admit to the crime you've been accused of?" he asked.

I glanced at the floor and then squarely at him. "As [the cartridges] ended up in my bags by accident," I said, "I take responsibility. But I did not intend to smuggle or plan to smuggle cannabis to Russia."

"But you understand that you broke the law," he went on.

Yes, but mistakenly, I said. "My career is my whole life," I told the court as I fought back tears. "I dedicated everything— time, my body, time away from my family. I spent six months out of the year away from everybody, and with a huge time difference." I'd always followed the rules, I said. My livelihood depended on it. "I was in a huge hurry," I continued. "I waited until the last minute because the whole time I was at home I was trying to recover from Covid. And there was just the stress and wear and tear of the season, plus the long flight, being jet-lagged."

The prosecutor paused and looked at the judge. "The question was a little different," he said. "Does she admit guilt?"

The judge asked me to address the question. "I understand my charges," I reiterated. "I do plead guilty because of the actions that have happened, but again, I did not intend to bring any prohibited substance into Russia."

No matter what I said, the prosecutor returned to his accusation that I knowingly smuggled drugs into Russia. On and on this went, with my team objecting, and with me sitting sullen in that cage. No need to badger the witness, Alex argued. I'd made my point clearly: I had no intent to break the law.

Intent. So much of my case came down to that word, six little letters, plain but powerful—but almost impossible to prove.

....

While I endured a couple of tough hearings, Relle faced a big test at home. On July 26, she began her intense two-day bar exam. From my cage, I sent love across the miles. "Do you want to say something to Cherelle?" a journalist asked me. "Good luck on the bar exam," I replied.

I made it back to detention at the start of a weekend. That meant we could watch what we wanted on TV. Good thing, 'cause I had no interest in talking. "How'd it go?" Alena asked. I shrugged, which she knew meant *horrible*. That evening I escaped into *Magnificent Century*, a Turkish series I'd gotten hooked on. It was based on the life of an Ottoman sultan, complete with backstabbing, cheating, and the sultan's wives all trying to kill each other. It became my new *Grey's Anatomy*, and bless Alena for translating every line for ninety minutes each weekend. Then again, it gave her something to do in a place where we had nothing but time and regret. "What do you think happened at the end?" she'd ask after we'd flipped it off. We could only guess. Lights out came before the final credits.

With my family's letters on hold during the trial, I pulled out ones I'd saved. "I'm doing all right," my mother wrote. "E.J.'s keeping me going. He's a sweetie. He sometimes walks me to my bedroom with his arm around me. Your grandma and Pa are watching over us from heaven. They're our angels. I love you to the stars and back. Hugs, Momma." I heard from Pops too, with basketball scores and blessings. "Laying across the bed at 4 a.m.," he wrote. "Haven't been to sleep, just listening to gospel music. I spend many nights like this. It'll get better when you're released. My faith in the Lord tells me you'll be home soon."

My favorite letter was from Relle. She'd written to me just before the trial. "As much as I want to scream because your return isn't happening on my timeline, I'm allowing God's will to be supreme over mine," she wrote. "Read Daniel 3:7–24. It's the story of Shadrach, Meshach, and Abednego, three Hebrews thrown into a fiery furnace because of their faithfulness to God. King Nebuchadnezzar came to witness their execution and was stunned to see a fourth man in the fire—the Son of God. That is our situation. We find ourselves in a furnace, our lives melting away. But Jesus is right here with us. He'll rescue us from the flames."

Lindz sent me campaign updates, along with personal love. Reverend Al Sharpton had teamed up with Relle, Sue Bird, and Nneka Ogwumike, the president of the Women's National Basketball Players Association, in calling for leniency in the verdict. The actress Kerry Washington wore a "We Are BG" shirt while guest-hosting *Jimmy Kimmel Live!* At the ESPYs, Nneka, Steph Curry, and Sky Diggins-Smith gave me a shout-out. "We urge the entire global sports community to continue to stay energized on [Brittney's] behalf, because Brittney isn't just on the Phoenix Mercury. She isn't just a member of her team in Russia. She isn't just an Olympian. She's one of us," Curry said during the broadcast. My WNBA teammates shined a light on the case by wearing jerseys with 42 on their backs at the All-Star Game in Chicago. Then *New York Times* columnist

Roxane Gay came to my defense in a piece titled "Brittney Griner Is Trapped and Alone. Where's Your Outrage?" "We are B.G.," Gay wrote. "We need to repeat that mantra until there is enough of a groundswell to bring her home. We are not free until all of us are free."

My mood shifted with every update, from elation at the headway to fear that "We're close" meant I should brace for devastation. While much of the news was delivered in letters, some was shared by Alex in quick convos during the trial. "LeBron James tweeted his support," he said after a session. *Amazing.* As appreciative as I was for all the good news, I couldn't truly take it in after hours of gut-wrenching testimony. I shifted constantly between gratitude and grief, hope and despair, three men consumed by flames and God showing up to save them.

16

NINE DEATHS

The prosecution's least credible witness came last. On August 2, it called the state forensic chemist who'd examined the cartridges taken from my luggage. This guy looked like a legit crackhead. His clothes were disheveled, his eyes glazed. "Do you have a record of the serial numbers of the instruments used to test the cartridges?" Alex asked him. "No," he mumbled. Also, the chemist's report did not include results of the second cartridge's examination. When Alex asked him why the second report was missing, he said it was because the department was short on paper—budget cuts. Alex's cross-examination of him revealed that he hadn't even heated the substance to the right temperature, which impacted the amount measured. So instead of the 0.7 total grams of cannabis oil the authorities claimed I had, it might've been 0.5 or less—which would have lowered my maximum sentence to five years rather than ten. Because this man half-assed his job, my full ass was on the line.

My team brought in Dmitry Gladyshev, a forensics expert who challenged the chemist's findings. He'd been in the field for decades and majorly outranked this young man. Dmitry analyzed a sample of what the customs agents seized from my luggage. Our expert's conclusion was as clear as the previous testing was flawed. "The examination does not comply with the law in terms of the completeness of the study and does not comply with the norms of the Code of Criminal Procedure," he told the court. The judge appeared unmoved.

Closing arguments and sentencing were set for August 4. With the verdict near, my friends took to social media. "Brittney Griner won 7 Russian Championships and 4 EuroLeague titles while playing for UMMC," my Ekat teammate Courtney Vandersloot wrote on Instagram. "We returned year after year and considered it a second home . . . I ask out of respect for the sanctity of sport, that Russia will have mercy and show compassion to BG as her trial ends." In an interview with Reuters, Las Vegas Aces head coach Becky Hammon—a former Russian national team star—pleaded for my release. "The time that she's served over there, enough's enough," she said. "I just ask the Russian government to do the right thing. It's never too late to do the right thing . . . it's time to send her home." Dee Taurasi and Breanna Stewart, two of my WNBA teammates, posted videos in which they asked for leniency.

I couldn't sleep the night before the verdict. I lay in my bed at county, staring up at the ceiling and wondering how my life would change. Alex and Maria came to county super early that morning, ahead of the midday proceedings. I rehearsed my statement for them. I'd mostly memorized it, didn't want to stand before the world while staring down at a paper. I still carried my notes, with my key points neatly handwritten. "Make sure you're clear that you had no intent to break the law," Maria reminded me. "And show remorse," Alex added. I wanted to present it perfectly, make my family and country proud. We've all seen the footage of someone getting arrested and acting a plumb fool. I was determined to be dignified. And though I doubted my statement would make a difference, I prayed it would.

The guards led me down to the Dungeon. Every cell was full on both the men's and women's sides. That made it smokier than usual, so much so that I almost passed out when I entered. The thick smoke matched my tee, a dark gray signaling how I felt. In the cell, I sat near a young Russian girl who was sniffling. We met eyes. I could see she was struggling emotionally and also that she had no food. I offered her candy and cigs, paid forward the kindness an inmate once showed me. I'd brought extra snacks anyway, knowing the day would be emotional. When the guards came to get me, I left a four-pack of Oreos on my chair. Many inmates left their food in the Dungeon, and we never touched each other's stuff. However sentencing went, I'd at least have my cookies.

The guards cuffed me and dragged me past the media. On day one, the press had been wild. On this day, it was outrageous. Reporters spilled over the roped-off area and shouted questions that sent shivers through me. "Brittney, how many years will you be sentenced?" someone yelled. "What labor camp will you be sent to?" I stared down at the floor and kept walking, not that I had a choice. During this final hearing, the judge allowed more reporters into the courtroom, including a few members of the American press. She also gave them permission to video record. I preferred it that way. I wanted the world to see me speaking, not just hear or read what I'd say. The judge pounded her gavel and called the hearing to order.

I stood. "Your Honor and other participants of the court," I began with a frog in my throat, "I grew up in a normal household in Houston, Texas, with my siblings and my mom and my dad." I paused to allow time for the translation, which gave me a moment to steady my voice. "My mom stayed at home and took care of me and my sister," I continued. "And my dad, he went to work and provided for our family. My parents taught me two important things. One, to take ownership for your responsibilities. And two, to work hard for everything that you have. That's why I pled guilty to my charges. I understand the charges that are against me . . . but I had no intent to break any Russian law.

I want the court to understand that it was an honest mistake that I made while rushing and in stress, trying to recover from post-Covid and just trying to get back to my team."

I clutched the bars. "The hard work that my parents instilled in me is what brought me to play for the best EuroLeague and Russian team here, UMMC. I had no idea that the team, the city, the fans, and my teammates would make such a great impression on me over the six and a half years that I've spent here, in Ekat. It became my second home, with my friends, my teammates, and my fans that I'd always interact with. I remember vividly coming out of the gym and all the little girls that were in the stands waiting on me. That's what kept making me come back here.

"I want to apologize to my teammates, my club, the fans, and the city of Ekat for my mistake that I made and the embarrassment that I brought onto them," I said as my eyes welled up. "I want to also apologize to my parents, my siblings, my own Phoenix Mercury organization back at home, the amazing women of the WNBA, and my amazing spouse. I've never meant to hurt anybody. I've never meant to put in jeopardy the Russian population. I've never meant to break any laws here." I stopped and looked directly at the judge. "I made an honest mistake," I continued, "and I hope, in your ruling, it doesn't end my life here . . . Thank you, Your Honor."

My body went limp as I sat. I exhaled deeply, relieved that part one of my nightmare was over. Regardless of what happened later, at least I got through that statement. My lawyers leaned back and whispered, "Good job." I nodded as my heart still raced. I was proud of how I did. It wasn't perfect, but that was part of what made it okay. I glanced at my paper only a couple of times, which allowed me to speak from my heart. The phrase *plead for your life* gets thrown around a lot, but luckily most folks will never have to. I pleaded with that judge like my future was at stake, because within a few hours, it would be.

My attorneys gave their closing arguments. Both beat the drum we'd pounded throughout the trial: my crime was involuntary. Maria reminded the judge of my positive character references and asked that they, and my clean record, be taken into account. She also emphasized that the confiscation of my phone and passport and my arrest violated Russia's legal procedures. Alex teared up as he spoke. "Brittney is a good person," he said with a quiver in his voice. He mentioned my charity work, said I was loved by my friends and teammates. "She's even won over some of the guards and fellow inmates in detention," he added. "As she left for trial, many of them shouted, 'Brittney, everything will be okay!'"—which they did. Over five and a half months of visits, Alex had become more than my attorney. He was and is a true friend.

After the prosecutor's closing message—I'd deliberately packed and smuggled cannabis into Russia—the judge called for a recess to deliberate. She'd retreat to her chamber for two hours, she said, review the evidence, and come to a decision.

The guards leashed me again and escorted me out. We'd passed through the press lobby and started down the stairs when the prosecutor came running up and tapped me on the shoulder. I turned around to see him waving his phone. "Picture?" he said, grinning. *Is this fool kidding?* He wasn't. I almost said no but quickly realized doing so might bite me in the ass. "Cool," I said, shocked that the guards were indulging this circus. Not only did they allow it, but they actually walked me outside to the back of the building so the prosecutor could get a scenic shot. They used our time out there as a cig break. "Don't smile," said the prosecutor as he moved close to me. He handed his phone to the guard, who took the picture. And hell yes: I smiled *wiiiide*, teeth and all.

In the Dungeon, the girl I'd met earlier was gone. So were my Oreos. I was pissed. If she'd been there, I would've gone off on her. I was so stressed I smoked a good six, seven cigs in a row. I stopped only because I almost ran out. I slid the few I had left in my pocket, saved them for after the verdict. Smoking got me through the first hour. The next one literally crawled by. I thought about Relle, probably by herself, watching the coverage and praying. I thought of *before*, my last trip home, that sweet Valentine's Day we shared. I thought of my parents, my entire tribe, knew they were hopeful in Houston. I thought about how many years I might get. *Five? Six? All ten?* I'd learned a few numbers in Russian, from *odin*, *dva*, and *tri* (one, two, three) to *vosem*, *devyat*, and *desyat* (eight, nine, ten). I tried to recall the pronunciations so I could listen for a number during sentencing. However much time I received, my nearly six months in prison would at least be deducted.

Back in my cage, I waited for the judge's return. That gave the prosecutor time to ask for another photo. "Don't smile on this one," he said as he leaned in and snapped. I smiled even wider. After the first pic, he probably realized that his standing with me cheesing wasn't a good look for him professionally. He only got away with either picture because my lawyers weren't there to intervene. I already felt like a spectacle during trial. His behavior reinforced that.

Alex and Maria filed in moments later, along with the additional journalists allowed in for sentencing. We all rose briefly when the judge entered, and then sat again. She hit her gavel and called the proceedings to order, or at least she tried. It took a while for the reporters to settle down. They were jockeying for the best view of me, so they could zoom in on my face during the verdict. The judge asked me to stand. I made my way to the front of the cage and clasped the bars. The translator stood near me.

The judge looked down at a paper and began reading rapidly in Russian. "Brittney Griner, the court finds you guilty of committing a crime, under Article 228.1 and Article 229.2 of the Russian Federation Criminal Code," she said without pausing. The translator leaned through the bars and whispered to me as she spoke. "The sentence, under Article 228.1, is one and a half years' imprisonment," she continued. When I heard the word *one* in Russian, I lit up before remembering my minimum was five. "Under Article 229.2 of the Russian Federation Criminal Code," she went on, "the sentence is a period of eight years, with a fine of one million rubles." *Vosem*. I gripped the bars tighter, wondering if I'd heard *eight*. "In accordance with Articles 69.3 and 69.4 of the Russian Criminal Code," she concluded, "Brittney Griner's final sentence is nine years' imprisonment, including a fine of one million rubles, to be served in a penal colony." One of the guards gasped. The translator swallowed hard before whispering the sentence to me.

Devyat. Gulag. Whoosh.

"Do you understand the verdict?" the judge asked. Every camera in that room was literally in my face, waiting for me to break down. I refused to give the Russian government the satisfaction. I stared at the judge with a dazed expression, biting my lip to hold back emotion. "Yes, I understand, Your Honor," I said.

I comprehended her words, but I froze at what they meant. I couldn't feel my face, my body, the air. I've lived with excruciating pain for most of my career, but in that moment I was numb. I thought I'd prepared for the worst. But nothing can prepare you for your world imploding.

The hearing lasted a half hour. The fate of my next decade was delivered in fifty-two seconds. I don't recall much after the judge's final gavel. Just like I'd stopped feeling, I'd stopped hearing. A few fuzzy details did come through, like my attorneys trying to comfort me. Alex held my hand and said, "Be strong." He and Maria assured me we'd appeal. I couldn't even process that promise. I was still stuck on *devyat*. My team and others lingered after the sentencing. I signed a bunch of paperwork while speechless in my cell.

Maria leaned through the bars. "Do you want to see your wife?" she whispered. I nodded. With her phone out of view of the guards, Maria dialed Relle on FaceTime. Relle was wrapped in a blanket on the couch, her face filled with tears she'd tried to wipe away. "Hi, babe" was all I got out before I lost it. So did she. "Babe, babe, it's okay," I said, pulling back the flood. "Everything's fine. We'll get through this." Nothing hurt me more than seeing Relle hurt. That was why I shifted from tears to tough. I needed to be her rock. We talked for a moment before I glanced at the guard, who winked in my direction. He'd noticed I was on the phone, which was against court rules. He let it slide. He'd been the guard who gasped when he heard nine years. He was as stunned as millions of others surely were.

Maria also called Lindz. "I'm proud of you," she said. "You did so well. Stay strong, BG. We'll get you home." I nodded and told her I was sorry. For the cartridges. For the trial. For everything.

Back at county, Maria and Alex tried to comfort me. I appreciated their compassion but was too stunned to take it in. I spent that night in a cell with two Russian ladies who spoke baby English. I'd seen them around detention but didn't know them. One looked like Callie Torres from *Grey's Anatomy*. She was in for swindling. The other was a Russian Meredith Grey. No idea what her charge was. Both were older than the actors they resembled, but the likenesses were undeniable. They didn't smoke, so I didn't either, out of respect. "How many?" asked the Callie look-alike. In the Yard, she'd heard my verdict was coming. "*Devyat*," I said, holding up nine fingers. Her eyes widened. "*Devyat?*" she squealed. I nodded and began to cry. Both women pulled me toward them, hugged me tightly as I cried. "Everything okay," I heard. They were lending me the strength I hoped I'd given Relle. "You smoke," they began urging, motioning as if they had cigs in their mouths. I declined, but they kept insisting. I ended up smoking every cig I had left.

That evening, the main guard made his usual ruckus, stomping through the halls. I strangely heard little of it. I was still in shock. In my mind I kept replaying that moment with my wife, the sorrow in her eyes, the tears in her voice. In the middle of the night a piece of paper slid through the peephole. A young guard who'd taken a liking to me had typed out a letter using Google Translate. "I am sorry for your nine years," she wrote. "I am sorry for my country. Don't worry, everything will be okay. You will go home." Her kindness, in the moment of my greatest weakness, made me tear up. Across the top of her letter, I printed the words *Thank you* and slid it back through the peephole. I then cupped my face in my hands and sobbed quietly in the dark.

....

When I returned to detention two days later, the verdict had started to sink in. The more it penetrated, the more I ached. My sentence was all over the news. The guards were talking about it. So were the inmates. Alena and Olya met me at our room door. "What happened?" Alena asked. She had, of course, already heard. She still wanted the scene-by-scene, which I gave her.

I didn't even try whispering in front of Olya. Much as I didn't trust her, I knew she'd overhear anyway. I shared the story but filtered out my feelings. If she was cozying up with the guard I'd seen her slip a note to, all she could report were the facts. Shitshow trial. Oreos stolen. A near decade of my life flushed away. "Everybody's been asking about you," Alena said. In the Yard, Tanya and others had shouted over the wall, "Tell BG sorry." A few second offenders from the other building also passed along a message. "Tell her it's political," they said. "This is bullshit. No one is ordered to pay a million rubles for the amount of cannabis she had." The $11,000-plus I could handle. My big heartache was nine years without Relle.

Alex and Maria tried to lift my spirits. During their second visit after the verdict, they brought some of my favorite foods: Honey cake. A Russian marshmallow treat. And this dish called cordon bleu, ham wrapped around cheese, and then deep fried with garlic butter in the middle. "We're already working on the appeal," they said. They'd known I'd be given time. The surprise was the amount. We'd hoped for the minimum of five years, and really thought we had a shot at it. My attorneys were as devastated as I was that I'd received the near max.

In a statement after the ruling, Alex and Maria expressed their horror. President Biden also condemned the verdict, calling on Russia to release me "immediately." He said, "My administration will continue to work tirelessly and pursue every possible avenue to bring Brittney and Paul Whelan home safely as soon as possible."

On my first night back in detention, the guards did their usual cell search. I filed from the room for roll call and faced the wall. "Griner!" the guard shouted. "Brittney Yevette," I mumbled. Later, I crept to the sink and stared in the small mirror above it. I studied my face, my blank expression, the joy gone from my eyes. *Brittney Yevette. One girl. Nine years. Lights out.*

17

TRANSITIONS

Letting go of hope is sometimes the most optimistic thing you can do. The release was gradual for me. In August I turned inward and processed my new reality. In September I turned anxious as trade talks reached a fever pitch. In October I turned thirty-two and just about lost it.

After the verdict, I started doing the math. Nine years was a long time. In Russia, it could easily be ten. "You've gotta tag on at least a year for the courts to finish the paperwork for your release," I heard from the other women. And that was assuming your files could be found. Alena knew of an inmate whose documents were lost for months. If I spent a decade in lockdown, I might never see my parents again, and especially Pops with his health issues. By 2032, my nephew E.J. would be twenty-four, grown up and long out of high school. I'd miss some of his biggest milestones, as well as those of other family members. My basketball career would be over. I'd be in my early forties and out of shape, would have to find a new way to provide for my wife. And Relle. She assured me she'd wait, but ten years was ridiculous. Every week I saw inmates getting served divorce papers. I was so scared Relle would leave me, or that she'd get me back and say, "Nah, this isn't it." Folks assumed my lowest moment was the verdict. My real nightmare was the possibility of losing Relle.

On August 10, Relle and I finally had our first phone call, aside from our quick FaceTime during trial. The conversation lasted five minutes before the prison phone cut off. We were lucky to get back on for another ten. The story of that call wasn't what we said. It was how much we couldn't.

Relle sounded like she was in a deep hole. "Can you hear me, babe?" I spent the first minute asking. I eventually made out a faint yes. Not only were we on different continents, but the connection from Russia to the embassy and then to Relle's phone made the line shakier than it would've been if we'd called direct. I never could truly hear her, but we carried on.

"How are you?" I asked, as if she'd actually tell me.

"I'm good," she said drowsily. It was the middle of the night in North Carolina, where she had an apartment during law school. "I'm over here sleeping with Marcel"—our miniature goldendoodle.

"I wish I was there," I said. She wished the same. Seeing each other on FaceTime was amazing, we agreed, but it made us miss each other more. I congratulated her on passing the bar. I asked about my family. They were devastated by the verdict but praying hard.

We drifted into small talk because the big questions felt too big to address in such a short time. Also, how do you sum up six months of agony? Not easily, which was why we kept things light. I could tell Relle was trying to be calm for my sake. The result was a stilted conversation. Also, we knew the Russians were listening. I held myself back from saying, "Yo, it's *me*! Can we keep it real?"

We did get to one serious topic. "Do you know anything about the offer?" I asked. President Biden had written that he'd put one on the table.

"I honestly don't know anything," she said. "I think it's just a back-and-forth thing. That's how it goes until there's a meeting of the minds."

We ended with a laugh. "You're lucky I picked up," Relle joked. "You're the only person I'd answer for after six months of silence."

As shaky as the line was, as strained as our conversation felt, it was great to hear Relle's voice. "I love you," she said. "I love you more," I told her. This time I didn't break down. After the verdict, I'd begun building a barrier around my headspace. It was the only way I could get through a decade in prison. Hope keeps you looking toward the future. I had to focus on survival.

········

Around the time of my verdict, Alena received her sentence. When she left detention, she told me and Olya she'd be back in six days. She wasn't. I worried I'd never see her again, though her stuff was still in the room. It was common for inmates to leave and not come back, no explanation. The guards would just clear out their belongings and move in the next inmate. After twenty days, Alena finally walked through the door. She was stone-faced.

"What happened?" asked Olya. I said nothing. I could tell by Alena's blank stare that she needed to be left alone. She ignored Olya's question and flopped down on her bed. Later, she started talking.

"My sentencing date got moved by a couple weeks," she said. Rather than bringing her back to detention, they'd kept her at county.

"So did you get a verdict?" Olya asked.

Alena nodded and teared up. "Eight years," she said.

Her husband had received the same sentence. Their max sentence had been fifteen years, I think. She'd hoped they'd get five but feared it'd be double digits. Eight was better than ten, but it's still nearly three thousand sunrises. Like me, Alena was scared she'd never see her elderly father again. Some inmates could pay their way out of prison early. The farther outside of Moscow your facility, the easier it was to bribe the authorities. I'd heard that some prisoners paid around $30,000 USD to cut their sentences short by years. It was supposedly under the table, but the wardens knew. Men were more likely to get that deal than women. The men did a lot too, machinery work mostly, but Russia relied on female prisoners to sew all its military uniforms and keep the facilities running. Alena didn't have the money to pay her way out. And in my case, even if I'd offered millions, I was going nowhere. The prison officials would've caught serious hell for releasing me. They might've even been killed.

Alena would appeal her sentence, she said, just as my team had for me in mid-August. When I heard the word *appeal*, I inserted *purgatory*. We lived between the hell of detention and the true Hades of the gulags. We didn't know how long we'd linger in detention, whether we'd ever be sent to the colonies. Nothing was sure but uncertainty. Little was in our control. That evening after lights out, I heard Alena crying in the dark. My heart broke for her.

With Alena and I stressed as hell about our sentences, we had no patience for Olya's prying. Our annoyance came to a head in August. As usual, Olya was quizzing me about my case. "Do you think you'll get traded?" she asked for the tenth time. "You know as much as I know, Olya," I snapped. Soon after, she left for a medical appointment.

"I know she's a spy," Alena said. "Remember the note she passed to the guard?" *Yup.* We'd heard there were spies all over the prisons. Inmates did favors for the guards and wardens in exchange for better treatment. I wasn't one hundred percent sure Olya was a spy, but this seemed like a good day to find out. I was fed up with her.

I stood guard at the door, peering down the hall through the peephole. Alena grabbed Olya's journal from the cabinet and flipped through it. Her mouth fell open. My name, in English, was on page after page. So was Alena's. She'd kept notes on dozens of our conversations, dating back to our first day in the room.

"Here she comes!" I said.

Alena slammed shut the diary and shoved it in the cabinet as we leapt onto our beds.

"Should we say something?" Alena whispered as the guard unlocked the door.

"Nah," I said. Alena nodded.

We changed our minds. Alena was so pissed that she shot me a look like, *I'm saying something*. I was so with her. We both sat at the table and asked Olya to join us.

"What's up?" said Olya, studying our frowns.

I glared at her. "Didn't I tell you I'd better never see my name in your diary?"

Her eyes widened. "Um, yes, BG," she said, sounding like a child.

"Have you ever written anything about me or Alena in your diary?"

She froze. "No, no, no," she said. Alena and I exchanged a look.

"Then why is my name all through your diary?" I said.

"It's not," she claimed.

"Go get your diary," I said. She did and laid it open on the table.

"What's this?" I said, pointing to *BG* several times on a page, close to Alena's name.

"I mean, I didn't write that much," she said.

Alena took over. For a good minute and a half, she told that girl off in Russian. By the end of her tirade, Olya's face was bright red.

"Get a marker and cross out our names," I told her. She sat there all afternoon blotting us from her pages. I asked her about the note she'd passed to the guard. She, of course, denied she had done it. "I'd better not hear you're talking about me to these guards," I said. Alena warned the same.

The next day, we got called to the warden's office. The guards had seen our confrontation on camera and wanted us to meet with the top warden separately. Olya went on her own. Alena came with me so she could translate.

"What's going on in the room?" asked the warden, a young guy in blue camo.

"Olya's spying for you all," I said. "She has my name all through her diary."

He grinned and nodded as if he knew. "Do we need to move her to another room?"

"Absolutely," I said. Alena agreed. We returned to the cell and said nothing to Olya about our request. She also shared nothing about her meeting. Behind the scenes, my lawyers asked the warden for Olya to be moved.

A week later my headache was over. Two guards showed up and ordered Olya to gather her stuff and move to another room. We acted surprised. I'm sure she knew we were behind it. Then again, inmates were often rotated. We'd only been kept together so my cellmates could serve as translators. Her replacement was Sara, a Spanish lady who spoke broken English. She was in her late fifties, with a Pilates figure and long curly blond hair, and had been charged with cocaine smuggling. She paced constantly and talked nonstop. She also put her used butt wipes in our shared trash can, right at the top. At least she wasn't a spy.

....

By the middle of August, I was still grappling with my sentence. My loved ones wrote. Every letter brought hope and anxiety, like one I received from Lindz.

"You know we can't say everything we want to, but negotiations are active," she wrote. "Governor Richardson's people know who is doing the negotiating and they are leaning into a separate channel. They have in-person meetings coming and they're keeping the heat on." Governor Richardson told ABC's George Stephanopoulos, "My view is optimistic, I think she's gonna be freed . . . I think it'll be two-for-two . . . Can't forget about [Paul Whelan]." That was on our side. On Russia's, various names popped up, and especially one in particular: Viktor Bout, a notorious arms trafficker known as the Merchant of Death. He was serving twenty-five years in a U.S. prison. "This quite sensitive issue of the swap of convicted Russian and U.S. citizens is being discussed through the channels defined by our presidents," confirmed Alexander Darchiev, a senior Russian diplomat. "The Russian side has long been seeking the release of Viktor Bout. The details should be left to professionals."

My team remained steadfastly optimistic. "Know that yes, you are coming home," Lindz wrote. I wanted to believe her, but two words reeled through my head: *Paul Whelan.* Though his name was part of these talks, the U.S. government and Governor Richardson had been trying to bring him home for more than three years. Same with many of the sixty-plus American hostages around the world. At various points the administration believed it was close to securing Paul's freedom. His family had stood by, praying for a reunion that still hadn't come. Everyone involved was well intentioned, yet he rotted away in a prison colony like one I was due to be sent to. Also, many hoped my role as a Russian sports star would expedite my homecoming. Clearly, that hadn't been the case. In every other letter, Pops wrote, "I believe you'll be home next month." I was thankful for the positive outlook, but I couldn't let myself believe as strongly as everyone else seemed to. Painful. Hoping and not hoping are both ways we protect ourselves. Hope gives us something to live for. Letting go steels us for cold reality. I told myself I couldn't expect a trade soon, maybe ever, but I kept an ear open for developments.

Two major ones arose in mid-September. Governor Richardson, who helped bring Trevor home, met privately with Russian leaders regarding a possible prisoner swap. That seemingly annoyed the Biden administration. A senior official told CNN that anyone "who's going to Russia is going as a private citizen and they don't speak for the U.S. government." That

BG at age eleven

BG and her dad, Raymond, in Houston in 2011

BG and her mom, Sandra, at a Phoenix Mercury game

BG and her family right before her jersey was retired at Baylor University on February 18, 2024

BG is escorted by guards into a cell on the day of her trial.

A letter-writing station at the Sports Bra in Portland, Oregon

Maria and Alex speak with the press outside BG's sentencing hearing on August 4, 2022.

Coaches Dawn Staley and Tara VanDerveer both wore BG shirts during the nationally televised No. 1 South Carolina vs. No. 2 Stanford game in late November 2022. Stanford set up letter-writing stations at the arena.

BG on the flight home from the exchange, with Roger Carstens and Fletcher Schoen of SPEHA, along with members of the U.S. State Department's flight medical crew, the U.S. Marshals Service, and the Department of Defense's Joint Personnel Recovery Agency

BG's first steps back on U.S. soil

BG and Cherelle's first embrace after BG landed in San Antonio after the exchange

Phoenix Mercury GM Jim Pitman, Cherelle, BG, Diana Taurasi, and Mercury president Vince Kozar after BG and Cherelle were picked up from San Antonio

BG and Cherelle in the hangar after landing at Kelly Field, Joint Base San Antonio, on December 8, 2022, surrounded by the U.S. government team supporting the recovery, including Personnel Recovery specialists from U.S. Army South and agents from the Department of Defense's Joint Personnel Recovery Agency, the White House, and the Office of the Special Presidential Envoy for Hostage Affairs at the State Department

BG gets up shots at the base in San Antonio in her first workout after being detained.

BG seeing Phoenix Mercury legend Penny Taylor, who called for BG's release during her Women's Basketball Hall of Fame induction speech in June 2022, for the first time after returning from Russia

BG at her first press conference after coming home, held at the Phoenix Suns and Mercury arena on April 27, 2023

BG and Cherelle kiss at BG's first Mercury home game in 2023.

BG and Mercury president Vince Kozar at BG's first press conference

Muralist Antoinette Cauley, Cherelle, BG, Neda Sharghi, and Arizona governor Katie Hobbs pose together in front of Cauley's mural outside the Footprint Center in Phoenix.

BG and Cherelle with President Joe Biden and Dr. Jill Biden at the 2023 White House Correspondents' Dinner

BG and Cherelle on the red carpet at the 2023 Met Gala

friction was potentially good for me. In the diplomatic race to bring me home, I was the grand prize. Governor Richardson's meeting intensified the competition. He and his colleagues said they couldn't comment on the specifics. *No comment* came up a lot in the headlines. Big things were happening, I heard, but no one could say exactly what. That made me anxious, the way I felt when I heard "Hang in there" or "We're close." *Time to celebrate or run for cover?* Couldn't think about it. That was why I retreated into my emotional cave.

Soon after the governor's secret talks, Relle and Lindsay met with President Biden in the Oval Office. Huge deal. I had no idea this meeting was even happening at the time. I eventually heard the details in a letter from Lindz. The meeting was scheduled for twenty minutes. It lasted two hours. "President Biden was warm and genuine," Lindz wrote. "He hugged Relle. The president and Relle sat in armchairs at the top of the two sofas and Jake and I sat across from each other like bookends to them. The conversation opened with the president talking to Relle. He expressed his commitment to getting you home as quickly as he can and his personal connection to loss and the importance of family. He was emotional but direct. He struck me as honest and told us more than I expected in terms of the details around the negotiations.

"We talked about how scared and alone you are. We also asked a lot of questions. I can't share the details, but know we asked all the hard ones. I came away with confidence that he'll do what it takes to get you home—even if the only deal he can make is a one-for-one. He asked what I needed from him and I said, 'I need BG home tomorrow.' He is working tirelessly to make that happen. The goal is to get a deal agreed to by the end of September. You are not going to a labor camp. Right now, negotiations are stalled, but hopefully with the UN meetings in New York this week they'll pick up." There was that word again—*hope.*

In October we lost the appeal to reduce my sentence. That didn't surprise me, but it still depressed me, right along with the weather. Skies became grayer, days shorter. Daytime temperatures fell to the forties, a sign of winter. *Will I be here for another?* To preserve my sanity, I chose to assume I would be. My prayer was that I'd at least be able to stay in detention. It was a hell I'd gotten used to after eight months. Alena felt the same. With our sentences in place, we dwelled less on rumors about the penal colonies. Too scary to talk about what might soon become real.

That month, I turned thirty-two. It was just another day, like the 242 previous miserable ones. There were a few bright spots I thanked God for. Alex and Maria showed up with a honey cake and a bunch of letters from family, Lindz, and WNBA players. Alena's dad brought her a birthday card to give to me. Relle sent a few humorous greeting cards that Alex delivered. "Babbeee," she wrote. "It's your birthday! Normally I'd have multiple gifts lined up for you and I hate I couldn't do the same this year. BUT . . . I always want to show you how deserving you are. So here's multiple birthday cards and prison gifts (snacks and books). I hope today you can think of all good things. You being born is a good place to start because my life wouldn't be as perfect without you in it. I miss you so much and love you like crazy. Happy birthday! Love, wifey." I broke down when I read what she'd written, tears of gratitude mixed with grief.

Around that time the judge granted another fifteen-minute call, and Relle and I talked again. This time around I was more honest with her, let the tears come. I felt alone. I felt scared. I felt sure I'd be there through winter. My baby tried to cheer me up. It didn't work. Soon after, Relle sat for another interview with Gayle King from CBS. She said our call was disturbing and shared the line I'd spoken to her. "My life just doesn't matter anymore," I'd told her. That was how I truly felt.

On the night of my birthday, I sat on the toilet and smoked a cig, thought about what I would have been doing if I was home. Pops and I would've probably gone deep-sea fishing, or me and Relle would've dashed off to Cabo San Lucas. Instead, I sat alone in the dark, my life reduced to ten feet of isolation, my heart aching for trees, sky, connection. I felt detached from the world and even from myself. That disconnection had hardened into cynicism. Maybe Relle was right. Maybe I should keep my head in the Word, count my blessings while expecting more. As that evening turned to morning and October stretched to a close, I tried allowing myself to hope. Soon after I let in that light, my world went totally dark.

PART IV

LABOR CAMP

It is said that no one truly knows a nation until one has been inside its jails. A nation should not be judged by how it treats its highest citizens, but its lowest ones.

—Nelson Mandela, anti-apartheid activist
and former president of South Africa

November 2022

Dear Mr. President Putin,

I hope you heard about me. I am a two-time Olympic gold medalist in basketball and a WNBA champion. More importantly I am also a proud member of the UMMC Ekaterinburg Basketball Club. Together with UMMC I won seven Russian championships and brought four EuroLeague basketball titles to Russia.

I am writing to you from Mordovia penal colony #2. I was sentenced to nine years in prison for accidentally bringing vape cartridges in my bag to Russia. Serving this sentence in Russia may mean that I never see my parents again. My father in particular, who is in his seventh decade, has health issues. Never in my life will I be able to play basketball again. My family and basketball are my life. Without them, my life will make very little sense.

I know I broke Russian laws and I am sorry. This was never my intention. I love and respect Russia and I spent more than seven years in your beautiful country. Yekaterinburg has become my second home and I love the Russian people. I hope many of them love me too. I pleaded guilty in court for my mistake and now I am humbly asking for your pardon.

I know you said on multiple occasions that sports should be outside of politics. You spoke about the sanctity of sports. I know that you love sports, Mr. President, and you yourself are an athlete. You are familiar with the joy of sport and the challenges that come with it. The history of sports in Russia is storied. The Russian Olympics and FIFA World Cup in 2018 are indeed among the best sports events of this century.

Mr. President, you are the only person on the planet who has the authority to help me. Please grant me your pardon. Please let me end the suffering of my family and hopefully return to the sport I love—the sport that has given me so much.

Sincerely,

Brittney Griner

18

OFF THE GRID

My road to prison began with a whisper. On the last day of October, a guard unlocked our cell door and waved Alena toward her. "Brittney will be moving soon," she said in a hushed tone. She'd overheard the warden mention it. She didn't know the date.

I teared up when Alena told me. So did she. The most harrowing episode of our lives had played out in detention, and yet it had become our comfort zone. I'd been there for eight months; Alena for much longer. We had our system down. We depended on each other for food when we ran short, daily conversation, gossip and games to pass the time, and the occasional shoulder to cry on. We always knew we had each other's backs. She was also the translator I trusted most, who every day helped me make sense of a language completely foreign to me. The thought of our parting filled me with dread.

Alena called her dad and asked him to get word to Alex, who rushed to see me the next day. "Which guard told you this?" he asked, glancing to be sure the visitation area guard was out of earshot. A new one, I said, young and cool. She'd taken a liking to me and Alena. Alex asked me to repeat what she said, not because he hadn't heard me but because he was shocked. He and Maria had hoped a trade deal would come right after the appeal. We'd prayed that, if I was transferred, the date would be in the distance. Now it felt hauntingly close.

We began preparing. That day Alex brought toiletries and salami. Alena and I made ten salami sandwiches and stuffed them in our fridge. Just like we didn't have a date—or know if I'd be moved—we also didn't know how long the transfer would take. "One girl was on the road to prison for six weeks," Alena said. *On the road to prison.* That was how inmates referred to the often treacherous transfer by train. Inmates weren't told well in advance if or when they would be transferred or where they would end up. Even once a prisoner was taken, his or her loved ones were given no intel during the transfer. They knew only that the prisoner would be off the grid for days or even weeks, often snaking across the country and stopping to pick up both male and female convicts. Alex told me I'd be allowed two bags that I'd have to carry myself. I stuffed a duffel with clothes. I'd fill another with sandwiches, dried meats, Mars bars, and one of my faves, Valentine's Day candy hearts. Alex returned the next day with more snacks, as well as a letter from Lindz. "This moment came faster than we hoped," she wrote. "Be brave. Send word to us however you can. We love you, BG."

Alena suggested I lighten my load. I'd collected more than a hundred letters and photos from home. I gave Alex the ones I wanted to save, along with my sudoku book, which wouldn't be allowed in prison. Everything else I destroyed because I didn't want Russia rifling through it. Alena and I ripped up page after page into tiny shreds and then burned them over the toilet with our cigarette butts before flushing them. I also got rid of clothes. Alena took a jacket. I sent one of my Nipsey Hussle shirts to Tanya through a nice guard. I kept my heavy Nike parka, snow boots, and warmest hoodies.

A few days after the guard's tip, the warden asked to see me. Alena came to translate. "You're moving," he said matter-of-factly. I stared at him, not sure what to say or feel. "Do you have questions?" he asked. "Where is she going?" Alena asked for me. He grinned. "That's above my pay grade," he said. Alena pleaded for more info. He finally let it slip that we wouldn't be at the same camp. Devastating. Though I sensed he knew, he did not reveal my camp's location or what day I'd leave. "It's close" was all he'd say. "It could be any day."

"Any day" turned out to be the next. Right after breakfast, the guard told Alena I'd be transferred in a few hours. Alena helped me zip my overfull food duffel. With the packing done, Alena and I lay on our beds and smoked while tossing an orange back and forth. "Don't cause trouble for the guards and you'll be okay," she told me. She also joked about her own uncertain road. "I'm going to end up with a girlfriend in prison," she said, laughing about the inmates who might roll up on her. "No, you're not," I said. "Just tell everyone you've got an American friend who'll beat their asses." Finally, around 3:00 p.m., the knock came. We hugged. We cried. We promised to stay in touch through Alex.

Six hours later I was still in the prison's front office. The train had been delayed. The square-box truck could take me to the station only when there was an ETA. So the guards cuffed me again and took me back to my cell. When I walked in, Alena looked at me like, *What the hell are you doing back?* Lights out came soon after, but we stayed up whispering, wondering, worrying. At 3:00 a.m. I heard barking and knew what that meant. Anytime guards moved an inmate after dark, they brought dogs, in case the prisoner tried to bolt. Alena and I teared up again and this time embraced longer.

A male guard cuffed me at the front and then handed me my heavy bags. He carried the boxed meal the prison staff had prepared for me. In the truck, he shoved me and my belongings into the tiny cage and attached my cuffs to a bar. I was the only prisoner. In the pitch-black I cried softly, scared of what was coming. We'd driven for what felt like two hours when we slowed. I heard a train whistle. Our truck backed into reverse.

The guard opened my cage and let me out. Our truck's back edge was inches away from the train car. The guard motioned for me to step over the gap. As I did, I glanced sideways and saw the long train. I entered a car for female inmates. Men were in separate cars.

The car was windowless and lined with cages similar to those in the square-box truck, but bigger. Each cage had three metal bunks built into its walls. The guard pushed me into a cage with two elderly Russians. We nodded hello, and I climbed onto the top bunk. The other women talked for a bit, showed each other photos of their children. I pulled out a picture of E.J. and faced it toward them. "Is your baby?" one asked in broken English. I tried to explain *nephew*, but they just stared. "My *sister's* baby," I finally said. They got it. We traded our verdicts by holding up fingers. One lady six, the other eight. They didn't seem surprised when I held up nine fingers. By then everyone in Russia knew my face and sentence.

I couldn't sleep. I stared at the ceiling, wishing I had my sudoku book. Near the back I'd eventually discovered a puzzle that Relle had solved when I first bought the book. She'd signed her name and the time it took her to complete the puzzle: ten minutes. It was the only real piece of her I had. When I felt down I turned to that page and rubbed her signature on my cheek. On the train, I longed for that page. I longed even more to hold her.

Five or six hours into the journey, I got hungry. I opened the boxed meal. It was filled with freeze-dried food, like army rations. I set it aside and reached for my salami sandwiches, ate two in a row. I'd brought water but didn't drink it yet. Alena had warned me not to guzzle because she'd heard some prisoners didn't have access to toilets on the trains. But I did. Every few hours a guard asked who needed to go. When I eventually raised my hand, he escorted me to an adjoining car. I squatted to avoid touching the filthy seat while a guard waited at the door. An hour later we picked up three female prisoners, who were pushed into the cage next to ours.

At sunrise two days later we stopped again. The railcar door swung open. This time when I looked sideways, I could see it was nighttime but little else. The guards led us into another square-box truck. Twelve or so men filed out of another nearby train car. They were shackled to each other by their ankles, chain-gang style, and led to their own van. An hour later we slowed to the sound of opening gates. The guards unloaded us in front of a building, dark and empty. *Maybe we'll be processed in the morning.* The women were escorted down one hall, the men down another, and me to my own tiny cell. I tried to ask why. "You American," the guard said. He flopped a stained mattress onto the bed, locked me in, and left while mumbling in Russian. *Am I doing my nine years in solitary?* I thought.

The next morning a man opened the door and held out sheets. He wasn't in uniform, so I guessed he was a guard's assistant. I pulled out a few short cigars I'd bought at the Market. They were a hot commodity in Russia, and I figured I'd use them as currency for favors. He grinned and took them. "Another mattress?" I said, pointing to the nasty one I'd endured. He nodded. He returned with a much cleaner one. Later, a guard took me outdoors to an area with uneven dirt and crumbling walls—their Yard. A male inmate was painting a wall. "You Russki?" he said. "American," I said. "Me speak little English," he said. My face brightened. "Do I stay here?" I asked. "No," he said, laughing. "This for men." We'd stopped at a male labor camp. I didn't know why. I was just relieved we'd move on. Soon after, the man went and got three of his friends. They came holding pictures of their children and asked me to sign, which I did. "Your country bring you home," one said. "You be okay." *Not so far.*

Back on the train, the journey continued. We picked up eight women in total before our last stop. At the time I wasn't sure how long the journey lasted—six, seven, eight days? I just knew it was dark and drizzly when I entered my new hell.

Correctional Colony No. 2—or IK-2—is in Mordovia, a region more than three hundred miles east of Moscow. The women's prison was part of the sprawling network of former Soviet-era gulags. Inmates referred to Mordovia as the Ass of Russia, and for good reason. The two dozen penal colonies there were known for horrid conditions, hard labor, and inmate torture. Winter temperatures dipped to five degrees below zero.

A row of guards met us inside the gates. They had AK-47s pointed at us, with barking German shepherds at their sides. They led us into a room with a small cell. Two female guards fetched us one at a time for a search as the rest watched from the cell. An Uzbekistani girl went first. The guards dumped her stuff on a table. They poured her sugar into her washing powder, broke her candy into smithereens, stabbed her bars of soap. I was called last. "Drugs?" asked the guard as she unzipped my duffel. I shook my head no. She cut open sealed packages of my salami, crushed my dry noodles, and set aside any clothing with color. Only black and white allowed, and just two tees and underwear. She tried to take my stack of boxers. "*Nyet,*" I protested, pulling down my sweats to prove my boxers were my underwear. With a scowl she let me keep them. Everything else she seized. "No Russki?" she asked as she searched. "*Nyet,*" I said, shrugging. She glanced at the other guard, and they burst into laughter. "*Nyet,* no Russki!" she repeated mockingly.

The guard motioned for me to remove my outerwear. I took off all but my boxers. The two women gazed at my body before making me rotate and do four squats. One scribbled notes as the other gawked. I was mid squat when the door behind me opened. I stood. I turned to see a Russian woman, forties, black hair, kind eyes. "I'm Ann," she said in perfect English. She said she was the inmate who oversaw the kitchen, apologized for finishing her shift late. "The guards want me to translate for you," she said. I was so overwhelmed with gratitude, I almost forgot I was half naked.

Once I'd dressed again, I followed Ann across a massive yard with a volleyball court at its center. The field was surrounded by several gated buildings. "That's where you'll stay," Ann said, nodding toward the buildings. Several dozen inmates gathered along the gates and stared as I walked by. "We all heard you were coming," Ann said, chuckling. It seemed everyone except my own family knew I'd serve time at IK-2.

We entered the admin building for a quick meeting with the warden, a short, balding man. He looked at me like I was scum. "Do as you're told and you won't have problems," he barked. After we'd gone Ann whispered that this warden had tortured a female inmate at another prison. Instead of being fired, he'd been sent to IK-2.

Our final stop was to pick up my uniform. The two elderly inmates who ran the shop looked me up and down and sighed, like, *We ain't got nothing to fit you.* All inmates were required to wear green corduroy uniforms. The jacket was like a Levi's button-down; the pants had a buttoned waistband. One lady fished out the largest uniform she could find. The hem on the pants ended at my shins. The jacket, surprisingly, fit my back, but rode up to show my stomach when I stood. Luckily, I was allowed to keep on my underclothes to shield me from the cold, especially since they didn't have an overcoat big enough for me.

I was given the required head wrap, similar to a hijab. The women tried to teach me how to wrap it, but I ended up tucking it in my jacket. There were no shoes my size, so I kept my boots. I waddled out looking like Steve Urkel, past twice as many inmates who'd gathered at the gates. With every gaze following me, I walked back across the Yard to quarantine, a small building filled with about twenty beds. My cellmates were the women who'd been with me on the train ride.

Ann left me with a guard. "I'll check on you when I can," she told me. Her job as head cook involved long hours. "Kate will come stay overnight with you," she said. Kate, a short woman with salt-and-pepper hair and a smile, showed up soon after. Her English was choppy but understandable. Of the eight hundred or so inmates at IK-2, Kate and Ann spoke my language best, Ann like a native. She was once an English teacher. She'd now been entrusted with a job she couldn't have ever imagined she'd have: translating for Russia's first female American inmate at IK-2.

....

Prison is more than a place. It's also a mindset. When I entered IK-2, I flipped a switch in my head. *I'm an inmate now*, I told myself. *I'll be here at least nine years*. I even rehearsed my release date: October 20, 2031. I knew that might change. Still, focusing on a goal would get me through the nightmare. As deeply as I cared for Relle and my family, I had to seal off that love to some extent. I'd still let myself miss them, but I would tuck away the tears. Softness would compromise my toughness, I felt. I adopted that mentality from day one.

Quarantine in Russia's prisons usually lasts two weeks, though it can vary from one facility to the next. Even before the Covid pandemic, new inmates were initially isolated and tested for various infectious diseases, from TB to hepatitis B. That sequestering became more important as Covid cases spiked worldwide. Russia's prisons were hit especially hard, with overcrowding, unsanitary conditions, and communal living ensuring rapid spread. I recall spending only one week in quarantine, maybe because my tests came back clean. During my time there, a guard came in the mornings and read a rulebook in Russian for two hours while I sat there bored. There were five other women. A pin on our uniforms displayed our names and one or more colors, from white and yellow to green and burgundy. The colors gave the guards your story at a glance: aggressive toward staff, suicidal, arsonist, swindler, runaway, on and on. I'd later hear that an elderly inmate, half blind, had tried to bust out of there with her cane. They hauled her back and slapped her with a new stripe. Mine was white, signaling drug-related charges. Same with others in quarantine, as well as Kate and Ann. Around campus I'd spotted the rainbow, including black for the most heinous crimes: Murder. Terrorism. Torture.

My initiation came at night. That was when Ann and Kate met me after their shifts. Kate assisted the deputy warden, whom the inmates called Mother of Dragon—tall, blue camo, sixties, caked-on makeup, and she breathed fire while waving her baton. Ann brought us cake that night, a perk of being the head cook. We huddled at the back as she and Kate gave me the lowdown, starting with rule one. "If a guard stops you," Ann said, "you have to tell them your crime and release date." She taught me every word of it in Russian. I practiced but never mastered what I needed to say.

They also described the grounds and other rules. All prisoners were housed in multilevel buildings called detachments, like a quad. Each was overseen by an inmate, the most senior in the group. "No handcuffs here," Ann said. The guards were watching but didn't escort prisoners through the colony, which revolved around the Yard. On one side was the cafeteria, where three daily meals were served: edible but still distasteful, aside from the honey cake I craved. Behind it was a church, a visitation room, an infirmary, and the Market. All could be visited at certain times on weekends. On another side was admin, where I'd met the warden. There was also an orphanage for the children of inmates who'd given birth while incarcerated. They could keep their babies there until the children reached two years of age. They were allowed (short) breaks to see them. Out of view was the Hole, for troublemakers. "Don't end up there," Ann warned. There were stories of women who'd been beaten bloody and then left for weeks in solitary.

Some requirements were like those at detention: 6:00 a.m. roll call, 10:00 p.m. lights out, beds made hot dog style, TV at designated times. Other rules differed: no smoking inside, and group exercise in the Yard. Three realities were new and awful. One was the bathroom. The second was my job. My building leader was the third. The stripe on her pin gave me chills.

19

NEEDLED

For seven days I was totally off the grid. My team had been told I'd been transferred but didn't know when or where. They also hadn't been prepared for the increasing dread they'd feel as one day rolled into the next. "I have no idea where you are or if you'll get this letter," Relle wrote to me before she knew I'd been taken. "I'm in shock and disbelief. I wish none of this was happening. We will find you, Babe, I promise." She'd heard the same stories I had, of inmates crammed in dark and dingy cars, rattling across Russia for sometimes months. Was I eating, sleeping, or even still alive? My family didn't know. That uncertainty intensified their anxiety.

Lindz and Relle had been running the campaign on little sleep and with heavy stress. By the time my transfer came, they were fighting through burnout. Relle retreated deeper into her prayer closet. Lindz developed vertigo. Back in September, recognizing the toll managing so many aspects of the campaign was taking on her and knowing the importance of every effort, Lindz asked Wasserman leadership for more support. "Whatever you need," Casey told her. The team launched another round of campaigning, complete with letter-writing stations at sporting events across the country. The agency's employees were working tirelessly. Many prayed during my seven days off the grid. On the eighth, I was found. Maria spent two days trying to locate me and reached out to numerous penal colonies. She finally networked her way to someone who whispered my whereabouts and confirmed them in a letter: "Yes, Brittney Yevette Griner is with us." My loved ones were relieved I'd been located. They were horrified at what I'd face.

Alex and Maria planned the long journey to see me while I moved into my quad. A short woman with black hair met me at the entrance. Through Ann, she introduced herself as Val, the building leader. Though she greeted me warmly, I knew she was trouble, starting with that stripe. Ann told me Val had once led a criminal organization. She pointed out people to be assassinated. In the outside world that made her dangerous. In prison that earned her respect. She'd been at IK-2 since 2008 and was the warden's right hand. Prison 101: Stay away from inmates in the boss's pocket. Val made that impossible. She tried to turn me into her bestie, probably to score points with the warden. She and Ann walked me through the quad, and Val stayed on my heels.

Our building had three levels. I was on the third. The floors were laid out like rectangular dormitories, with a common room at the center. In one area was a small kitchen. In another were cubicles, one per inmate, for personal items and sealed food. Nearby was a huge closet for our bags and uniforms, since nothing could be kept in the sleeping area. Each floor had three massive bedrooms, with fifty women scattered across them. My room had twenty inmates. When I entered, they all just stared. No one spoke English, and Val spoke very little. She shooed several women out of her way and directed me to my bed. Before my arrival she'd arranged for me to be in her building, rather than Kate and Ann's, as well as to have me sleep next to her. The room was crowded with mostly bunks. Even the singles were crammed together. I was relieved to see that the inmate welders had created a longer bed for me. You could socialize only with the women on your floor. And you'd catch hell for wandering to other floors or quads.

The bathroom was a special hell. There was no hot water at IK-2. If you chose to shower—and most didn't—you heated water in an electric kettle and poured it in your personal bucket. The shower was a tiny, tiled stall behind a folding screen. I was too big for the stall. So I squatted behind the screen, scooped water over my dreads, and tried to get clean in the stream. Meanwhile, the restroom buzzed. It was one big open area with four toilets facing each other and six sinks shared by all fifty of us. I saw a lot I didn't want to see. Some women popped in tampons as they sponge-bathed at the sinks we used for brushing our teeth. And the room reeked, as did most of the women. You could never get truly clean in that pigpen. Also, we sat knee-to-knee while taking dumps. The scene was disgusting.

Val put a bathroom hierarchy in place. The guards allowed building leaders to do mostly as they wanted. Val hogged the restroom for herself at 5:30, a half hour before lights on. All others shoved in whenever, allowed ten minutes max. A week into my time there, Val began insisting I rise early and use the bathroom while she did. She also demanded that her main minion, a sweet woman named Sveta, heat my water for me. I resisted on both fronts. Much as I detested the filthy, chaotic bathroom, I hated even more being controlled by Val. The women shuddered at her icy stare and closeness with the warden. She could make your life hell, everyone said. I didn't want to become known as her evil twin. I also didn't want to be seen as some entitled American who couldn't even heat my own water. I eventually gave in on the early showers but did my best to keep my distance otherwise.

No luck there, because Val was also my boss. We all had different shifts depending on our jobs. Our weekday routine after wake-up: All prisoners in the Yard by 6:30 for twenty minutes of exercise in the bitter cold. We'd be out there doing arm circles, '60s-style calisthenics, while shaking snow off our head wraps. Then it was over to breakfast by 6:55, with a timed twelve minutes for your meal, to ensure all eight hundred of us got served before work. After porridge, we raced back to our quads for roll call. One guard was assigned to each building. With a chalkboard list in hand, the guard shouted out your last name—"Griner!"—and you responded with the rest of it—"Brittney Yevette!" Once your name was called, you lined up behind the guard, until everyone in your building had been accounted for. Afterward, we raced back to our quads to gather anything we'd need during work, like the (prohibited) candy bars we stuffed in our pockets and the (allowed) electric kettles for hot water. Between 8:00 and 9:00 a.m., we rushed across the grounds to the metal detectors that were at the entrance to the massive building we worked in. Guards shouted, "Get in one line!" and shoved us around with their batons. Once we made it through the detectors, we stormed toward our stations. If you didn't complete your work, there'd be consequences.

Russian labor camps are called that for a reason. All inmates work ten-, twelve-, or fifteen-hour-or-longer days. Those with jobs like Ann's worked around the clock. Ann oversaw all meals for the inmates and also personally served the prison officials. Kate, assistant to Mother of Dragon, also lived on call. While her job had an upside—darting around campus to run errands— the big downside was never getting a break from the meanest warden on campus. We earned a few rubles an hour, around 25 cents. It was basically slave labor.

I worked in sewing. We worked in a factorylike building, with row after row of Soviet-era machines. There was no ventilation and little heat. No bathroom breaks were allowed. We knew to empty our bladders during the allotted twenty-minute lunch break. Each group was given a quota, around five hundred military uniforms a day. Teams who failed were berated. A girl near me was sewing so fast she stitched together her fingers, which meant she bled onto the garment and slowed production. Her leader yanked the material from her hand, threw it on the floor, and screamed for her to pick it up and continue. If you cut yourself, you just dealt with it, no whining or stopping.

I'd never been much of a sewer. My grandmother, mother, and aunts all sewed and crocheted, so I grew up surrounded by the craft. I also did some sewing in eighth-grade home ec. Not my thing. I wanted to be outdoors, running around, not struggling to thread a needle with my big ol' hands. So when I heard I'd be in sewing, I thought, *This is gonna be a long nine years.* I had no say in the matter. None of the new inmates did. During quarantine we were given psych evaluations. If you passed—and I did—you were told, "You're sane, so we expect you to work." The next stop was the warden's office. He called us in, one at a time, and said, "This is going to be your job. Do you understand?" You had to verbally respond that you did. The vast majority ended up in sewing because that was where Russia needed the most hands. The labor camps were basically military uniform sweatshops.

For once, my size brought me a little luck. I was way too tall to fit at the sewing machines, so Val made up a job for me: clipping threads from buttons using mini scissors, like the kind used to cut nose hairs. The buttons had been freshly sewn onto jackets made of stiff waterproof material. Once I'd cut off stray threads, I used a large damp sponge to wipe off the powder markings the sewers had used as guides. Lastly, I buttoned the jacket from top to bottom, which was slow and frustrating because my fingers are big. Same thing with the thread clippers: my fingers didn't fit though the scissor handles. The job sounds simple, but it wasn't for me, and I had the bruised hands to prove it. My "training" involved Val showing me how to do the task once and then looking over my shoulder for a couple of days. The hardest part was standing hunched over a worktable for hours. My knees swelled; my back throbbed. That was my first job. My next would bring a whole new round of danger.

Evenings brought dinner, TV time in the common area, and calls from each floor's phone room. Val ran that show too. She and other longtimers hogged the phone lines first, and others got however much time was left. Newcomers in our building got no calls their first year, simply because Val said so. Even if she'd let me use the phone, I could've called home only with outside permission. Foreigners' calls had to be set up through an embassy. That took forever.

While the women battled for phone time, I caught up on my soap, *Magnificent Century*. Without Alena to translate, I could hardly follow it. I missed my friend. Between the end of work and lights out, I mostly sat by myself and read the Word. I was surrounded by women, dozens more than in detention, but I'd never felt more alone.

....

My lawyers came to visit about a week into my time at IK-2. I was overjoyed to see familiar faces and fought back tears when I spotted them. Visitation took place in a small room. I had to get there before their scheduled visit so I could be searched. After stripping to my boxers, I dressed and entered the room with a camera above. A guard stood nearby, monitoring our conversations more closely than they'd done at detention. Also, Alex had to hold up any letters to the divider and have me read them. In prison, all letters were the take-back kind.

Alex and Maria brought news from home. Midterms had come and gone, which cleared the path for trade talks, they felt. Lindz was in constant touch with the White House and SPEHA. "President Biden has made public statements about his commitment to getting you home and he's at the G20 this week," Lindz wrote in a letter Alex held up. "Putin isn't there but Russian officials are, so there will be conversations." My lawyers reiterated how much they still believed I'd be released, though they were saddened at how things had unfolded. Our fight for my freedom was now happening amid the reality of my imprisonment.

Pops sent Scriptures for me to cling to. Relle tried to lift my spirits with her usual humor. "Your side of the bathroom misses you," she wrote. "When I turned on your sink water barely came out. I may need to move over to that side for my face washing. Head up, champ. I love you. One day this will all be a memory." That day, in my head, was October 21, 2031.

Once I finished my week in quarantine and moved into the quad, Kate and Ann visited when they could but far less than they had initially. Their jobs kept them busy. I begged to be in their quad, which was for the most well behaved. I was told I'd have to be at IK-2 for two years before I could even apply. Ann tried to pull some strings to get me in, but Val's strings were longer. She'd convinced the warden to keep me near her. Even from afar, Ann and Kate became my sanity. They were also my passport around the colony.

"Do you want to see the pets?" Kate asked me one weekend on her way to do an errand.

"Of course," I replied, with a face that said, *What pets?*

As we walked to a remote area of the grounds, she explained that some inmates' work was to raise rabbits, to be sold to local farmers for prison income. We arrived at a building where she pulled back a tarp. My eyes widened at the sight: dozens of rabbits as big as cats, in cages stacked up as tall as me. There must've been fifty bunnies back there.

"They sell *all* these rabbits?" I asked. "Only the ones we don't kill," she said. I stared at her. "If the prison's short on food," she said, "they slaughter the bunnies." The inmates running the farm were these old USSR-era types who'd grown up killing animals with their bare hands. I'm sure I ate rabbit and didn't know it. Our cafeteria was filled with food I didn't recognize.

Kate got me out of my cell while Ann gave me the hookup. The colony cook knew everyone. Soon after I arrived, she took me to a different Sveta from the girl in my quad who was forced to heat my water. This Sveta was less than five feet, with long blond hair, and she was the sweetest person you'd ever meet—super girly. She was the master seamstress who made all our prison uniforms. She took quick measurements and soon delivered two uniforms—one for work, another for weekends, with the purpose of reducing funk—plus an overcoat. She also made me pajamas, mittens, and extra scarves. "How's my big friend?" I'd joke when I saw her. "How's my little friend?" she'd reply. She didn't know English either, but I taught her that phrase. My new uniform at least covered all of me. Still, it'd be no match for a Russian winter.

20

FROZEN

After three days in sewing, I could hardly stand. It was one thing to hoop for hours. You were on the move the whole time. It was agony to crouch over a knee-high table all day. "I need to get out of there," I told Ann. I also wanted to move away from my assassin boss, who continued brownnosing me while browbeating my teammates.

On the one hand, Val kissed up to me. On the other, she tried knocking me down to size. She was the big dog on campus and made sure no one forgot it. When she came into a room, everyone shut up or scattered. If she wanted a spot on the couch, she ordered whoever was in it to get up. In the quad one weekend a lot of us were watching TV in the common room. Val had one girl rubbing her feet while she kicked back. Val got up to go to the bathroom, and I went to get something from my cubicle. On our return to the TV room, Val bumped into me, on purpose and hard. I shoved her to the floor as the other girls stared. She pretended to laugh it off. Me too. I even helped her up from the floor, like, *My bad*. But we both knew her bump was no accident. It was Val's attempt to assert her dominance.

While that didn't work in this case, her other tactics did. She once snitched to the warden that I'd skipped dinner. All meals were required, but I'd stayed in because my legs were sore and swollen from work. The warden called me into his office and reprimanded me, while Val took pleasure in her power.

My job already sucked. Dealing with Val's passive-aggressive games made it suck harder. Ann and I went together to ask the warden if I could do different work. "Tell her she'll get no special treatment," he barked at Ann while hardly looking at me. I didn't expect to be coddled. I just wanted to survive my nine years without ending up in a wheelchair.

We next tried our luck with one of the deputy wardens, this tall woman who had played volleyball back in the day. The sport was huge in Russia, even bigger than basketball, and many guards and wardens were retired athletes. "Her knees and back are killing her," Ann translated. The top warden was out that day, and this deputy, though stern, seemed more understanding than he'd been. I asked if I could work in welding. In eighth grade I had lived for shop class, loved working with my hands. Too dangerous, she said, since no one on that team spoke even baby English to explain how to use the power tools. Not knowing Russian might cost me a limb. Feeling desperate, I showed the deputy warden my blistering hands, and she agreed to find me another role. That was how I got moved from sewing to fabric cutting.

My new crew was made up of second offenders. It was unheard of for a new inmate to work alongside the vets, who follow their own rules to some degree. It was also unheard of to have a six-nine American in a Russian labor camp, so concessions had to be made. My new task seemed just as dangerous as the one I might've done in welding. I sliced large pieces of fabric using a spinning blade. If we got an order for military jackets, for instance, me and another inmate would grab a huge fabric roll, hoist it onto a big table, roll out the amount of fabric needed for a jacket, clamp it down, and then lower the rotating blade to cut it. For an order of a hundred jackets, we braved the blade a hundred times. After cutting, we'd place a big stencil on each fabric piece and mark it with chalk. The sewing team would eventually use those markings as a guide in assembling the garment. We'd then count the pieces, bundle them, and haul them to the next building. Everyone in my group cut, bundled, and hauled, but I did the most hauling because I could lift heavy weights. I'd carry two huge bags at a time, one on each shoulder.

Our machine looked left over from Soviet times. It was basically an old table saw, no shield, rusted. Lose concentration and you might lose a thumb. Several of the thirty women in my group were missing fingers. My partner had a long scar on her face, starting near her eye. My boss, Olya (every other woman in Russia was Olya, since family names got passed down), once badly injured her hand when the blade broke and shattered in a thousand directions. One of my teammates spoke a tiny bit of English, so she tried to translate. Alex had given me a traveler's dictionary that I took to work. But it had phrases like "Where's the nearest restaurant?" and "How do I get to a nightclub?" rather than "How do I keep from killing myself with a blade?" "If you hear a boom," my teammate told me, "duck." It was difficult to cut some of the fabrics, like the slippery material used for lining. I had several close calls but never lost a finger. Still, my hands were horribly bruised.

Our group had a quota. I never knew what it was, probably because Olya kept us ahead of schedule. The second offenders didn't play. They'd figured out how to work smartly so they could get out of there no later than 7:00 or 8:00 p.m., even with breaks factored in. Olya, like nearly everyone at IK-2, couldn't go an hour without a cig. That meant we got frequent smoke and bathroom breaks, unlike the sewing teams. We'd be out in the brutal cold, puffing and shivering. Back inside, Russian pop music blared from Olya's boom box as we worked. Music helped the time pass, but the work was still grueling—we must've done a thousand or more cuts a day. At least I got to do it with old-timers who weren't closely watched by the guards. Though the conditions were awful, I was grateful to be busy. One of the agonies of prison was having nothing to do but mourn.

Shortly after I started my second job, I got sick. Not surprising. The extra layers Anna and Sveta got for me made me warmer than I would've been otherwise, but definitely not *warm*. When I inhaled, I felt like my breath had frozen in my lungs. My hands were always freezing, my head cold. Our morning exercises were required even in blizzard conditions. The snow that constantly gathered on my head would melt and make my wrap damp. Same with my uniform. Also, we were required to hand-wash our clothes in the bathroom sinks and then air-dry them either on clotheslines outside (they'd freeze) or on the radiators. That was if you could get a spot on one of the few radiators in our TV room. Val had first dibs. She decided who else got a spot—her henchwomen—and some never did. Val allowed me a place on the radiator to lay out my wet socks and underwear, but they never got dry. What was worse than being cold was being wet *and* cold. That was why I got ill.

And then there was my hair. My dreads had become knotted over the months. At IK-2, they froze together. My iced locs started molding beneath that damp wrap. And because I had no hair dryer, my dreads took three days to fully dry after I showered. During exercise on frigid mornings, I could literally feel a head cold coming on.

To make matters colder, at one point the entire prison lost electricity, like I'd heard it once did in another penal colony. That temp dropped so fast. It started on a Saturday and lasted three days. Though we didn't have to work, we did endure hours in our cold, dark quad. I had on every piece of (damp) clothing I owned. Luckily, no fights broke out, and no one tried to escape through the unlocked gates. The guard dogs were still wide awake. Some inmates took advantage of the cameras being off by hugging up with their girlfriends on other floors.

I tried to warm up by helping Ann cook for the colony. In a field near the kitchen, she and her team made our meals over makeshift campfires. I carried half a cow from the deep freeze to the field. My lawyers had been concerned I'd be given the prison's toughest jobs because of my size. True. The guards once had me shoveling snow and breaking up ice around a building and were shocked at how quickly I got it done. Though my attorneys were right, I wanted the difficult jobs. They took my mind off the bleak big picture.

The physical exertion probably weakened my immune system. That, plus my wet hair and uniform and the power outage, broke me all the way down. I felt like I was dying. I didn't get tested for Covid. I don't know why. The nurse in the infirmary took my temperature, which was high, and then gave me Theraflu and sent me back to work. I felt exactly like I did the first time I had Covid: heavy chest, sore throat, hard to breathe. My team had connected me with two local attorneys, Natalie and Yury, to help with any issues that arose, since Alex and Maria were so far away. They couldn't do anything legally for me, but they did check on me frequently and update Alex and Maria on all aspects of my life at IK-2. Natalie and Yury didn't know English (we talked through a translator), but Natalie dropped off medicine and other supplies. Bless her. She also visited me while I was sick, just so I could get out of work. I laid my head down on my side of the partition and took a nap. The next day I felt so crappy that Ann begged a guard to let me out of work. He initially said no but finally caved. We weren't allowed to stretch out on our beds during the daytime, even if we were sick. That morning, I hadn't been able to get out of bed.

I'd just gotten on my feet when I got yelled at by Mother of Dragon. "You *will* learn Russian," she told me. Starting in quarantine, she and the warden kept saying I wouldn't get special treatment. "No one's going to keep speaking to you in English," she said through Ann. I just stared at her. Even if I'd learned Russian, I wouldn't have given her the satisfaction of hearing me speak it.

Around that time I celebrated Thanksgiving alone, jailhouse style. I bought a smoked turkey leg from the Market. In my quad's kitchen one night, I deboned the turkey and made rice, put both in a bowl, and poured soy sauce over them. I thought about Relle, Mom and Pops, my whole family gathered in Houston for the holiday. I ached that I couldn't be with them.

....

My locs kept freezing after I recovered. I started thinking about making it through the coming winter and possibly eight more. The damp mop on my head would make that tougher. In late November I decided to cut it off.

You know a Black woman only when you know her hair journey. The two are tightly interwoven. When I was in elementary school, my mom tried to lay down my hair with thick grease. That lasted two minutes. Soon as I started running around and sweating, my thick mass of curls frizzed up. And getting it combed out on the weekends was an ordeal. I'd be on the floor between Momma's knees, with her yanking her pick through it and me complaining. A few times she tried to flat iron it. Same thing: my curls quickly made a comeback.

My mother has thinner hair than I do. I have more of my father's texture. I'd see Mom in the bathroom, twirling her brush through her strands. I once tried that when I was in middle school. The brush got stuck in my hair. I had to get it cut out and then rearranged how I did my pigtails to cover the short patch. Luckily my hair grows fast. Later, when I was in eighth grade, my sister SheKera gave me a box-kit relaxer. I just wanted to see what my hair would look like chemically straightened. "It's going to burn," she warned as she slathered on the cream. "Let me know when you feel a tingle and I'll rinse it out." I guess my pain tolerance is high because the tingling felt good to me. But then it got warmer, and then hot, and then hotter, and I finally said, "Yo, it's fire now." "When did it start burning?" she asked as she rushed me under the faucet. "Ten minutes ago," I said. I didn't just get burned. My scalp was covered in patches. SheKera sprayed olive oil sheen spray all through my crown.

In high school I wore braids or had my hair pulled back in a giant poof ball. Occasionally, I'd pick it out into a big 'fro, Angela Davis style. Then, at the end of my freshman year at Baylor, I started locking it. Dreads are a commitment—if you don't like them, you've gotta chop off all your hair to start again—so I began slowly. I did two-strand twists in the front, with braids still in the back. From then on I just kept twisting the front with Jamaican beeswax and thinking, *I like this.* The next year I twisted it all. By the time I met Relle, I had a nice full head of locs. I loved the Rasta vibe, total freedom. I also loved how easy they made my life. I didn't have to think much about my hair. I could just hoop.

After almost twenty years with dreads, I was ready for a change. They were breaking in a few places. If I pulled them, they'd snap off. For two years before my detainment, I'd been going back and forth on whether to cut them. My reservation: the shape of my head. I have a dip in the back that my long hair has always covered, and I worried about how I'd look close-cropped. Also, me and my dreads had history: coming out with Pops, the WNBA draft, my rise at Baylor, my love story with Relle. I'd worn them short, long, in-between, and even dyed super blond. Together, we'd been through the good, the bad, and the devastating. Now I was facing the sick and frozen. They had to go.

In prison I needed permission to chop my hair. Ann helped me write an application to give to Mother of Dragon, told her I needed to cut my locs for health reasons—I'd keep getting sick if I kept them. She agreed. There was a salon at the colony. The prisoners' families could drop off hair products, a rule two inmates I'd seen around the colony take advantage of. I nicknamed them the Twilight girls because they looked like legit vampires from *The Twilight Saga:* platinum blond hair, skin so pale they could've been Edward Cullen's sisters. In the salon, the stylist was Val's girlfriend, Jenya, an older lady with a short, blond cut. She had a nice little setup: barber chair, hair tools, pictures of hairstyles on the walls. And she did it all, from perms and buzz cuts to color and curls. Still, when I sat down in her chair, she looked at my dreads like, *What do I do with* this?

I showed her a picture of my nephew E.J., who had the short fade I wanted. I gestured for her to snip off the locs. A dread at a time, the old me fell to the floor. She then put a guard on her clippers and—*bzzzz*—raked the vibrating steel over my scalp. I couldn't see while she cut. I just had to trust her. Later, when she turned me around to the mirror, I thought, *Not bad.*

Since arriving at IK-2, I'd been frozen, sick, got my hair chopped off. The girl I once was now lay in a heap of dreads on the concrete floor. But the true me, the survivor, remained. I'd always thought of myself as someone who could endure almost anything. At a labor camp in Russia in the dead of winter, I found out just how tough I was.

21

TAKEN

Relle and Lindz pursued every avenue to get me home. Like my attorneys and others calling for my freedom, they didn't know if I'd ever be traded. They just kept working as if their lives depended on it, because they knew mine did.

At *Glamour*'s Women of the Year Awards in New York, Relle used her platform to shine a light on my imprisonment—and to roll out our campaign's new phase, focused on letter writing. "I've spent the last eight months riding waves of grief and, to be honest, just total disbelief," she said. "I can't believe that I'm standing in front of you today, living without my favorite person, my greatest love, biggest support, and sanctuary. Language truly fails to capture the excruciating pain that stems from having a loved one held hostage." She ended by asking the audience to write letters of support for me and to share them on social media with the hashtag #WeAreBG. "Together, let's show BG and the entire world that love will save the day," she concluded. From this event and dozens of other letter-writing stations the team set up, thousands of emailed letters poured in.

Lindz was also working her strategies, like finding a direct line to Putin. Basketball avenues were not proving fruitful, but she knew he valued sports. Fiona Hill, a former official at the U.S. National Security Council and a Russia expert, had advised us to focus on protecting the sanctity of sports and to emphasize the important role they play in positioning Russia as part of a global community. Lindz and our team created a list of athletes whom Putin cared about. Near the top was the legendary MMA fighter Khabib Nurmagomedov, who another Wasserman client, the Olympic medalist in fencing Ibtihaj Muhammad, had brought to Lindz's attention. Khabib was a Russian citizen and friendly with the Russian president. Maybe he could appeal to Putin for my release while building a humanitarian legacy for himself—that was Lindsay's hope. To connect with Khabib, she first tried his agent, then asked the owner of the Las Vegas Aces to introduce her to UFC president Dana White, who has publicly supported President Trump. But politics wasn't the topic. Connecting with Khabib was. They arranged a call with that understanding, but Dana had other plans.

"I've just gotten off the phone with Trump," Dana told Lindz.

"So what did you talk about?" she asked.

"President Trump is thinking about getting involved in bringing Brittney home."

Pause. "How?" she asked.

"He's considering flying to Russia to get her," he said. He added that the president might soon speak publicly about his intention. Trump had just launched his 2024 presidential campaign. Bringing me home could be a political win.

Lindz weighed the news and decided to call the White House to relay what she'd heard. If President Trump planned to get involved, the White House needed to know. She got two different responses: One senior official received the news calmly and thanked her for passing it along. Another was clearly unhappy, asking why Lindz was calling Dana. Maybe that official knew something my agent didn't about how close a deal was. Or maybe the revelation lit a fire under the White House to get me home.

Meanwhile, my team had created a spreadsheet of candidates the Russians might trade. Would it be a one-for-one deal or a twofer? Anything was possible, but they pushed for me and Paul Whelan for two Russian prisoners. Over the months of my detainment, my team and the Whelan family stayed in regular contact, and Lindz worked closely with Paul's attorney, Ryan Fayhee, along with Trevor Reed's lawyer, Jonathan Franks. Uniting in our message made it stronger: every American hostage, regardless of background, deserved to be brought home.

After my verdict, Relle planned a TV interview alongside Paul's brother, David. That plan changed when Queen Elizabeth died and the media spotlight shifted. Still, our families worked arm in arm. Many speculated about who the Russians might trade. Roman Seleznev, the hacker serving a twenty-seven-year sentence, was a possibility. So was Vadim Krasikov, an assassin in German prison for life after murdering a Chechen fighter. Viktor Bout was on every list. If a swap happened—and that was still an *if* in November—the arms dealer loyal to Putin would almost certainly be part of a deal. I didn't care what prisoner I got swapped for or who brought me back to America—Biden, Richardson, Trump, or former NBA player Dennis Rodman, who'd said he would try to cut a deal. This prisoner wasn't picky. I'd take any path home.

....

Ann showed up at my workplace and told me to follow her to the main building. The date was November 29. The reason for the summons was unknown.

"There are some people here to speak to you," she whispered as we walked. The deputy warden and three men Ann didn't recognize had told her to quickly bring me to them. The guards had sealed off the building, she said, and weren't letting inmates in. "Everyone's acting weird," she told me. "If they ask you anything, be careful." I nodded and entered the building.

The head warden was out sick that day. The deputy warden, the tall one, was seated across from two of the men. Another sat off to the side. All three had on nice suits and expensive watches. I assumed they worked for FSB, Russia's security agency, but no one introduced them. Ann and I sat. "The U.S. Embassy needs to speak to you," the deputy warden said to me via Ann, who translated. "You'll need to take the call here in my office, on speakerphone. The call will be recorded." I nodded and swallowed hard.

Moments later, on the deputy warden's desk phone, two men introduced themselves as officers from the U.S. Embassy. I recognized one of the voices and felt relieved. It was the Consular Affairs officer who'd visited me in detention.

"There's a trade deal on the table to bring you home," one of the officers said. I leaned closer to the phone. Ann and I exchanged a surprised look.

"Really?" I said.

"Yes," he said. "It's still early, and you'll need to keep this very quiet. If the news breaks before Russia wants it public, that could jeopardize the deal." I must've agreed. I was so astonished I couldn't hear myself speak.

"Do you have any idea who you'll be traded for?" asked the officer.

"Yes, I have an idea," I said. "Can you tell me?"

He couldn't say, which made me wonder why he'd asked. "Can you guess?" he said.

"Viktor Bout," I replied.

Silence.

"You're thinking in the right direction," he finally said. He wouldn't confirm it but didn't need to. The whole world had heard Viktor would likely be part of any trade. The officers didn't say when I might be released or give other details. They just wanted me to know my freedom "might" be close. They reiterated that this must stay hush-hush.

The deputy warden and the FSB men filed out to a nearby office to debrief. I leaned toward Ann and softly squealed, "I might be going *hooome*!" She smiled and put her finger to her lips. The room was likely bugged, she whispered.

The deputy warden and two of the FSB agents returned to the office. The third man hovered in the hall. One of the agents in the office, the apparent leader, began speaking in perfect English. He measured every word.

"Yes, there's a possible deal," he said. "But in order for it to work out, your country has to do all the right things." I stared at him like, *Such as?* He pressed his lips together. "You need to pay the fine of one million rubles right away," he said. He then underscored what I'd already heard: I could not say a word. He also told Ann she couldn't share the news with anyone, including Kate. He knew the three of us were tight.

"If I can't tell anyone," I said, "how will I arrange the payment? I have no direct access to my finances from prison." He stared at me like the thought hadn't occurred to him and then huddled briefly with the others. "You can tell your lawyers but no one else," he said.

I was bursting with questions: When might the deal go through? How much time would I have to prepare? How many bags could I take? And for contacting my lawyers, would the warden approve a call from the quad? The leader didn't truly give answers, but the little he said was apparently too much for the agent listening from the hall. He came in, tapped his colleague on the shoulder, and said, "That's enough." The deputy warden further shut me down. "Stop asking questions," she said.

The lead agent made one last request: he asked me to write a petition of pardon to Putin. When I'd first arrived at IK-2, my team had spent hours helping me carefully craft a private petition of pardon to the Russian president. That letter, however, was never sent or made public. We were saving it for the moment when Putin's receipt of it might have the most impact. This possible trade deal arose before we had to make that move.

But in order for Russia to agree to a prisoner swap, these agents told me, I'd have to address their president directly. The agent handed me a paper with tiny Russian script and told me to copy it in my own handwriting on a separate piece of paper. I sat there for an hour and painstakingly wrote every word, with no idea what I was writing. Ann later told me what the letter said. It was a confession. I'd been forced to tell Putin I "repented" for my crime, as if he were some kind of deity. That struck me as weird, but I didn't care. Given what I'd endured, I'd write anything to get out of his country.

The deputy warden dismissed us, and Ann walked me back to work. Every inmate we passed stared at me with a question on her face: *Are you going home?* In prison there were no secrets. The moment three strangers had arrived at the colony, trade rumors began flying. "Is it happening?" one girl came up to us and asked. Our silence answered. We kept our promise not to tell Kate, but that was pointless. By the time I got back to work, my teammates knew about the meeting. They'd heard it from others in the building. I feared the agents would accuse me of blabbing and that any deal would be off.

How do you go back to cutting fabric when your mind has just been blown? Carefully, so your anxiety doesn't cost you a finger. I wanted to believe what I'd heard but also felt I couldn't trust it. Part of me knew my freedom had to be close because the Russians were demanding money, though they could've taken my $11,000 and kept me in prison. Another part of me realized this had to be legit because the U.S. Embassy was involved. Still, there I was, at a labor camp in the middle of winter. Until my feet were on U.S. soil, I couldn't exhale. The meeting felt like progress, but it wasn't yet time to celebrate.

That night I couldn't sleep. The next morning I stumbled to work dazed. *Oh my God, this is happening*, I thought. A moment later I'd push down that feeling and convince myself, *They're playing me*. After work I was allowed to call Alex. He was so shocked he got quiet at first. He'd known talks were progressing but had no idea a deal might be close. He and Maria arranged for the money to be wired from her firm. It was sent to the transport department of the Ministry of Internal Affairs in Sheremetyevo Airport.

After the money was sent, the Russians got quiet. That intensified my anxiety. Had they changed their minds? *You've got nine years,* I told myself after three days of silence. *You just got here a few weeks ago. You'd better focus on your reality and get a routine down.* If I got out of prison right after serving my sentence, that'd be a perk. And if I was freed any earlier, that'd be a miracle. *Chill, BG,* I coached myself. Because the moment I leaned into excitement, I'd get hit with, "You're going nowhere." While Russia said nothing, a battle raged inside me. I was worried. I was fearful. I was a mess.

A full week after the U.S. Embassy's call, Ann came to my job again. She was beaming. "It's happening," she whispered excitedly. I studied her face. "For real?" I said. "Stop messing with me. I've still got five more hours of work." "No you don't," she said. "I've been told to take you to the main building so you can fill out your exit papers." I dropped the fabric I was about to cut and left without a word to my coworkers. They stared. They knew.

That afternoon I was told I'd be released the next day. I could take the belongings I'd brought, as well as my uniform. On the night before my departure, I gave away almost everything: food, clothes, hair products, toiletries. Several of the girls stopped in to say goodbye. "You fly home?" one girl asked. She held up her hand as if it were an ascending plane. I nodded, and we laughed. Many of the inmates brought me photographs of their children. They asked me to sign, and I happily did.

Even some second offenders came through, though they could've gotten in trouble for leaving their quads. Just before an inmate's release, Ann said, the nice guards relaxed the rules. One girl's freedom was every girl's celebration. Ann and Kate dropped in too. Ann brought honey cake she'd made during her shift. The three of us embraced as they wished me well, said, "Don't ever come back here." As a parting gift, I gave Ann the earnings I'd received from human resources. For all my long hours I earned less than a hundred bucks.

My final hours at IK-2 mirrored those of my first: my tattoos were photographed, my belongings were searched, I did squats in my boxers. Once I had dressed in my uniform again, a guard held up a camera and motioned for me to follow him. All over the colony he snapped photos of me. Playing cards in the common room. Lounging on a couch with Ann. Making my bed in the quad. Having lunch in the cafeteria with a coworker from the second-offender group. Every one of those photos was staged. Some were eventually released. In the propaganda pictures things look clean, orderly, even pleasant. The reality was the opposite.

I left IK-2 right around lunchtime on Friday, December 2. I wasn't told where I'd be taken. *Are we going to an airfield for me to fly home?* I wondered. *Am I boarding a train to Moscow to go to the U.S. Embassy? Does my family know I'm leaving prison today? Has the story hit the news?* Just like during my arrival, I was kept in the dark about everything. I also had no translator. The guards led me from the front gates and captured my departure on video. In the footage I look exhausted, because I was. I hadn't slept the night before. Too anxious. I left wearing my uniform and carrying my two duffels.

I signed some last documents before climbing into a van. Instead of the usual square-box truck, this van looked like the kind used to transport handicapped passengers. I was caged but not cuffed. Though I was the only passenger, four guards climbed in. On a small cot in the back, I bumped along for seven, eight hours before we finally slowed down. In silence and pitch-black, the guards unloaded me in front of a massive brick building. It looked like another prison. I glanced around. "Moscow?" I asked the guard. He nodded and led me toward the building.

At the entrance my fear came true: I was back in a labor camp. I didn't know it then, but this was a large men's prison near the capital. I was led through the metal detectors as I tried to figure out why we were there. I recalled the overnight train stop on the way to Mordovia, but that was to get to captivity. I thought I was on my way to freedom, but was I? And if I was being thrown back in prison, how long would I be there? Would I ever make it home? The uncertainty was more than unsettling. It was terrifying.

A male guard gestured for me to follow him as two other guards held up the rear. Hauling my duffels, I struggled up one steep staircase, and then a second and a third. By the fifth, I was out of breath. By the eighth my legs and lungs were on fire. I stopped and put down my bags, but the guard behind urged me on. We must've climbed ten, twelve floors before we finally arrived at another security checkpoint. The lead guard motioned for me to set my bags near a scanner. "Take toothbrush and underwear," he said. I quietly did as I was told as my insides screamed, *Yo, what the fuck is going on?* After I'd removed a few items, a guard shoved my duffels through the X-ray machine and then left with them.

The other guards took me to an office. "This is where I stay?" I kept asking. One guard ignored me as he filled out a form with my name on it. Another gave me a blank stare. I held up nine fingers in the face of the third. "*Devyat* here?" I asked. "Yes," he said. My heart pounded. "Yes?" I squealed. He repeated his answer. "How long?" I asked. *Silence.* "I stay here *devyat*?" I asked repeatedly, my tone growing irritated. All three tuned me out. I squelched tears as I was searched as I'd been upon entering IK-2: squats in my boxers, pics of my tats. I was stone-faced but losing it internally. I thought I was getting traded. Instead, I was getting rebooked.

I don't know what time it was when a guard finally led me to an empty cell. It felt late, sometime after 9:00 p.m. He turned his skeleton key in the lock and gestured for me to enter. He handed me a mattress and left. I glanced around. The room was about six by eight feet. There were two sets of bunks, a small table, a kitchenette with a sink and cabinet, a barred window covered in dust, a tiny camera above the door. The toilet was a hole in the ground but pretty clean. Since guards never cleaned the cells, the last inmates must've been neat. In a corner were a small TV and a remote. I'd heard male prisoners controlled their own channels, those lucky bastards.

At 6:00 a.m. the lights flickered on. Sprawled on a bottom bunk, I was still dressed in my IK-2 uniform, had nodded off with a feeling of dread. A guard barked in Russian from outside the cell but didn't barge in for a check. Moments later a tray slid through the door, porridge and goat's milk. I lumbered from bed and sat at the table, ate while wondering what the day would bring. I hadn't been taken to quarantine or given a different uniform. Those seemed like signs my stay would be temporary. But *how* temporary? Back at county I'd been held for weeks with little information. I felt like I was back there, in those painful hours before Alex arrived. I had no translator. No phone or watch. No human contact. At least at IK-2, I had quad mates. As horrible as that place was, work and community made it survivable. In this place I'd die of isolation.

I turned on the TV and channel-surfed, relished the simple luxury of controlling *something*. The programs were all in Russian. Still, I found a few shows Alena had once translated for me, tried to recall the storylines. Around noon, a guard showed up and ordered me to follow him. We climbed stairs to the roof until we finally reached the Yard, a steel enclosure of about thirty individual concrete cages with a ceiling made of bars. It was patrolled by a guard with a machine gun walking above on a suspended sidewalk. I could hear men yelling between the cells but saw no one from my cage. I sat on a bench and smoked for an hour, tried to get the guard to take me back to my cell. It was cold as hell out there. I also felt like a dog that had been taken out to piss.

The second day went mostly like the first: TV, Yard, isolation, plus having my fingerprints taken. The whole time I was freaking out and wishing I could call Alex. Was this some twisted joke? Had the deal been called off? In place of answers I had anxiety, and it increased by the hour. After fish and potatoes on night two, I pounded on my door to get the guard's attention. I was crouched near the peephole when he flipped it open, and I shouted, "What is happening?" He yelled a Russian obscenity, slammed the peephole, and stomped off. I cursed back at him. I didn't care if I got punished. Being held without explanation was its own cruelty. Yet it couldn't compare to what was coming.

On the third day I was taken to the infirmary for medical tests. I saw women for the first time, medics darting from room to room. A guard locked me in a cage within an exam room. In came two nurses, one fresh-faced and smiling, the other wrinkled and stoic. The younger one spoke a little English. "Blood," she said, gesturing for me to stick my forearm through the bars. I refused. I wasn't giving blood until someone told me why I was there. "How long do I stay?" I asked. She smiled and shrugged. "Nine years here?" I pressed.

Just then, the elderly nurse pulled my arm toward her. I yanked it back. I made such a scene that two guards ran in, which was what I'd hoped for. I wanted every official in that prison to know I needed answers. The move was pointless. After a shouting match translated by the younger nurse, the guards insisted, "You have to give blood." Exhausted and emotional, I held out my arm and allowed Russia to take one more part of me. Afterward the older nurse rammed a swab up my nose and down my throat for a Covid test. She smeared the swab across a card with my name on top. She also smeared on a dab of my blood, next to my fingerprint.

Back in my cell that evening, I escaped into the World Cup. On December 6, Portugal put a beating on Switzerland, 6–1. I went wild cheering, grateful for a joyful distraction. Soon after, I had another bristly exchange with the guard who'd cursed at me. I'd banged on the door, asking for my lawyer or the warden. He told me to shut up. I was preparing for lights out when the peephole flipped open. A paper fell in. I picked it up and looked at it. Two sentences were handwritten across the top: "You leave tonight. Be ready." Adrenaline coursed through me.

I gathered my few items and threw them in a plastic bag. *This is happening*, I thought. No guard had ever given me a note like that. He'd likely been told by his superiors to relay the instructions, and realizing that made me trust the note's message. And if it wasn't true, I still needed to believe. For months I'd tried to protect myself by keeping hope in a corner. On this night I let it in. I had to or I would've gone crazy.

Lights out came. I lay on the bed, one foot on the floor, ready to jump up. I nodded off but kept trying to wake myself. I didn't want to be dead asleep when the guards arrived, but I was also legit exhausted. Hours later, sometime before 6:00, a guard beat on the door. I threw off my covers and leapt up as he looked in through the peephole. I gave a thumbs-up, like, *I'm ready*. He mimicked my gesture. Moments later I heard boots approaching. When the door opened, four guards in full camo stood at attention. I followed them to a staircase, where another three guards waited. The fact that I was surrounded, seven to one, reinforced in my mind that this was real.

We entered a large cold room. One guard led me in, and the other six followed. An older man holding a clipboard introduced himself as a doctor. He spoke crude English. "Check," he said. I added the word *out* in my head. He looked me up and down, and his eyes stopped on my arm tattoos. "Gang?" he asked. "*Nyet*," I replied. He wrote on his clipboard sheet. "Scars, medical problems, drugs?" he asked. No, no, no. "Shirt," he said, gesturing for me to remove my top. I took it off and laid it on a table in the corner. The doctor began photographing my upper body. "Pants," he said a moment later. I reached for my shirt to pull back on. "No," he said, "leave there." I reached again for my top, but he backed me away. "Leave, leave, leave," he ordered. The room was freezing; I was already topless. He insisted I get butt naked.

The guards stared as I removed my pants but left on my boxers. "Off," the doctor ordered. I looked at him, dumbfounded. *Off?* "Everything off," he reiterated. In shock and humiliation, I removed my boxers. Then my socks. Even my glasses. I didn't cover my privates, nor did I cower or tremble. I just tried to escape my body, pretend I wasn't there. Two guards exchanged a glance. The rest gazed. I sensed they expected me to fall apart, some weak-ass American. I stood tall as the doctor snapped photos and motioned for me to rotate. *Front. Back. Side. Click.* I felt like weeping but had no tears left.

22

THE TRADE

I left the men's prison after four days—and after 293 days of incarceration. The morning of my departure I was stripped of my dignity. The guards also seized my notebook with my IK-2 quad mates' Instagram handles written in it. My uniform was taken as well, which actually gave me hope. I must've been leaving the penal colonies, since uniforms were required there. I layered up with clothes I pulled from my duffel: a hoodie, red coat, and gray skullcap. There was one more good sign I was truly coming home: I noticed my blue passport jutting from my case file, which a guard held. I'd last seen it in February.

The prison was connected to what looked like a county clerk's office. The guards led me there, and we waited in a hall. The young nurse who'd drawn my blood stopped in. "Am I going free today?" I asked her. "Yes," she said with a smile. "You just have to sign your pardon papers." *So am I going home today? How will I get there? Was a trade deal finalized?* I had these and other questions but didn't ask them. She'd answered the one that mattered. I wanted to celebrate in that hall, but I squelched the impulse. *Not home free till you're home,* I told myself.

The guards led me out front, where three FSB agents waited. They had on tactical gear and looked muscular enough to fight off a grizzly. They took my bags and loaded me into the van's back row, no cuffs. They sat up front. No one told me where we were going. From my window I watched Moscow pass. It was so early that few cars were on the road. We picked up another agent, a woman. We also stopped at a gas station with a convenience store. "Do you want coffee?" the one agent who spoke English asked. "I'll take water," I said. Anything could be stirred into coffee. Bottled water was at least sealed.

We drove to an area near the Kremlin. "Do you know this building?" the English-speaking agent asked, pointing. I nodded. "That's Putin's palace," he said, chuckling. I fake laughed. *Are we going to see the president?* I began worrying. I recalled the repentance letter I'd written to him. Maybe he needed something else from me, a signature or just a meeting. Stressful. I didn't want to see him if I didn't have to. We circled around the Kremlin three times but didn't stop. I don't know why I was taken there. It could've been a reminder I was still under Putin's control, or just an expression of national pride.

The sun was up when we arrived at an airfield on the outskirts of Moscow. The agents led me to an awaiting plane and gestured for me to follow them up the jet bridge stairs. Though my heart raced, I stepped slowly, not quite believing where I was. A flight attendant met me at the top. So did a translator. He introduced me to two men onboard, Russia's version of SPEHA. I was then seated in the bulkhead, near a reporter from Russia's state media. He pointed his camera at me.

"What's your mood?" he asked me in a thick accent.

I laughed nervously. "Happy," I said. The whole car ride there, I'd promised myself I wouldn't show the Russians how excited I was, but in that moment I couldn't help it.

"Are you ready for our flight?" he asked.

"Yes, I'm ready," I said.

"Do you know where you're headed to?"

"No," I replied.

"You're flying back home," he said.

I paused. "To the U.S.?" I asked.

"Yes," he said. "Everything will be fine."

This was the first confirmation I had that I was headed to the United States. I still didn't know the route. Trevor Reed's exchange took place in Istanbul, Turkey. I wondered if mine would too. I also didn't know the details of the deal, a twofer or a one-for-one. I'd hoped to see Paul Whelan on my flight. My heart sank when I didn't. *So will I be traded for Viktor Bout?* I had no clue.

Up in the air the English-speaking FSB agent struck up a conversation with me as his colleagues gathered around. I could tell he was the jokester of the group, laughing when the others were dead serious. In my head I called him Mr. Funny Man.

"Do you have anybody waiting for you at home?" he asked.

"My wife," I replied. The translator told everyone what I'd said.

Mr. Funny Man bugged out his eyes. "Your *wife?*" he said.

I nodded.

"Why a wife?" he asked. "Why not a man?"

"Because I'm a lesbian," I told him.

"Is that legal?" he asked.

"Yes," I said.

One of the diplomats, who'd overheard us, laughed and interrupted. "Oh, he just wants a visa," he said, nodding toward Mr. Funny Man. Clearly, I wasn't his ticket to America.

"I know some people," I said, smiling. "You're tall. I bet I can hook you up."

We'd flown two hours when we began descending, too short a time to be in Istanbul. I peeked out my window and saw mountains, greenery, countryside. "We're landing to refuel," the diplomat told me. He must've seen the question on my face because he added, "This is Dagestan"—the homeland of the MMA fighter Khabib Nurmagomedov, he said.

"Where are we going?" I asked the translator.

Abu Dhabi. Four hours more. And please, he urged, eat.

I declined. I'd survived for months without getting poisoned, couldn't chance it on this flight. Instead, I sat worrying about what might still go wrong, like our plane crashing into a field. For weeks I'd been having nightmares like that. I'd be flying to America when my plane would suddenly nosedive, or we'd get blown from the sky by a missile. I'd wake up sweating and remember where I was, trying to forget both tragedies. My growling stomach interrupted that spiral. An hour into our flight, I caved to the scent of steak and potatoes, which the others were enjoying. I'd gotten hungry enough to take a risk but still sniffed before I bit in. The meal was tasty, five-star compared to prison fare.

After eating I began wondering, *Does Relle know I'm on my way home? What will it be like to see her? Will she be happy but also mad about this whole mess?* For nearly a year she'd been on her own, holding together a home without me in it. I was scared about how so much time apart might have changed her, me, our dynamic. I also thought about seeing my parents again. I knew Momma would cry her eyes out. I was stressed over Dad's condition. Even before I left for Russia, I'd noticed him slowing down. I felt nervous about what state I'd find him in.

As we descended, the agents asked if they could get me anything else. *Yes, the last nine months.* We landed in Abu Dhabi just before dusk, then sat on the tarmac. I was anxious. I was giddy. But I was now fully believing this trade was happening. We taxied to another area of the tarmac. Moments later our jet bridge lowered and a man climbed to the entrance. Inside he spoke with the two diplomats for a while. He then walked toward me.

"My name is Roger Carstens. I'm with the U.S. Department of State," he said with a broad smile. *Roger.* For months I'd known his name but not his face. I exhaled when I realized it was him. "I am here on behalf of President Joe Biden and Secretary Antony Blinken to take you home," he said. He handed me a "We Are BG" pin and said, "There are a lot of people who are dying to see you come home and they gave me this pin to wear when I met you."

He explained how the trade would unfold. "You are going to be on a U.S. plane in less than five minutes," he told me, with a confidence that relaxed me. He said he'd get off the aircraft we were on and that I should gather my stuff. He explained that I'd be brought off the plane and walked to the center of the tarmac. "We'll say our thank-yous and then we're gonna get you out of here." He mentioned the prisoner he'd flown there with, and that I'd likely cross paths with him, but didn't say his name. Before returning to his plane, Roger asked, "Are you ready?" I stood. I was.

The Russian cameraman got off our aircraft first. I waited for the go-ahead from the diplomats. "It's time," I finally heard. I made my way down the jet bridge. Two agents followed with my duffels. Across the tarmac I spotted Roger with a man I couldn't initially identify. Both groups walked toward each other. I soon realized the prisoner was Viktor.

The Merchant of Death looked nothing like the menacing villain he'd appeared as during his prime. If I'd seen him on the street, I would've passed him thinking he was just another middle-aged man. I'd seen photos of him following his 2008 arrest, that killer expression and no hint of remorse. On the tarmac he seemed like a shell of himself, gray mustache, ruthlessness muted. He looked at me, I looked him, and then he reached for a handshake. "Congratulations," he said as we shook. "Good luck on being home." I instinctively wished him the same.

Unlike my bruised hands, Viktor's hands were soft. So were the creases on his face. He'd spent much of his sentence doing artwork, I'd heard—painting portraits of cats. I'd spent mine with a table saw. We released our grip. I was left with a sick feeling, like death, all over my palms and beyond.

Air Force BG—that was what my flight home should've been called. From the moment I boarded the jet, the crew catered to me. A medical team tended to my cuts and bruises and took my vitals. A SEAL psychiatrist trained to work with military personnel returning from traumatic situations gently talked me through how I'd be cared for in the coming days. We'd fly to a military hospital for a full mental health assessment, she said, and I could choose which facility. Brooke Army Medical Center in San Antonio made sense. I'm from Texas, my family's nearby in Houston, Relle could easily get there from Phoenix. "I've got a bag packed for you," the psychiatrist said. We'd stop in London to refuel and then fly to my home state.

A flight attendant offered me steak and a Coke. I accepted because I could. The cut was twice as thick as the one from the Russians and was followed by an amazing dessert. Roger and his colleague Fletcher had heard I loved Lemonhead candy. They'd stocked the plane with it, as well as with sudoku puzzles. I reclined in a swivel chair and popped the candy, with the crew gathered around me. "Don't you want to sleep?" Roger and the others kept asking. I didn't. Conversing in my language felt centering, after months of feeling lost in translation. I initially struggled to recall words. I couldn't think of the word *similar*, for instance. That was because I'd spent so long trying to convey things simply to non-English speakers. I'd lost some fluency. I'd lost a lot.

I shared a few harrowing stories with the crew, like the train ride to IK-2. But honestly, I wanted to talk about anything *but* Russia. Along with the psychiatrist, there were three U.S. Marshals with special ops and combat experience on board, and I learned that Fletcher and Roger were both U.S. Army Rangers. Roger was Special Forces and a Green Beret. I've always been fascinated by anything military-related, so I probed them for war stories. I also asked Fletcher and Roger about their work. "What are some of the countries you've gotten people out of?" I asked. Afghanistan. Myanmar. Nigeria. Venezuela. And, they hoped, more to come. If Pops had been there, he'd have wanted every detail, I said. They laughed knowingly. They'd enjoyed many long conversations with my father during my detainment. Their shared fight for my freedom had brought them close.

During the London layover at a private airfield, a lady who worked there lit up when she saw me. "Oh my God, can I have your autograph?" she asked. *Of course.* She'd played basketball back in the day and had followed my career. She'd also been one of the many who'd prayed for my freedom, and now there I was at her workplace. We posed for a photo as she repeated, "I can't *believe* this!" It was cool. It also foreshadowed my coming reality.

"Let's get you on the phone with your family," Roger said. I called my father from a line onboard and got his voicemail. "I've been traded, Pops," I said in the message. "I'm on my way home. I bet you'll wish you would've picked up!" I tried him again later. "Man, I'm just striking out today," I said, laughing. I now know the old man was asleep. My ordeal had him wiped.

Relle picked up on the first ring. "Hi, babe!" she said with emotion in her voice. She'd kept her ringer on and was expecting me to call. "So you know where I am right now?" I said. *Hell yes.* Two days earlier she'd been summoned to the White House to see the president. The agenda hadn't been revealed. "Pack a bag for BG," Lindz told Relle. My agent had just had drinks with the SPEHA team and sensed my freedom was close. When Relle arrived, she was greeted by President Biden and Vice President Harris in the Oval Office. "BG is on her way to San Antonio," he'd told her. Relle was still in shock.

I finally lay down to rest on a couch. The SEAL Team 6 guys played cards and told more stories, laughed and reminisced. I fought fatigue so I could soak in the tales. Sleep ultimately won. A while later, I awakened to the sound of the captain's voice through the intercom. "We are now entering U.S. airspace," he announced. I sat up with tears in my eyes. I was home.

PART V

HOME

When you're told you're not good enough, you tell them, "Not only am I good enough, I'm more than enough." When they say, "Send her back home," you tell them, "I am home. I am the foundation of what we call home." When they tell you that you're angry or nasty, you tell them that they're mistaken: "This is me. This is me being resolute and standing firmly in my truth."

—Angela Bassett, award-winning actress and icon, speaking at Black Girls Rock

BG

You're the best, my love 😇

Say more lol! 😇 🖤

Nah, scratch that, Relle . . . you're the most BEAUTIFUL woman in the entire world. 🌎 Wow, I'm so happy I get to wake up next to you for the rest of my life

Awww, you're sweet! I'm honored I get to wake up next to you FOREVER 🖤

BG and Relle at home together in Phoenix on Christmas 2022 following 293 days apart

23

GROUND SHIFTS

Roger told me Relle would be waiting on the tarmac in San Antonio. She'd been whisked there from D.C. on a private White House plane after meeting with the president. My family would arrive later. On my flight's last leg I thought only of my wife—seeing her, touching her, holding her again. For ten long months I'd imagined the experience, and also convinced myself not to. *Nine years.* Dreaming of coming home any sooner made the finish line feel further away and only lengthened the agony. And now there I was, preparing to glimpse her, believing and yet stunned. We began our descent at 3:30 a.m. San Antonio time. I felt the plane drop, the cabin pressure increase, my heart race faster with each dip. At thirty thousand feet, I gazed out at the clouds. At twenty, I gripped my seat. At ten, I saw the tarmac and held back emotion. The wheels at last touched down.

My hands shook as we taxied. Eventually, we pulled up to the hangar. "I can see your wife," Roger said. I squinted through my window but couldn't spot her from my side. "You want to trade seats?" he asked. *Absolutely.* When I caught sight of Relle,

I lost it. There she stood, tears flooding her cheeks, standing on an X out of the news media's view. I pressed my face to the window. She waved, and I wept harder. She was surrounded by supporters, an American flag behind them. The jet bridge lowered, and an additional medical team boarded, did more checks. "Ready to hug your wife?" Roger asked after five minutes. *Yes* was lodged in my throat.

I approached the door. *Don't slip down these stairs*, I told myself, not wanting to add a fall to my ugly-cry. I stepped carefully at first, stairs one and two, but the desire for Relle's touch overtook me. I leapt down the last few steps and darted across the tarmac. I pulled my wife close, enveloped her body, squeezed her more tightly than I ever had before. We cried and cried, tears of exhilaration, 293 days' worth of longing stored up. Our hug lasted a full minute. The others looked on, dabbing tears, but Relle and I were oblivious. On that tarmac it was just us two. "Sorry if I smell like cigarettes," I whispered in Relle's ear. "You don't," she whispered back. "But, honey," she said, "let's get outta here." The real first hug awaited. Lindz and I embraced, and she said how much she'd missed me, introduced me to the small army who had fought for my freedom. There were twenty or so supporters gathered. I hugged and took photos with most. A cameraman brought in by my team captured the cryfest. That hangar floor was covered in tears.

A private lounge had been prepared for Relle and me. We couldn't get in there fast enough. My favorite snacks were lined up on a table: Skittles, Junior Mints, Flamin' Hot Cheetos. But Relle was the only snack I wanted. I sat on a couch and pulled my wife onto my lap, released the final floodgates as we smooched. We touched each other's cheeks, eyelashes, noses. Relle slid the beanie off my head. "Oh my gosh, you look so different!" she squealed, running her palms through my curls. "Do you like it?" I asked. Yes, she assured me, peanut head and all, I'd always look cute to her. Relle was, of course, still fine as hell, more gorgeous than she'd been years ago at Baylor. She had braids down past her butt, just as I like them. Still, great as she looked, I sensed the toll our nightmare had taken on her. She was exhausted. We were still in our bliss a half hour later when a knock came. The hangar staff would begin work soon, at 5:00 a.m., we heard. We'd need to pause our reunion until after my medical checkup. We'd be apart for the next twenty-four hours while the team supported my reentry—a post-trauma protocol for newly freed hostages. I'd spend eight days total on base.

Three white vans were waiting to take me to the base hospital and Relle to her room on campus. Two of the vans were decoys, intended to keep the media gathered nearby from knowing my exact location. In the hospital, the medical team led me to a private wing, with no other patients on the floor. I traded my clothes for a blue and white gown, slipped onto a large hospital bed actually long enough for me. I've never received a more complete checkup. In and out came the doctors and nurses, as kind as they were thorough. One implanted a port in my arm for IV treatments. Another examined every inch of my skin, cleaned up my bruised hands after the beating they had taken in the labor camp. X-rays were done on my chest, heart, abdomen, lungs. I was tested for every imaginable infectious disease. For two hours I got poked and prodded. Doctors discovered I was anemic and badly dehydrated. It's a miracle my lungs were okay after smoking like a freight train for ten months.

That was just the physical assessment. The SEAL Team 6 psychiatrist I'd met on the flight teamed up with another to check on my mental health. After patiently guiding me through some of what I'd experienced, they prepared me for what could be coming: symptoms of PTSD. Hearing a door bang shut, for instance, might remind me of my cell door slamming. "You may experience mood swings, sudden anger and irritability, insomnia and nightmares, or feel a strong desire to withdraw," they told me. "And after trauma and extended family separation, it's common for family dynamics to shift. Your wife has survived without you for nearly a year. Now that you're home, she may need you less—or she might expect you to do everything."

These experiences were common, they said. They promised to support me then and after release. They also advised me not to watch or read news coverage of my ordeal. Possibly triggering. I nodded but flipped on the TV set as soon as they left. I'd just spent nearly three hundred days with no control. Reaching for the remote was my way of reasserting it.

Also, I was curious as hell about the coverage and eager to hear English. All the news channels were reporting on my homecoming. It was strange seeing myself on blast. I'd known the world was following my story, but for months I'd felt alone in the horror. And now my private heartache was playing out globally. *Jarring.* I wished I'd followed my therapists' recommendation, but curiosity got the best of me. I did finally move on to other news by scrolling through my iPad. Ketanji Brown Jackson had been sworn in as the nation's first Black female Supreme Court justice. Serena Williams had hung up her racket. Drake had dropped a new album. The second *Black Panther* movie was out. Nancy Pelosi's husband, Paul, had been attacked with a hammer in his home. I read and I reeled. I'd missed so much.

At 11:00 a.m. I began asking for my wife. I understood the team's recommendation for gradual reconnection with loved ones. Some hostages have severe PTSD after years of extreme torture and isolation. The transition from hell to freedom can be overwhelming. I asked the psychiatrists to bend the rules; Relle's presence, I felt, would be part of my healing. They agreed and called her. By noon she was curled up with me in that bed, doing her best to avoid my painful arm port. We cuddled into the overnight hours, filled in all the details we hadn't been able to divulge in letters. We didn't go deep that first night, just work and family and a play-by-play of Relle's graduation and bar exam. We also didn't nod off. We'd already lost ten months. We were determined not to miss another minute of each other.

Pops and Carlo arrived the next morning, just before my transition from the hospital to a residence on base. Mom and E.J. were recovering from Covid with help from my sister Pier, so our in-person reunion would have to wait. Relle and I were up and dressed when my father and brother walked in. We all hugged hard while fighting tears. "Do you know how much I missed you, girl?" Pops asked. *For sure.* "You almost gave me a heart attack," he joked. I kept the humor going. "All right, big man, you're looking good," I said, patting his belly. He swore he'd been exercising, but we both knew damn well he probably hadn't been. Pops had spruced himself up for my return, wanted to be the strong dad I relied on. But I could tell my ordeal had weighed heavily on him. His slight limp was a sign of the stress he'd endured. My homecoming lifted the burden. Same with Momma. When she and I connected on video, she cried her way through a pack of tissues. But after her tears came relief. Her baby was home—finally.

The residence was a beautiful little retreat house set up like a bed-and-breakfast. The psychiatrists came through frequently to monitor my progress and hear more of what I'd survived. I teared up while completing a homework assignment they gave me. I'd been asked to draw each of the cells I'd been in, as well as the prison grounds. Sketching that first cell at county broke me. That isn't because it was the filthiest I'd endured, but because of the way I'd felt there: like I wasn't a person. I was ripping up T-shirts for toilet paper, trying to clean myself as a way to feel human.

In the residence, each day brought fresh tears as family showed up. SheKera and her daughter, my niece Niyah, visited. So did my uncle Tony and aunt Evelyn, as well as my cousins Jasmine and T.J. Janell Roy, my friend who was like a sister, also came to embrace me. In between all that hugging I ate—a lot. When I'd left for Russia ten months earlier, I'd been a muscular 250 pounds. During detention, and especially as our trials approached, Alena and I went crazy eating: salami, condensed milk, muffins, noodles. I hadn't had a scale, but I'd seen the stomach flab forming. During the long workdays at the penal colony, I dropped that flab and then some. I came home at 222, small for six nine. My family helped fatten me up. Jeremy

Cassano, SPEHA's family engagement coordinator, had been assigned to help us with whatever we needed. We had that guy picking up takeout around the clock, from Whataburger (best in Texas) to Smoke Shack BBQ (meat so tender it fell off the bone). Then, during my last night in San Antonio, Relle and I dined out at Pappasito's Cantina. The quesadillas were fire. So were the Flamin' Hot Cheetos I'd been downing all week. My fingertips were bright red and burning—aka Cheeto Fingers. Between the Cheetos and the barbecue, I'm sure I packed on at least five pounds.

I cut into the calories with exercise. On base I did a short workout, the first time in months I'd been in a gym. I kept it basic—crunches, planks, biceps curls—and was still totally out of breath. By then I'd (mostly) stopped smoking cold turkey, no cigs on the base and sporadically from then on. I've probably had fifteen cigs total since I've been home. Luckily, I didn't go through nicotine withdrawal—no symptoms. Still, after I'd spent ten months smoking a half pack or more a day, my cardio capacity was shit. I found that out when I hit the basketball court on base after that first workout. I did some shooting with Relle, who can play. Back at Baylor, I coached her intramural basketball team. At first it felt strange just to hold the ball, but it also felt amazing. I'd missed it. I got more and more winded as Relle and I did some one-on-one. As we were wrapping up, I dunked on her, just to see whether I could. That. Hurt. Like. HELL. When I stretched up toward the rim my back cracked, every joint in my body screaming for help. But I still made the dunk. I also made a mess of my back. It ached for days.

We left San Antonio on December 16, nine days before Christmas. Ahead of my departure I got a clean cut. The barber for the San Antonio Spurs edged me up, refined my new style. I almost fell out of my chair when the barber spread that Spurs cape on me . . . The Phoenix Suns and the Spurs had been rivals for decades. But he did a good job on my drop fade. I decided then I'd keep it short on the sides and back but grow out the top.

For my final journey home, I knew my team had arranged a private flight. The stunner was who I'd share it with. Dee Taurasi, my Mercury teammate, came bounding down the steps of the plane's jet bridge and threw open her arms. We hugged and cried and rocked back and forth. Phoenix Mercury president Vince Kozar was also there, along with then GM Jim Pitman. Best. Surprise. Ever. The Suns lent us their jet. During our two-plus-hour flight I shared pieces of what I'd been through. It felt so freeing to talk, particularly to Dee, who'd played overseas far longer than I had. "That's so Russian," she kept saying as I told my stories: shitty prison conditions, inmate spies, a letter of repentance to Putin. I relished our joyful reconnection. What was home but feeling known, understood, loved.

....

Back in Phoenix me and Relle got another surprise, this one upsetting. We'd known we couldn't initially return to our home. Our address had been made public during my trial. Not everyone was happy I'd been freed, and it takes only one nut to detonate your world. We'd need to stay in a temporary house, Relle had been told while I was in Russia. We thought we'd be in an Airbnb for a few weeks, but once in Phoenix, we heard we'd never move back to our place. We'd assumed that once the story died down, we'd carry on as before. But our *before* was no longer safe. We'd have to sell our home and look for another.

The harassment began while I was still in prison. Soon after the verdict, Relle was pulling up in our driveway when a journalist, along with a film crew, stormed her car door. "Can you answer questions about the Brittney Griner case?" the reporter shouted in her face. Relle said nothing and rushed indoors, feeling frightened and violated. When I heard about the incident, it scared me even more than it did Relle. It was my responsibility to protect my wife. I couldn't from where I was, which made me pissed with myself for the predicament I'd put us in and determined to shield her as best I could. Following that incident, dozens of threatening letters showed up in our mail-box and at the Mercury's practice facility. "No way should you have been traded for Victor Bout," someone wrote. "I hope you sleep well at night knowing the Merchant of Death is on the loose. Thousands will now die because a lesbian basketball player was freed." Another wrote that Paul Whelan, a respect-able marine, should've been traded instead of "a gay nigger." The contempt was terrifying, our hypervigilance warranted.

Still, the loss of our home was a major blow, especially for Relle. Though we'd owned that house for five years, we'd never settled in. I was overseas for long stretches and Relle was in law school in North Carolina, so we spent only summers there together. During my detainment, Relle had finally put the last touches on our nest. Whether I came home in one year or nine, she wanted my reentry to be smooth. We were grateful to have a temporary place and, more than that, each other. Also, stuff is just stuff. And yet our surroundings and belongings orient us. We feel grounded in our living rooms, bedrooms, havens. And when that's missing, there's a deep sense of displacement, as I'd just experienced for 293 days. Relle absolutely hated it. She is orderly by nature, needs systems to stay centered. Our team had moved a few items from our home to the Airbnb, but the new house felt nothing like us. I went from surviving in a box to living out of boxes, finally home and yet homeless. In the Airbnb that first night, Relle broke down as I held her. "I'm not okay," she sobbed. Her tears weren't just about our uproot-edness. They were a show of vulnerability after ten months of necessary strength.

Other transitions followed, like having full-time security. The upside was that we felt safe. The big adjustment was our loss of privacy. The security team was in and out of the house. When we arrived at the Airbnb, the guards were putting up cameras, securing the perimeter, checking doorbells. We didn't have much choice when it came to hiring security—our situ-ation required it. It wasn't like a six-nine ex-hostage who was all over the news could lie low. My conspicuousness made us a target. Relle had also become recognizable. For months she'd given interviews in her effort to bring me home. She'd also addressed the world from a White House podium on the day of my release. With the president and vice president beaming behind her, she said, "Over the last nine months, you all have been privy to one of the darkest moments of my life." And now the world was privy to our whereabouts. That made us vulnerable.

I did all I could to ease the transition. With our security team, I established a rhythm with the hope of keeping Relle sane. The guards would be around but still give us space, follow us in Target from a distance. As I stepped up for my wife, I quietly dealt with regret. Anyone who doesn't believe in regret probably hasn't been thrown in a Russian prison. I didn't deserve the hell I was put through, and yet my forgetfulness on that February morning had cost us dearly. The whole time I was locked up I was scared Relle would be mad at me once I got home. She wasn't. But she was disappointed in my carelessness and reeling from its consequences. She had forgiven me. And no one would insist more loudly that my treatment was cruel and unjust. But that awareness did not shield us from the aftershocks of our crisis. When your world is violently upended, you don't just mourn your immediate losses. You also grieve a future that no longer feels possible, the peace that might have been.

Our first evening in the Airbnb, I did a body flop onto the queen bed. Not my bed but still a blessing, plush with spotless sheets I'd never take for granted. Laying on that mattress felt like resting on a cloud, with no metal springs gouging into my back. And my shower that night was euphoric: a steady stream of clean, hot water flowing over me. When I first got in there, I instinctively rushed, a habit I'd picked up during prison's timed showers. *Yo, slow down,* I had to remind myself. I stayed in there a good half hour. Same thing with eating. I loved savoring my food and hadn't been able to in the labor camp. Once home, I lingered over meals while thinking about Paul Whelan. He would've given anything to be in my place. During negotiations for his release, the Russians offered President Biden a one-or-none deal: either trade me alone, or risk leaving us both wrongfully detained. As challenging as my transition was, I was thankful to be home and praying for Paul.

We spent Christmas in our temporary house, with our new lives under construction. Cuddled on the couch, we watched *How the Grinch Stole Christmas* and *Home Alone*, as well as *Frosty the Snowman* and *Rudolph the Red-Nosed Reindeer*. Back when Relle and I began dating, I'd tease her that she hadn't seen the old-school holiday flicks and coaxed her into watching them. That became our annual tradition. She also got me into her princess love stories. When she'd flip one on, I'd be like, "Nah, I ain't watching that." An hour later I'd be looking over her shoulder at a character, going, "Wait, he's doing *what*?" That Christmas we watched them all: chick flicks, classics, and also *The Wiz*. Dorothy had found her home. Mine was Relle.

24

A HOUSE DIVIDED

During the holidays, I rode the adrenaline high of finally being home. In the new year I started crashing. My first PTSD sign was insomnia. I'd lie in bed for hours reliving my nightmare, starting with that security checkpoint search and ending with getting stripped and humiliated. I couldn't turn off my brain. When I did finally fall asleep, I'd have one nightmare in particular. Something had gone wrong with the trade paperwork, and I had to return to Russia to straighten it out. Once I was there, officials hauled me back to the penal colony. The dream felt so real my body believed it. I'd wake up shivering on top of drenched sheets.

Even before this ordeal, I'd been a night owl. Some of that was my nature, but a lot of it had to do with my circumstances. I first played overseas in China in 2013. I'd be up on my Xbox in the middle of the night, adjusting to the time difference and coping with the isolation. I got in the habit of watching TV and playing video games in the wee hours, distracting myself from my loneliness. After prison, my go-to escape didn't work. In fact, it became a trigger. When insomnia hit, I'd tiptoe off to another bedroom to watch TV. Minutes later I'd feel anxious. In detention my world was my bed: I woke up in it, lay on it all day watching TV, went to sleep in it after lights out. I'd always loved watching movies, have over five hundred downloaded on iTunes. But watching them alone, on my bed in the shadows, made me feel I was back in prison.

I began withdrawing. I was over the moon to be home with Relle, and yet I'd gotten used to being solo. Though I'd been surrounded by inmates at IK-2, the language barrier sealed off my world. I was also more of an observer than a talker. That became truer by necessity while I was detained. Relle and I talked a lot when I first got home. But after the initial burst of stories, I shared less. The memories were too painful, and I could see they made Relle ache. She wanted to process the sorrow with me and encouraged me to keep talking. My instinct was to protect her heart as well as my own. If I'd been in our house, I would've escaped to the garage—my sanctuary. But I had none of my tools in the Airbnb, and the space wasn't set up for my usual hours of tinkering. Rather than tinker or talk, I shut down. Much as Relle loved me, she couldn't understand my particular pain of being held captive in a foreign country. The psychiatrists in San Antonio tried to get me to open up by asking compassionate questions. I didn't feel like talking.

In January I connected with Alex for the first time since I'd been freed. After a round of virtual high fives, he asked, "How are you doing?" I gave the rote answer I'd been giving to everyone: fine. I wasn't ready for a deep dive. I wanted to remain in day one of my freedom, bask in the exhilaration and stay above the heartache. Alex updated me on Alena's whereabouts. She'd sent word through her father that she'd been assigned to a penal colony pretty close to Moscow, which meant her dad could visit often. I was relieved and happy for her. I wanted to reach out and will one day. But especially when I first returned to Phoenix, thinking of Alena reminded me of the hell we'd endured. I'd made it home, yes, but a part of me felt lost in Russia. And some of my belongings were still there. On the evening of my detainment in the redbrick building, I slid off my chocolate-diamond wedding ring and asked Alex to hold it for me. Once home, I began wearing the simple gold band I'd gotten engaged in. The other is still in Russia, an unrecovered item amid so much left behind.

On the one hand, I wanted to forget what I'd been through. On the other, I couldn't turn away. I stayed on my iPad, clicking through the coverage. After hooping year-round for eight seasons, I was jobless when I first came home, which gave me hours to sit and read. I did so initially because I was eager to see the headlines unfold. But later, it became my way of affirming, *This actually happened.* The longer I was home, the more surreal my imprisonment felt. I'd click on a video of me speaking from that courtroom cage, or the one of the trade with Viktor Bout. When I'd see my face, I'd be a little surprised but also strangely relieved. My head wasn't playing tricks on me: Yes, I'd been a hostage. With that fact reconfirmed, I'd view news reports and social media. Horrible idea. Many applauded the president's success in negotiating my freedom. Just as many said I should've been left to rot in Russia, while others called the deal "one-sided" and said Paul Whelan, the marine, should've been traded instead of me. I was used to the negativity. An Instagram poster once called me a "gay bitch nigger" and said my mom should've strangled me at birth. Once you heard that, not much else stunned. But what did surprise me after my release was the amount of vitriol. Its prevalence nearly broke me.

Even before my ordeal, America felt increasingly divided—politically and racially. In the streets and around kitchen tables, folks were voicing sharp disagreements. The dissent wasn't new. We have a long history of protest that our democracy depends on. What felt different was *how* we protested—with the kind of venom I saw on my message boards. People weren't just disagreeing; they were attacking one another's humanity. The Internet's anonymity made the cruelty more possible.

Before my imprisonment, I'd raised my voice by taking a knee. Breonna Taylor's and George Floyd's murders sliced open a wound as old as our homeland. My protest was decades in the making. I knelt for the Scottsboro Boys, the teenagers falsely accused of raping two white women and sentenced to death in 1931. I knelt for the thousands lynched in the Jim Crow era. I took a knee for James Byrd Jr., Amadou Diallo, Sandra Bland, Ahmaud Arbery. I knelt because the values signaled by our flag didn't align with how Black people were treated. Along with my teammates, I dedicated the 2020 season to social justice. Black Lives Matter was our point. Kneeling was how I then chose to make it. At the time, I was criticized for not standing during the national anthem. That backlash intensified after I regained my freedom. Some asked how I could have "disrespected" the nation that brought me home.

My kneeling was a sign of just how much I love our country. My ancestors helped build this nation. My father spent his career defending it. I take pride in being American, especially after being imprisoned in a country where public dissent can get you killed. Here, freedom of speech is our right. Exercising that right makes me more of an American, not less. Sit. Stand. Kneel. Protest. The beauty of our homeland is that we have a choice.

....

Those first months of my freedom were a struggle for Relle. I'd always been her anchor, but with me wobbly, she had to lean elsewhere. Her refrain became "I'm not okay." She needed a total shutdown: no cooking and cleaning, no laundry, no being the doting wife or superwoman. On top of caring for me, she was also at a career crossroads. As she awaited her bar exam results, she started looking for work at a law firm. She'd been respecting my need to withdraw, and she likewise needed space for her own healing—a chance to cry without feeling like she was bringing me down. In January, she found a three-day program for brainspotting therapy, a treatment for healing from trauma. She booked a villa at the program's resort in Phoenix. In addition to daily therapy sessions, she enjoyed massages.

When she returned, her spirit seemed lighter, so much so that she set up ongoing cognitive behavioral therapy with a local counselor.

I was okay with Relle not being okay, but I couldn't initially make the same admission. My condition confessed it for me, though. I moped through my days, exhausted after not sleeping well, lamenting how purposeless I felt. In prison I'd had an all-consuming focus: the fight for my freedom. At home I felt adrift, with no reason to get dressed. I was depressed yet refusing to use the word. Saying it aloud would've felt like defeat. *Pull it together, BG,* I told myself. *You're home, so you should be happy.* The San Antonio therapists were still in touch, but I knew I needed local support. So I looked up a counselor I'd worked with years earlier. I'd lost her number, so I filled out her company's online intake form. "Why are you seeking counseling?" was the first question. I paused. "I just got swapped in a prisoner exchange with Russia," I wrote. "I think I should talk about this." Five minutes after I submitted the form the counselor called me. She'd followed my story and thought about reaching out but didn't want to overstep. I teared up in our first session, told her I'd let down so many. Relle had forgiven me. So had my family. But while I'd signed the pardon papers and left Russia in my past, I carried the guilt. "Give yourself grace," the counselor encouraged. That was hard to do when you were still living with the consequences of your mistakes. But I kept talking, and she continued holding up a mirror.

Relle and I braved our first outing during MLK weekend, at an annual event celebrating Dr. King's legacy. Once home, I just wanted to do something normal, whatever that word now meant. As soon as we were spotted, hundreds bombarded us. The crowd was so thick we couldn't take a step. The festival organizers graciously lent us a golf cart. They paused their event and welcomed me onstage. I said how grateful I was to be home and was turning to leave when the organizer posed the question on everyone's minds: "Can you tell us a little about how hard it was in Russia?" From the sidelines Relle yelled out, "She can't answer that!" I got offstage fast. My wife knew that wasn't the time or place for me to begin opening up. She was protecting me. When I rejoined the crowd, many shouted, "BG, we're glad you're home!" and "You're a miracle!" Dozens approached us with brimming eyes, told us we'd inspired them. We posed for picture after picture, signed autographs till our hands were numb. Relle recalls the experience as "beautifully overwhelming." Me too. What a privilege to be seen as an inspiration. Still, it was an adjustment at a time when we were dealing with so many. And it was surreal.

That weekend was another demonstration of how dramatically our lives had shifted. Before my imprisonment, I was known in the ESPN crowd and somewhat beyond. During and after my ordeal, all the major networks aired my story. In August 2022, I was on the cover of *Time* with the headline "Brittney Griner and the Fight for Freedom." The next spring, the magazine named me as one of the 100 Most Influential People of 2023. *So humbling.* My story put important issues in the spotlight: pay inequity for female athletes, the plight of American hostages around the world, the realities of being Black and gay in a nation where both groups are marginalized. My presence itself was a message of hope. The crowd's warm reception that weekend blunted the sting of the negative posts I'd encountered. The experience reinforced for Relle what she still calls her transition: a rebirth. Over the years I'd gotten used to standing out, in sports and for my stature. The attention was new and uncomfortable for her. "I have to let go of the old me," she said. "There's no 'normal' to go back to." The question was how to embrace our new reality. We're still learning to do so, doing better on some days than on others.

I knew Relle was right. Still, I kept hoping I'd wake up in my *before.* All my interactions jolted me from that fantasy. People meant well. "I'm so glad you're home," I heard a lot. I appreciated the sentiment. But a moment later I'd be thinking, *Why the hell wasn't I home? Oh right: I was locked up.* Or someone would say, "I can only imagine how tough it was." That innocent comment would have me reliving the horror and struggling to sleep that night. One of the hardest things to cope with was the *unsaid*. People would be like, "Welcome home," and then stand there with a question on their faces: *What the hell happened over there?* Inside I was going, *Just fucking ask me*. I preferred the directness to the awkwardness, but then again, bluntness was also triggering. Emotionally, I was all over the map.

I was scattered, in part, because I felt useless. My team told me to take my time. But the truth was I had too much time. I didn't do R&R well. In spring 2023, I returned to the place where I'd always felt most like myself. I had to get back on the court.

25

GROWING SEASON

I knew I wanted to hoop again after that San Antonio dunk. The move threw out my back but also raised my hopes. *I've still got it*, I thought. I hadn't been so sure after ten months of salami and cigarettes. "When can I get in the gym again?" I asked Lindz in San Antonio. We agreed I should postpone workouts until after I'd been home for a bit. Whatever the timeline, I was sure I wanted to stay with the Mercury. I appreciated how passionately my team and the league fought for my freedom. If the Mercury still wanted me—and that was an *if* given that no one yet knew exactly what shape I was in—I'd wear my purple-and-orange jersey with pride.

The *when* of my return was a wait-and-see. And what I saw was that I'd be a wreck if I didn't get back to balling. I spent December and the first half of January locked in a safe house—that was how sitting around that Airbnb felt. Of course, I had freedom to move, but I was missing a strong reason to do so. I gave myself one in late January. That was when I showed up at my team's training facility for a workout, to assess where I stood physically. Before my detention, I could bang out three sets of biceps curls, twenty reps per set, with a fifty-pound dumbbell in each hand. I grabbed the thirty-five-pounders, thinking I'd ease back in. After struggling through two reps, I was like, *Ain't no fucking way*. I had to go down to the twenty-pounders, and even that was a challenge. I also tried a plank, which I used to be able to hold for forty-five seconds. I was shaking after ten. I'd lost core strength and muscle. I'd lose far more if I returned to the couch.

I felt defeated after that workout but also determined. My sense of failure pointed me toward what I craved, a strong reason to move forward. The road to the court would be brutal, but the alternative was staying mired in depression. Having a goal to work toward would keep me from constantly looking back. I talked it over with Relle, Lindz, and the GM and coaches. They were aware of my condition. They also knew I'd work like hell to dramatically improve it. They'd support my return at any point and emphasized I should think it over. By February 21, I'd thought long enough: I re-signed with the Mercury for the 2023 season. The team and I mapped out a one-hundred-day conditioning plan leading up to training camp on April 30.

As I whipped myself back into shape, I stepped more fully into the world. A few weeks after the MLK event, Relle and I took in some golf at the WM Phoenix Open (I fangirled so hard when I met Tony Finau). The next day we cheered on the Philadelphia Eagles at the Super Bowl in our city. Soon after, we appeared at the NAACP Image Awards, where I was humbled by the crowd's ovation. "I want to thank everyone," I said, "and let's keep fighting to bring home every American still detained overseas." That last part was a big reason I ventured into public: to keep the spotlight on Paul Whelan and other hostages. Another reason was to find joy.

In the lead-up to the season, I also got LASIK eye surgery. For years I'd been balling half blind. I'd always been chicken to undergo the procedure, but I knew I needed it in order to play my best. I dragged my feet in scheduling it, but Relle got me in the doctor's office with a grin and an ego play. "After all you've been through, are you going to let some little procedure scare you?" she said teasingly. *Hell no.* The surgery was pain- less and just ten minutes per eye. Afterward, I went home and slept. I woke up at midnight with perfect vision, wishing I'd had the procedure years earlier. The world went from blurred to vibrant.

With new clarity, I hit the gym hard. The priority was rebuilding my muscle mass and cardio fitness. I trained five days a week, thirty to forty-five minutes a session, with our strength coach. My teammates Dee, Soph, and Shey Peddy were often at the gym; our training slots overlapped. During that off-season, just the four of us were in Phoenix. Many WNBA players live locally only during the regular season (in modest housing pro- vided by the club) and then leave for their home cities during the off-season. Others play overseas like I did, to supplement their salaries. Soph and Shey welcomed me as warmly as Dee had in San Antonio, with hugs and tears.

In those first weeks the trainer mixed up the cardio work- outs. Some days I hopped on the bike; other days I jumped in the pool (on an underwater treadmill, I'd run, jump, and pump my arms, using water as resistance for building cardio capacity). And in every session I lifted, starting with those twenty-pounders and working my way up to the thirty-five- and forty-pounders. (It'd take me all season to hit the fifties again.) If my teammates were in the weight room we'd dance our way from the bench to the leg press with Beyoncé, Guns N' Roses, or Dre blaring. We'd trade high fives through gruel- ing lifts. The pain was unreal, the improvements slow. Every couple of weeks I'd be lifting and think, *This doesn't hurt as bad as before.* Still, I crawled home aching: hands, hips, neck, knees. I had new respect for the athlete I'd been before my ordeal, how diligently I'd worked to stay in peak condition. You don't realize what good shape you're in until you're . . . not.

After lifting, I hit the court. That dunk in San Antonio almost took me out. So did my first hoops in Phoenix. Just catching the ball and putting my arms up to make the shots was agonizing. My body recalled the motion of shooting (muscle memory), but my aim was completely off—though at least I could now *see* the rim. One of the coaches put me through a drill: make five hundred shots (jumpers, layups, hooks, mid-rangers, three-pointers) from various spots on the court. After the first fifty shots I was gassed. For the next hundred-plus, it took all the stamina I had just to get the ball up. *Stamina*—it's critical for athletes, and especially for ballers. When you're dog tired, the first thing to go is your mind. And if that level of exhaustion hits during a game, it slows your reaction. You see your opponent trying to drive past you, but you're too beat to get between her and the basket. You're using all your energy just to stay upright. I eventually made my five hundred shots, but it took twice as many attempts as it would've pre-prison, and also twice as long—an hour. The whole time my arms were screaming.

Diminished muscle mass was the main reason. I finally understood what my teammates who'd lost muscle mass after surgery had gone through to get back on the court. I'd had my share of serious injuries and been in casts and wheelchairs, but I was lucky to have never needed reconstructive surgery. I'd witnessed many players fight their way back after, say, Achilles tendon repair. They were off their feet for so long following surgery that their muscles atrophied. They literally had to learn how to walk all over again. Something similar happened in my case. My movements felt restricted. I couldn't stay light on my feet. My mind knew what to do on the court, but my body couldn't keep up—a frustrating disconnect. The only solution was to move: slowly, consistently, and despite the pain.

My improvements were so gradual I contemplated pausing my comeback. I felt my weak performance might hurt the team. By training camp that April I'd come a long way but was still playing far below my own high expectations. In team practice I'd miss shot after shot and cuss. My teammates were super encouraging. "It's okay," one would yell out. "Just keep shoot-

ing." Afterward my coach and GM would pull me aside. "We
didn't even think you'd be here, and look how much progress
you've made," they'd say. "Most players wouldn't even have
tried to come back this quickly. You've worked your ass off. It's
a miracle you're even here right now." I nodded and thanked
them as two words reeled through my head: *I suck.* I'd limp
home from practice and tell Relle, through pants, "Yo, I can't
do what I normally do. Maybe I shouldn't play this season."
Sticks and stones might break my bones, I said, but dunking
just might kill me. I joke my way through hard times a lot, and
the tougher things are, the sillier I get. "Babe, it's going to be
fine," Relle assured me. The season would have the last laugh.

In the weeks ahead of the season, I felt like I was on a freedom tour, with special outings all over the country. Though I
was still struggling with insomnia and other PTSD symptoms,
the deep depression of early January had mostly lifted. I was
excited to attend some once-in-a-lifetime events, to have a reason to dress up after months of funk and hoodies.

That April, at the White House Correspondents' Dinner,
Relle and I hit the red carpet. The last grand entrance I'd made
was at the start of my trial. Then, I'd been terrified and alone.
Ten months later with Relle on my arm, I beamed as we entered
to applause and hugs. We were hosted by Gayle King and her
CBS team and sat at their table. Gayle put us at ease with her
warmth and humor. During my detention, she'd supported
Relle on and off camera. Dozens flocked to our table to talk
with Gayle, the mayor of Who's Who. Al Sharpton stopped by.
I finally got to thank him for his advocacy. I also enjoyed meeting NBA star Kyle Kuzma and Winnie Harlow, the inspiring
supermodel with vitiligo. And for the first time I met President
Biden and expressed my deep gratitude for his fight to bring me
home. "This one did a fantastic job," he said, nodding over at
Relle. "I'm proud of her."

Days later I attended the Met Gala as a guest of Anna Wintour herself. Calvin Klein dressed my wife and me in custom looks. We reveled in the experience, starting with our walk up those iconic red-carpeted steps. Photographers flanked the staircase, clicking and shouting out stars' names. We'd seen that entrance a million times on social media and couldn't believe we were there. Lil Nas X was near us at the entrance. "Welcome home, BG," he and others said. I couldn't get over folks recognizing me. I'd just dapped up Dwyane Wade when he held up his phone for a FaceTime. "I just had to show my daughter what the Met Gala looks like . . . One day she could be here." A dope dad, a tearjerker moment, and I got to be there for it. Relle almost fainted when she saw Idris Elba. "Baby, say something to him," she whispered as she squeezed my arm. I gave him a handshake and then introduced Relle. She was blushing so hard she could barely say hello. "Are you serious?" I teased her once we walked off. We now have a running joke. "When I walk in a room," I remind her, "you'd better pass out like I'm Idris."

Back in Phoenix and ahead of the season, I had a news conference, my first time speaking publicly since coming home. I paced beforehand, super nervous to talk openly about myself rather than basketball. The pressroom at the Footprint Center was more packed than I'd ever seen it, and it made me wish my league got that much coverage regularly. It took my becoming a hostage for the cameras to zoom in. Once I sat, I thought, *I'm good . . . not gonna cry.* Moments later I teared up. "How have you found the resilience personally to be here with us?" asked Holly Rowe from ESPN. "I'm no stranger to hard times," I said with a crack in my voice. "Just digging deep, honestly. You know you're going to be faced with adversities throughout your life. This was a pretty big one, but I just kind of relied on my hard work getting through it."

My emotion caught me off guard. For months I'd been dealing with my anguish alone, in my head, in a cell, in the dark. It felt vulnerable to now share it with the world. It's painful to reckon privately with your heartache. It pierces even more deeply when you hear the anguish in your own voice. That day, part of me felt like retreating. A bigger part of me was relieved to pull back the curtain. My emotion made headlines. So did my declaration that I'd never again play overseas unless representing my country—which, if chosen, I'd be honored to do at the Paris games in 2024. And I wouldn't be afraid to travel abroad. I knew that the same country that brought me home would protect its Olympic athletes.

The season kicked off on May 19, on the road against the Los Angeles Sparks. In the locker room beforehand, Vice President Kamala Harris greeted me with open arms before speaking with both teams gathered. "Thank you for all that you did in supporting Brittney," she said. "A team is a team is a family." Billie Jean King and Magic Johnson watched from the stands, along with more than ten thousand fans in the arena and millions who tuned in to ESPN International. The crowd roared as I entered. Many wore 42 jerseys and waved "We Are BG" signs. I stood for the national anthem, teared up at its new meaning for me, stood proudly for the reason I once knelt, because I cherish my homeland. I was sincerely thankful for the outpouring of support. When you've been freed from your greatest nightmare, you live in a posture of gratitude with little room to express other emotions. You feel overwhelmed at times, as I did on that evening. I was there to compete and also to celebrate, and mixing the two felt foreign. With all my heart I wanted to soak in the love, and did. With all my heart I wanted to withdraw, and couldn't. Two contrasting desires surged inside, threw my emotions off balance.

I carried those feelings through the season. Pops, Mom, and my entire Houston family flew in for my inaugural home game on May 21. It was the first time Relle and I had hosted the full tribe, and I loved seeing everyone. After my isolation in Russia, I'll never take a hug for granted. We lost that game, just as we had the first, but my family's presence lessened the sting. So did the fans who'd traveled far and wide to see me. Then and throughout the season, some flew all the way from Europe. One woman came from Alaska. And all came wishing me well, often gathering along the tunnel leading to the locker room to wave hello. The groundswell of attention was a reminder of my shifting identity, from hooper to former hostage, athlete to spokesperson. In my quiet moments I whispered gratitude to God for helping me to use my heartache for a larger purpose.

Those first losses set the tone for the season, which quickly went from disheartening to disastrous. I was playing like crap, and I knew it. It's hard to settle for good enough when you know you're capable of much better—especially when you're under a microscope. The world was watching, more eyes on the WNBA in part because of my return. That was a good thing. But feeling scrutinized when you're at your lamest is also hard. At halftime from the locker room I'd text Relle, who was at courtside. "Do I look tired out there?" I asked. No, she assured me. Strange, since I felt like I was dying, limbs heavy as I gasped for air. On the sidelines my coaches encouraged me, but I cringed at my missteps. I appreciated the kindness but also longed for candor, which was how I talked to myself. I sucked, but then again, I didn't, I'd realize when I saw the stats. Because even during a season I'm not proud of, I led the team in average points per game, blocks, field goal percentage, and other metrics. I was also chosen to play in the annual All-Star Game. The stats didn't lie, though my spirit contradicted them. I was still reckoning with deep feelings of shame.

The season was an emotional roller coaster. Our league is tight-knit, with a lot of us having played together on various teams at home and overseas. Every stop brought tight hugs and tears. In Indiana, I loved seeing Emma Cannon. We became close when she hooped for Phoenix. The coach of the New York Liberty, Sandy Brondello, used to coach the Mercury. She'd also once been the assistant coach of my Ekat team in Russia. In New York, Sandy and I, as well as my many friends on the Liberty, lingered on the sidelines to catch up. I was in constant homecoming mode, at once loving the confetti and ducking to avoid it. That was also true during competition. Ahead of every game, We Are BG–themed footage blared on the jumbotron: the campaign, the WNBA camaraderie, the monumental push to bring me and others home. The first few times I saw the video, I took it in. But as the forty-game season unfolded and our losing streak lengthened, the constant reflection made it tough to get locked into each game. Before tip-off, I'd listen to music to get hyped for the on-court battle, Moneybagg Yo blasting through my headphones. Soon after I'd run into the arena and, boom, my wrenching past would be right back in my face, throwing off my focus. The video was a necessary reminder of the American hostages still detained. I will not rest until Paul Whelan and others are home, will always remember the pain of feeling forgotten. That's why I stayed quiet about my edginess over that footage. Still, my spirit registered it.

Throughout the season we dealt with one injury after another. Soph badly hurt her jaw, Dee crushed her left toe and struggled with a hamstring injury, and Shey sustained a concussion and had to be carried off-court on a stretcher. That last one scared us. Then in June, during a game against the Seattle Storm, I went down with a hip injury. Soon after, my other hip started acting up, my knees were killing me, and I was having overuse problems with my calves. All that dampened my hope that we could turn the season around. I was sidelined for the second half of that game, as well as for the next three, all of which were double-digit losses. My bruises weren't just on court. In private I grappled with anxiety and a recurring nightmare that my pardon had been overturned and I was back in a Russian hellhole. Our losses intensified my angst. My sense of personal failure created more of the same. Then, around that time, a deep fear came true, that I was home but still not safe.

On June 10, my teammates and I were walking through the Dallas airport, on our way to board a flight to Indianapolis. Relle was traveling with me but checked in separately and planned to connect with us onboard. We rode down a long escalator, turned right, and out of nowhere some jackass got in my face, yelling. "Was it a fair trade for the Merchant of Death?" he shouted. "Is it true you had sex with Vladimir Putin?" My security stepped between us and urged the man away. Others around us stared as we stood stunned. My guard called the cops, and we ducked behind a wall until they arrived. As we huddled, I could feel my jaw clench as anxiety overtook me: *Where's Relle?* I rang her. No answer. Tried again. No answer. I feared that, after lunging at me, this guy would find my wife and accost her. When Relle finally answered, I exhaled, told her to stay alert. The cops arrived, and we filed a report. We later learned the man was a right-wing YouTube personality, angling for provocative footage. The police escorted us to our flight. But while the dust had settled, the damage was done: I was rattled. We all were. My teammate Brianna Turner is often mistaken for me in public. What would happen if someone else attacked us? Would one of us have to die before our league took seriously our pleas to fly private?

"The safety of Brittney Griner and all WNBA players is our top priority," the league said in a statement after the incident. It didn't feel that way. For years we'd been insisting on charter flights, as NBA players were granted. You can't just roll up on LeBron in the airport. The same should be true for WNBA players. And after my return home, my team made the case that I should fly privately for safety reasons. The league understood our concerns but initially said private flights would give me an unfair advantage—an edge I believe every female athlete should have. Throughout my career, you might've spotted me on commercial flights, my giant ass squeezed in a middle seat. That happened a lot. I'd sometimes pay to upgrade myself just so I'd have legroom. Even that upgrade left me cramped. Rather than arriving ready to compete, I'd be aching and hunched over. One year the league flew me to the All-Star Game in a middle seat, coach. Rather than feeling like a star, I felt like an afterthought. I'm grateful the WNBA allowed me to fly private for the rest of the season. The Mercury paid for it. But there's no guarantee me or my teammates will fly private in the 2024 season and beyond. We've been told the choice is about money. It seems like it's about devaluing women, and especially women of color. Approximately 70 percent of WNBA players are Black.

In July, my frustration came to a head. In a road game against the Washington Mystics, our opponents didn't have to beat us. We beat ourselves with mistake after mistake, leading to a searing 84–69 loss. I played as well as I could but felt powerless to turn things around. After, in the locker room, I punched a wall in frustration. One of my trainers rushed over. "Are you okay?" she asked. *Nah*, but I gave my standard bullshit answer: "I'm good." "Let me see your hand," she said, examining it. My knuckles were red and bruised. "Come on, BG," she said compassionately, like *Don't make this worse.* She was right—I was hurting. My outburst wasn't just about that game. It was about a season that felt doomed, on the heels of another still crippling me.

The meltdown prompted me to step back for two games to focus on my mental health. By then I'd moved on from the therapist I'd reconnected with in January. After a few sessions I sensed I needed something different, though I wasn't sure what. I connected with another counselor, who gently led me to a new level of awareness. I came in for a session one day and rattled off a bunch of reasons I was angry with myself, from missing my wife's graduation to feeling like a detriment to my team. My carelessness was still costing me.

"Do you have other emotions aside from anger?" she asked.

I paused. "Sometimes I get really sad," I said.

"What are you sad about?" she asked softly.

"It's fucked up what I went through," I said.

She nodded as I got choked up. "Yes, you made a mistake," she said, "but that doesn't make all that transpired after okay. Did you purposely mess up?"

"No," I mumbled as a tear escaped down my cheek.

"If a friend made a mistake that impacted you," she said, "how would you react?"

I might initially be upset, I said, but I'd let it go. I'd get that it wasn't intentional.

"That's what I hope you can do for yourself, BG," she said. "Forgive yourself."

That was a breakthrough. Since I'd gotten home, I'd heard repeatedly, "Have grace for yourself." I had a hard time absorbing that lesson. The grief I felt bumped up against any grace I tried to show myself. But when the therapist helped me step outside my mess and see it as a friend would, something clicked. My screwup was the biggest of my life, and it came with a steep penalty. Still, I was allowed to be furious about how I was humiliated, the absolute horror of what I endured. Russia stripped me of my humanity. Rather than giving myself permission to admit that sorrow, I'd been cursing after missed hoops. More than angry, I started to see, I was sad.

That realization was so eye-opening that I wanted—and needed—to dive deeper. Because just having that understanding hadn't kept me from slamming my hand against a wall, and my sadness was popping up all over the place. I've seen *The Notebook*, a romantic drama, a thousand times. I'd never once cried. I watched it during that season and bawled my eyes out, releasing tears I'd suppressed for months. I was like, *What the hell is going on with me?* Trauma. I told my therapist I wanted to do intensive therapy at a PTSD recovery center. She encouraged it. So after that locker-room flare-up, I booked a spot at a three-day residential program in Tucson. I wish I'd vetted it more thoroughly.

From the moment I checked in, I felt like I was back in prison. The small room reminded me of the one I'd been in during detention. No electronics were allowed, so they took my phone, said I'd need permission to use theirs. They also seized my snacks and candy, no clue why. My first meeting with the therapist was a giant red flag that I was in the wrong place.

The counselor, fit and in his forties, held a clipboard with my intake form on it. "So what happened to you in Russia?" he asked. I shared a bit of what I'd survived, his eyes widening with each sentence. "I can't believe it," he kept saying as he jotted down notes. "So what else did the Russians do to you?" I told another story, and he kept requesting more. When he set aside his clipboard and leaned forward in his chair, I thought, *This dude ain't trying to help me. He's trying to get the damn scoop.*

Things slid further downhill. The program was advertised as specializing in PTSD recovery but seemed focused on drug and alcohol treatment—great, just not what I thought I'd signed up for. I'd hoped to be with other trauma survivors opening up about their experiences and how they were coping. Instead, the staff tried to get me to go to a Narcotics Anonymous meeting—sharing, yes, but centered on substance abuse. I did meet a couple of military vets struggling with PTSD, but they were there for drug addiction. I knew trauma and addiction often went hand in hand. I also knew I had to get the hell out of there.

I'd arrived in the morning. By sunset I was asking to call Relle. The staff said I could if I used a phone card, reminiscent of the prison I'd just left. I figured the line was recorded, so I got right to the point with Relle. "Hey, hey, hey . . . listen real quick," I whispered, the triple *hey* my distress signal. "Call our security guy and tell him to come get me right now." When he arrived later that evening, the guards at the gate wouldn't let him in. He insisted that he be allowed to see me, and they threatened to call the cops on him for trespassing. He caused such a commotion that they finally relented, while sending a counselor to me. "Did you call to go home?" the therapist asked. Yes, I said, and told him why, starting with that claustrophobic room. "Do you want to sleep on the couch in the common area?" he asked. I'm six nine and grown as fuck—I'm not sprawling out on some nasty couch that'll kill my back. He got it, and I got out of there. Days later I returned to the court for the August 5 game against the Seattle Storm. I scored twenty-two points. We still lost.

Relief—that was what I felt when the worst basketball season of my career limped to a close. And I do mean limped. In our September 8 game against the Las Vegas Aces, I tripped during a drive to the hoop while being double-teamed, fell awkwardly, and twisted my ankle during the second quarter. The pain was so intense I struggled to get up. I slowly stood and staggered to the sidelines, where I stayed for the rest of the game. I watched as we racked up our tenth straight loss, in a season with thirty-one of them. With that defeat, we also ended the league's longest active streak of playoff appearances, ten in a row. It was the first time since I joined the Mercury in 2013 that we didn't make the playoffs. I was as physically run-down as I was emotionally fragile. "Not happy with my performance overall this season, no matter what happened or what I went through," I told the press afterward. "Next year will definitely be different"—I hoped. My on-court game would depend on my mental one.

26

HOME TO ME

Though I couldn't wait for the 2023 season to end, at the same time I dreaded the break. I feared I'd spiral back into depression, with long stretches of silence and heartache. The breather turned out to be a gift. For the first time in a decade, I didn't dribble my way from a WNBA court straight onto one overseas. No China. No Russia. No suitcase to mispack. Just me and Relle in our new home as we got our houses in order—emotional and spiritual, professional and personal.

In August, as the season wrapped up, we moved into the place we'd purchased. It was exactly the haven we'd prayed for, tucked in the desert mountains and surrounded by cacti and quiet. Everything about it said *chill*, from the woodburning fireplace out back to the view of breathtaking sunsets. And I loved the huge garage. I'd taken my time with setting it up right, getting cabinets put in and wall clips to hang stuff. Though, like me, it was a work in progress, the space needn't be finished to serve as my sanctuary.

Our change of address coincided with a temporary shift in roles. Relle landed a job at a law firm; I supported her from home. I was so proud of my wife for passing the bar the spring before. I already knew she was smart. She proved she was also tough, crushing a major exam in the middle of our biggest nightmare. Her new firm specialized in family law. I specialized in housekeeping. While Relle was on the clock, I was making beds, sweeping floors, running errands. I love grilling but can't cook worth a damn, so I had takeout ready when Relle got home. Over dinner I proudly rattled off what I'd done all day, as she beamed and teased me: "I feel like I have a house husband." What she had was a partner with a purpose. When I'd first returned from Russia, she did nearly everything around the house, just as always. By stepping up for her—for us—I stepped past the uselessness that dogged me in those early weeks home.

My big brother, Carlo, kept me company. He embraces the YOLO life and flew in from Houston just to hang. He hadn't even booked a return flight: he just wanted to be near me for as long as I needed. I loved having him close. I couldn't remember the last time I pulled up on my brother daily, just catching up over lunch and laughing our asses off. His presence was a safety net, a buffer against depression. He stayed a week, but his healing presence lingered. So did the memories Relle and I gathered throughout that fall. For my birthday in October, I celebrated thirty-three years of life and more than three hundred days of freedom. Relle and I vacationed at a golf resort with sweeping views of the Newport Beach, California, coastline. I played eighteen holes while soaking in the sunlit horizon, a contrast to the shadowed confinement of my birthday the previous year. On that trip we also went offshore fishing, surrounded by blue waters as far as we could see. We caught enormous dorados and yellowfin tuna, with Relle passing me the rod to reel in the big ones.

Back at home the following month, we nested. Over Thanksgiving we ordered pizza and played games into the early-morning hours, my one and only and me in an Uno square-off. A shelf in our closet was crammed with vintage games, from

Operation and Candy Land to Monopoly and Life. They were a throwback to old-school fun, a reliable source of laughter and rejuvenation. Soon after, on December 8, came the anniversary of my freedom. "I can't believe it's been a year," I told Relle. In some ways the time had flown by amid the season's whirlwind. In other ways it crept, with nightmares on sweaty pillows and memories of that courtroom cage. I was wide awake for the misery. Yet the experience now felt otherworldly, like it had happened to some other girl in some other life, on a planet far away. The day my mom went into labor with me, her mother said, "That child's gonna be known all over the world." My grandma Irene didn't mean that in a bigheaded way. She was just repeating what the Spirit had whispered. She had no idea how tall I'd grow or that I'd hoop or be the first American woman thrown into IK-2. She has, sadly, passed on, but her prediction chills me. I'll go down in a frightening chapter of geopolitical history, in a book I wish I could slam shut. When I shared that with Relle, she nodded and hugged me. The moment reflected my new way of grieving: expressing what I felt instead of bottling up those feeling inside and brooding.

The off-season was emotionally and physically restorative for me. Between housekeeping, hosting, and travel, I rested a lot. That was easier to do than it had been when I first came home, largely because I was so exhausted from the season and still recovering from injuries. But there was a bigger reason: My rest involved connection. With Relle. With my brother. With nature and my surroundings. That bonding was available when I'd first returned from Russia, but it took time for me to be ready for it. Time may not heal, but it does pass—slowly, quickly, with certainty. For me, its passing has brought relief. It has created distance from my ordeal that has lessened its agony. The further away I've gotten from the terror I survived, the less distressing it has felt. I still have flashbacks to the penal colony, but they're fewer now. I still tear up and struggle with rage, yet the meltdowns are further apart. I haven't been fully healed, voilà, like magic. Trauma recovery isn't immediate or linear. There are stumbles forward and backslides. Healing is usually measured in years. During that off-season, my progress was about opening my heart, to my loved ones and my surroundings. Time's passing had unburdened my spirit just enough for me to begin accepting their support.

My emotional journey has continued in therapy. During the season, I bounced around to different counselors, gathered ideas for coping with trauma. I had a couple of sessions with a therapist specializing in PTSD. "Trauma changes the brain," she said. That was what the therapist explained to me, and this was what I heard: I experience the world differently after surviving all I did. Someone cutting me off in traffic, for instance, has always pissed me off. Pre-prison, that would've registered as a six out of ten on my rage-o-meter. After, it was a twelve-plus. I'd speed ahead of the driver while cursing up a storm, an outsize response connected to my rewired brain.

Though I valued that therapist's insight, I ultimately returned to the counselor who helped me see how sad I was. About three times a month, we get together. And for a long time to come, I'll be healing. My therapist isn't pushy, which is one reason I like her. She tells me what's available in the field of PTSD recovery and then backs off. She suggested I look into Eye Movement Desensitization and Reprocessing (EMDR)—a treatment known to bring relief to some trauma survivors. I'm fascinated and may eventually try it. My therapist also prescribed sleeping meds, which have helped me get deep rest. When I first came home, I used them on nights when I tossed while recalling IK-2 but needed them less over time. Now I take them only when I'm on the road, when unfamiliar surroundings trigger anxiety. This is okay and normal, my counselor assures me. "When it comes to trauma recovery," she says, "there's no 'shoulds' or prescribed timelines." There's just me, feeling my way through a slow-but-sure process, searching for lasting calm.

As I turned the page on the 2023 basketball season, I began looking toward the next. For years I'd used my overseas play as training for the WNBA season. With Russia now in my rearview mirror, I'd need another way to stay in shape. I found one with the help of the Mercury's new coach, Nate Tibbetts, who was hired in October 2023. Nate previously served as assistant coach for the Orlando Magic. He was brought in by billionaire investor Mathew Ishbia, who'd purchased both the Mercury and the Suns the same month I came home from Russia. Under Mathew and Nate's leadership, everything felt new—including my prep for the 2024 season.

Dee, Soph, and I started off-season training earlier than usual. It was optional, and I'm glad I had the choice in light of the previous season's wreck. We eased into workouts. In October, between my vacations and holidays, we lifted weights four days back-to-back and three days off. Then, in December, we transitioned to both lifts and court time five days a week. That schedule continued in the new year. So did separate qualifying camps and competitions for the U.S. Basketball Women's National Team, ahead of the Paris Games. The Olympic team will officially be chosen in July 2024. When you put on a Team USA jersey, you play your heart out. That was what I did at the 2016 and 2020 Games, in Rio and Tokyo. And if I'm chosen, that's what I'll do in Paris. The USA has won seven consecutive golds. France could be the backdrop for an eighth.

With my pro-ball prep underway, Relle and I began strengthening our financial foundation. I was in Russia for the same reason nearly half of WNBA players still play in countries like Australia, Turkey, Italy, and even Russia: to boost our salaries, which are dramatically lower than those of NBA players, and with a smaller revenue share in our league's profits. I know I'm blessed to have earned what I did while abroad. I also know most folks would be stunned if around 80 percent of their income suddenly went up in flames, as mine did. Relle and I have always been careful investors, so we're fortunate to be on solid ground. And yet even as we give thanks for that stability, we're working to further solidify it. We're exploring business ventures. We'll see what the future holds while trusting the One who holds it.

....

Before I left for Russia, Relle and I had decided we'd look for a church home. We found one soon after my return. The place just fits us: casual clothes welcome, stuffiness not, online and in-person services offered. We love both. The key teaching resonates with me: that I'm more flawed than I can know and more cherished than I can hope. We also enjoy the style of worship. It resembles that of Maverick City Music, the contemporary gospel group Relle and I keep on our playlists. The inspiring music reeled us in. The uplifting sermons keep us there.

One Sunday the pastor shared the biblical story of Job, in a message that hit home for me. Job had been blessed with wealth, family, friendships, God's favor. During a test of his faith, Job lost everything, including his children. Still, he wouldn't turn his back on the Almighty, even when he broke out in sores. He did, however, question his Maker: Why was this happening? The Lord responded with a rhetorical question: "Where were you when I laid the earth's foundation?" (Job 38:4, NIV) God was reminding Job that He built the universe. He not only understood Job's circumstances, but He also had designed the world they existed in. In that knowledge Job could rest.

While I was in prison and now that I'm home, I've often wondered why this whole mess happened, beyond the simple fact of my hurried packing. Big picture, why did my path take this turn? I may never have an answer, but I'm clear on what God told Job: I can relax in His Sovereignty and timing. When trials come, like the big one I endured, it's tough to wait patiently for God to help. I wasn't patient in Russia. By nature, maybe I never will be. But it eases my anxiety to remind myself that the Father created time. He's got this. He's got me.

A better question than why my ordeal happened is how I'll use it. That's my focus on this side of my nightmare. I can't unsee what I witnessed and experienced in Russia, can't rewind the clock to my *before*. But I can use my darkest moment to shine a light on American hostages all over the world. On equal pay for female athletes and understanding of LGBTQ+ people. On the experiences of Black women, whose expressions of anger, while no different from anyone's, brand us as always irate. I didn't ask for this platform. I had no say in what I look like. But I stand tall in this body and on this stage. I still ache when I hear, "Is she a man or a woman? Doesn't she have a dick?" What I have is a hope that we can be gentler with one another, that we can imagine how it feels not to fit.

I came home with that hope and with some new apprecia-tions. I used to think I was grateful for my life. I wasn't. I got caught up in "I hate going to the gym," complaining how an exercise killed me. So often in detention, I'd think back on my whining. I'd sit in that cell, fearing for my future, wishing I could run suicides and have my lungs on fire. Other times I'd dream of enjoying a sunset with no bars in the way. I missed clean water from the faucet. I missed seeing my full face in a mirror big enough to reflect it. And more than any posses-sion or experience, I missed my loved ones. I knew I cherished them. I might've hugged them more tightly if I'd known I soon wouldn't be able to.

That awareness makes me think back on a day, years ago, when Relle and I went furniture shopping. We'd bought our first home. In the store, Relle picked up a candle she liked; I insisted on another. She preferred medium-height table lamps; I wanted tall ones. I honestly didn't care, had never been into decorating. My dissent was about control, and it was petty. I gave her hell just 'cause I could, not realizing I'd robbed us of happiness. That's what unnecessary friction does: replaces the pleasure that might have been. Instead of sharing a laugh, you're rolling your eyes and stoking tension. I recalled when we recently bought furniture for our new place. Totally different experience. I gave no opinion on the throw pillow colors, the style of the couches, the height of the lamps. Relle was in her bliss choosing what she wanted, and I was in my bliss watching her enjoy it. These days I settle disagreements quickly. I served a lot less time than I feared I would. I plan to make my extra time joyful.

....

Now that I'm back in the States, I think a lot about what home means. In Russia, I knew home by its absence: Isolation. Fear. Sadness. Confinement. My deep sense of disconnection brought clarity about what I most crave and yearn to create. Home is love. Home is rest. Home is stability. Home is freedom and connection, the opposite of *whoosh*, a big exhale after 293 days locked up. Home is holding Relle close while watching a cheesy flick. Home is choosing not to grumble and always giving thanks. I once kept track of time by the rattle of the Moscow train, a sound I heard every morning as I stirred awake in total darkness. My days are now measured by the laughs I share, the loved ones I frequently embrace. I'll linger longer than I used to.

Relle and I are expanding our home. Before I left for Russia for the final time, we decided we'd start a family soon after Relle finished law school in 2022. My imprisonment delayed that plan but did not change it. In fact, after our nightmare, we were even more sure we wanted to welcome a child. Time doesn't pause, and nor will we. Soon after my last game of 2023, we did our first round of IVF. It was successful. Relle is pregnant, and we're ecstatic. We pray our family will soon grow to three.

In this season of expectation, I'm getting outdoors more. Soon I could be cradling a little one to sleep—best to do some roaming now. Nature has always been my home, no walls or ceilings, just boundless and renewing sky. I feel most liberated when I'm off-roading in Bulldog Canyon, an hour east of Phoenix, blaring music from my Jeep's radio, exulting in the Sonoran Desert. I enjoy being away for short stretches, knowing civilization is within reach. Sometimes I'll stop and walk barefoot in the dirt. Other times I'll just reflect in silence, thank God for bringing me back to Relle. A while later, I'll climb back in my Jeep to crawl over rocks and squeeze between trees. Driving soothes me. Creation centers me. Back at our place I'll build a fire in the yard, quieting the dogs as I watch the sun lower. I do that every chance I get, gaze in awe at the wide, orange sky, dappled with pinks and purples. I can sit there for hours, remembering all I'm blessed with. That's home if there ever was one, me by the fire and at peace.

BRING OUR FAMILIES HOME

I broke down when I heard that ten American hostages had been freed from Venezuela in 2023. A year earlier, almost to the day, I had landed on U.S. soil, just as they did. Knowing the horror of my ten-month ordeal, I could only imagine the torture they'd endured during years of imprisonment. I cried because I recalled exactly how it felt to emerge from a seemingly endless nightmare. Coming home was evidence that the world hadn't forgotten me.

Today, fifty-seven Americans are as desperate as I once was. That's how many publicly disclosed hostages there are as of early 2024, according to the James W. Foley Legacy Foundation (JWFLF). That organization and one of its key partners—the Bring Our Families Home Campaign (BOFH)—sprang up from unimaginable horror. When James W. Foley was kidnapped and murdered by ISIS in 2014, his family turned their pain into purpose by advocating for American detainees. In 2022, the BOFH Campaign came together when loved ones of U.S. hostages linked arms with an emotional message to President Biden: Use every available tool to #BringThemHome.

The families were demanding an audience with the president, yes, but they were also asking to be *seen*. They fear, as I once did, that the world has moved on without them.

Before my experience in Russia, I was largely oblivious to the deep grief of hostages and their families. I rarely heard about American detainees and had no idea there were dozens of them in at least fifteen countries. The few times I did see a snippet on the news, my sadness disappeared almost as quickly as it arose. Hostages were *over there*, seemingly someone else's concern. And then one February, *over there* became my here and now. My loved ones promised I wouldn't be forgotten.

The BOFH Campaign helped them keep that promise. Three months into my ordeal, the family members of detainees launched their movement with a demonstration in front of the White House. That gathering was about more than my imprisonment. It was about moving their loved ones' names from an afterthought to a priority for the president. It was about combining their individual pleas into one shrill, unignorable scream. It was about ensuring that the world understands that hostage diplomacy does not discriminate. When overseas, any American, regardless of race, religion, or political affiliation, can be violently forced into captivity. Our citizenship alone is enough to make us targets.

Neda Sharghi, who helped launch the BOFH Campaign, knows that all too painfully. Her brother Emad, an American citizen, was visiting Iran, his birth country, when he was forcefully taken captive in 2018. Emad was thrown in prison and designated wrongfully detained by the U.S. government. In a relentless push for his freedom, Neda rallied alongside the family members of other hostages. One was Elizabeth Whelan, the sister of Paul Whelan, the marine wrongfully detained since 2018. While Paul and I were still in Russian custody, Neda pleaded with President Biden on behalf of U.S. detainees. "We are tired. We are scared. We are angry," she wrote on X. "We want our innocent loved ones home."

Neda and other BOFH Campaign families stood firm. They did so, in part, by displaying a mural depicting eighteen American hostages—a way to keep our horror in the headlines. In July 2022, as I sweltered in a cage during my trial, the campaign unveiled the fifteen-foot mural, which spanned the length of an alleyway in D.C.'s Georgetown. The black-and-white mural, designed by the artist Isaac Campbell, was made by mixing flour, water, and sugar to form a nontoxic, biodegradable glue. The mural would deteriorate with time, like detainees' conditions. My face was on the mural. So were those of Kai Li and Mark Swidan in China; Shahab Dalili in Iran; and Majd Kamalmaz in Syria. Majd, a therapist from Virginia, was taken hostage while checking on an ill relative. The husband, father, and humanitarian has been there since 2017. The D.C. mural was just the first. Three additional paintings have gone up in cities where detainees have a tie to the community—Houston, Denver, and my stomping ground, Phoenix, at the Footprint Center. WNBA players helped to install it, and many visited it and posted pictures of themselves alongside it through the 2023 season. That mural was unveiled the April after I came home. The murals are part of a larger movement that I pray continues.

I was so inspired by the BOFH Campaign that when I returned home, I joined in the partnership that Relle, Lindz, my team, the Mercury, and other WNBA players had initiated. We all linked arms in the crusade to keep U.S. detainees in the spotlight. Throughout the 2023 season, the campaign's logo was affixed to our home court. Footage played before games highlighting the campaign's work and featuring the families of those detained. The Mercury also hosted a letter-writing station at which fans could send encouragement to hostages, as well as letters pressing their elected officials to act. We then took our support on the road by welcoming the families of detainees at our away games. I have hugged so many on the sidelines.

Our calls for action have lit a fire. In 2023, President Biden signed into law National Hostage and Wrongful Detainee Day, observed annually on March 9. That bipartisan legislation included the creation of the Hostage and Wrongful Detainee flag, a bright yellow beacon amid the darkness detainees endure. For me, every day is hostage day, each hour a reminder of what detainees can't get back: time with their families. When your life has been stolen, you stop counting in months. You instead count in memories you're not making. Your connection to time comes in the mail, in stories from those whose lives are moving forward.

During my lowest moments in prison, letters lifted me. My family's notes in particular pulled me through. Yet as heartening as those letters were, I'd think, *They're supposed to say encouraging things.* Not so with strangers. That's why receiving notes from people I didn't know meant so much. I'd linger over letters from midwestern moms and military vets, from high school athletes and WNBA fans. I also received support from Russians. Some offered to add money to my books so I could buy things from the Market in prison. Others cracked me up, like the Don Quixote–type character who wrote to me faithfully. Along with poetry, he sent me a picture of himself sporting a handlebar mustache. In it, he was bareback on a stallion that was up on its hind legs. Not the typical support letter, but it gave me a much-needed laugh.

Connection to the outside world—that's what I ached for during my ten months of isolation. It's why I tell those who want to help U.S. detainees to start by picking up a pen. Write to your fellow Americans and let them know you're with them. And keep that pen handy for reaching out to the family members who are part of the BOFH Campaign. The battle to bring home a loved one is often a lonely one. Knowing that someone, *anyone,* stands with you makes that fight feel less wearisome, as it did for my wife, Relle. The letter itself isn't magic. It's the acknowledgment of a hostage's humanity that restores hope.

Before my ordeal, if someone had told me to write to Congress about a U.S. detainee, I would've thought, *That crap don't work*. It does. When we flood the mailboxes of public servants, they're forced to pay attention. No single tactic will get hostages home, but several together might: an avalanche of letters, petitions signed by millions, repeated phone calls to our legislators. We know advocacy makes a difference: thirteen of the eighteen detainees pictured on the BOFH Campaign's D.C. mural are now home, including Neda's brother Emad. After more than five harrowing years of wrongful detention, Emad was freed from Iran in September 2023.

Every time a hostage comes home, I feel immense joy and relief. I also feel more determined to see all U.S. detainees united with their families. My loved ones shined a light on my case, but I was fortunate some already knew me through basketball. Hostages like Zack Shahin are hardly talked about. He has been imprisoned and tortured for fifteen years in Dubai. During my first season home, his family met with me at the Wings game in Dallas. They said Zack feels so abandoned by his homeland that he's been on the verge of suicide. I'm proof that when we raise our voices, Zack and others can be prioritized. I implore our president to meet with Zach's family, and the families of those detained. But more than that, I urge our leaders to bring home all U.S. hostages by any means necessary. Each is an American who deserves what I now cling to: freedom.

I also hold tight to small pleasures. Hot showers. Long walks. The sun on my face and the wind at my back. Now that I'm home, the simplest things have become the most important: people I cherish, work I love, and a fresh season that fills me with hope.

....

Learn more about the BOFH Campaign at BringOurFamilies Home.org and follow them on X and Instagram: @bofhcampaign and #BringThemHome.

These American detainees in the BOFH Campaign and beyond are still rallying for their freedom:

- David Lin from California, detained in China since 2006
- Zack Shahin from Texas, detained in the United Arab Emirates since 2008
- Austin Tice from Texas, detained in Syria since 2012
- Mark Swidan from Texas, detained in China since 2012
- Shahab Dalili from Virginia, detained in Iran since 2016
- Kai Li from New York, detained in China since 2016
- Majd Kamalmaz from Texas, detained in Syria since 2017
- Paul Whelan from Michigan, detained in Russia since 2018
- Andre Khachatoorian from California, detained in Russia since 2021
- Evan Gershkovich from New Jersey, detained in Russia since March 2023

ACKNOWLEDGMENTS

During a tender moment in *Grey's Anatomy*, Cristina tells her close friend Meredith that she wrote down her name as an emergency contact ahead of a medical procedure. "You're my person," Cristina says to her bestie. Those three words make official what they've shared but never voiced: an unbreakable bond.

Before Russia, I knew Relle was my person. During my detainment, I discovered I also had a massive village. Hundreds came together to pull me through the horror. My friends and family leaned in from the other side of the world. So did scores of others who'd never even met me. I tear up when I think about the many hands that helped bring me home. It's humbling. In some ways it's easier to give than to receive. When you offer help, you're the valued contributor. When you accept, you're vulnerable. And yet that vulnerability creates a connection that expands your heart. My heart remains wide open in this new season. I'm filled with gratitude for those who showed me kindness in my hour of greatest weakness, starting with those closest to me.

Relle, my beautiful queen, we've known each other for more than twelve years, six of them in marriage. When I'm ecstatic, you're the first person I want to share my joy with. And during my low moments, you're the only one I want to be around. There you were, fighting for me, when you should've been focused on graduating from law school and passing the bar. You did both with such grace, even as you campaigned to bring me home. I've always known you're extraordinary, and now the whole world knows it too. I truly wouldn't have made it through this ordeal without you as my guiding light. During our years together, I've often told you that you saved me by showing me a better way to live. During our ten months apart, you saved me yet again, as you prayed me back into your arms. I love you, babe—forever.

Dad, my big guy, my Superman—I appreciate you. As I write this, I'm getting choked up at all that you mean to me. Thank you for telling me I didn't bring dishonor to our family. Thank you for being the solid rock you were when I was growing up. You're strong, you're steady, you move forward even when things get tough. Thank you for showing me how to do the same while carrying myself with dignity. I could've sat around sulking in Russia and stayed focused on *This is so unfair*. The fact that I kept moving was all you, Pops. Thank you for your example.

Mom, I don't know anyone more compassionate than you. No matter what someone has done to you, you've always responded with kindness. Thank you for teaching me how to love people even when they're not the nicest toward me. Thank you for offering others grace in a world that could use more of it. While in Russia I was so worried about you. Our family has often joked that you're as soft as a marshmallow, but I discovered you're a true warrior. I'm as grateful for your tenderness as I am for your strength—both of which brought me home.

DeCarlo, thank you for always keeping it one hundred—totally real with me. You've been more than a great big brother and close friend. God blessed me with an amazing father and then He also gave me you—a second dad. When I was growing up, you used to tell me about the hard times you'd lived through. The experiences you shared helped me survive my ordeal. We both hurt during those months when we couldn't talk. But each time I got a letter from you, I felt like you were right there beside me. Thank you for checking in on everyone while I was away. And thank you for having your phone ready during my call with the family. You were the first one on the line that night, and you've always been there to show me the right way to go. I appreciate you.

My sister SheKera, aka KK—you had the tough job of making sure Dad didn't try to get on a plane to Russia and bring me back home. Thank you for making sure Pops was good, and that everyone else was too. You played counselor for our family, and I appreciate you giving so much of yourself for us. Also, I know it was hard being in front of a camera, asking for help to bring me home. Thank you for doing that for me, as well as for keeping our Houston tribe intact. And to my niece, Niyah: I love you so much, and I also loved every picture that you drew of me.

Pier, I call you my little sis even though you're older than me 'cause I was always bigger. Growing up we were at each other's necks, but I knew then what I still know: we've also got each other's backs. I love you, sis. Thank you for writing to me so often while I was in Russia. Your letters were the best. You honestly shocked me, lol. . . . I never knew you were such a good writer. You kept me up to date with everything happening, and I appreciate you for that. Thank you, too, for looking out for Mom and E.J. And to my nephew E.J.: I am proud of you for stepping up as the man of the house for your mom and for Nana, your grandmother.

Janell Roy, thank you for being a loyal friend since our days growing up in Houston. I call you a friend, but I count you as family. I'm blessed to have you in my life.

While many rallied for my freedom, a few led the charge. At the helm with my wife, Relle, was my agent, Lindsay Kagawa

Colas—executive vice president of Talent and The Collective at Wasserman. Lindz, choosing an agent was a tough decision in 2013. I remember you saying to me, "I'll be there for you during good and bad times." I now know I made the right decision, because you've been a steady companion. Thank you for all the hours you put into bringing me home, as well as for the time you've invested in me throughout my career. You're an amazing supporter. And to your husband and kids, thank you for lending Lindz to my cause, well beyond normal working hours.

During Lindsay and Relle's battle to bring me home, a mighty village stood with them. I'm grateful to the entire Wasserman team for pouring endless resources into my campaign, and for becoming my second family. Under the masterful leadership of Casey Wasserman, the core We Are BG team spent long hours overseeing my campaign. Tracy Hughes, Annie Takahashi, Mike Pickles, Laura Waters-Brown, and Calder Hynes—you were the heartbeat of the crusade. Thank you for all the early mornings and late nights. I also appreciate the phenomenal efforts of others at Wasserman and beyond: Rica Rodman, Carmen Dittoe, Molly Oretsky, Topher Hegngi, Mary Pryor, Sky Dickinson, Maverick Carter, and the team at Uninterrupted, Luke Bonner, Devin Lars, and Joy Oladokun. The words *thank you* fall short in conveying my sincere gratitude.

I'm grateful to my Russian legal counselors, Alex Boykov and Maria Blagovolina. You worked tirelessly on my case and did everything in your power to reunite me with my family. Alex, you were more than my lawyer—you became a friend. Though I had a lot of love coming in from family, I was alone in Russia. You made me feel less lonely. I enjoyed our fun conversations about rock 'n' roll and the blues, and I'm still shocked you'd heard of the Chitlin' Circuit! Thank you for hanging out with me for hours. When I met you, I didn't know what to expect, but you ended up being a gem and a blessing.

Maria, thank you for representing me so well. You were a sounding board and a safe space when I needed to talk about things I felt comfortable discussing only with a woman. Your calm presence gave me a sense of reassurance that all would be okay. When I was sick, you were warm and supportive. Sometimes you'd tell you me, "My daughter says hello." That little comment meant so much, because it reminded me that I was not just a prisoner but a person. Thank you for that gift and many others.

I survived detention with the help of friends. Alena, you kept me sane through my low moments, even as you were dealing with yours. Thank you for making sure I didn't fall into deep depression, or at least that I didn't stay there. And more than that, thank you for giving me a sense of home when I was thousands of miles from mine. I also appreciate your dad for giving me a birthday card, as well as for passing messages to my lawyers. I wish you well and hope to see you on the other side when you're free.

Ann and Kate, you helped me so much during my time in the penal colony. Thank you for teaching me what I needed to know to stay out of trouble. You weren't just my translators, you were my guardian angels. Thank you for all our little pow-wows with snacks Ann brought for us. And when I got sick, you both took great care of me. You made the toughest experience of my life a lot more survivable.

My village grew during my work on *Coming Home*. Kim Witherspoon, I couldn't have asked for a more brilliant literary agent. Thank you for championing my story, and for your long hours and late nights. I've relied on your publishing expertise and appreciate your strong leadership. I'm also grateful to your team at InkWell Management, and especially your associate Maria Whelan. Thank you as well to Jon Liebman, chairman and CEO of Brillstein Entertainment Partners. Your representation is invaluable.

To the team at Knopf: Thank you for giving me the platform to share my story with the world—and for your understanding when I needed time and space during my first year home. I'm particularly grateful to Reagan Arthur, publisher; Maya

Mavjee, president and publisher; and Todd Doughty, senior vice president of publicity and communications. Your commitment to excellence is known around the globe. I'm grateful to have experienced it firsthand.

Jordan Pavlin, thank you for believing in my story. Your discerning edits made *Coming Home* stronger, and your warmth made this journey a joy. Thank you for being the book's first reader and an enthusiastic advocate. I'm also thankful for your assistant editor, Isabel Yao Meyers, as well as for the many behind the scenes who helped bring this narrative to life.

Michelle Burford, my co-writer: You had a clear direction for this book from the start. You were so passionate about my story and making sure we never compromised my voice and memories. You said you'd ride me during our conversations and that there'd be long nights. Well, consider me a Clydesdale horse lol! Thank you for hearing me and pushing me. No one else could've delivered what you have. Your creativity made *Coming Home* blossom.

My basketball family is as wide as it is supportive. Thank you to Cathy Engelbert, the WNBA commissioner, and Adam Silver, the NBA Commissioner, for standing with me through my crisis. I'm also grateful to Nneka Ogwumike, president of the WNBPA; Terri Jackson and the entire WNBPA staff; Travis Murphy, who oversees the NBA's relationship with the State Department; Vince Kozar, president of the Phoenix Mercury; Jim Pitman, former general manager of the Mercury; my Mercury teammates, as well as my WNBA and NBA community; Jim Tooley, CEO of USA Basketball; and Carol Callan, the women's national director of USA Basketball. I'm particularly thankful to Dawn Staley, my former coach during the Tokyo Olympics and the head coach of the South Carolina Gamecocks. While in Russia, my greatest fear was that I'd be forgotten. Thank you for reminding the world of me daily on social media. You spoke my name to anyone who would listen. You also forfeited your visit to the White House to get my wife a meeting with President Biden. You're a force and a friend.

Also, a heartfelt thank you to Tara VanDerveer, head coach of Stanford University's women's basketball team, and Nicki Collen, head coach of the Baylor Bears. Thank you for keeping my story in the headlines.

I'm genuinely grateful for the support of my former team in Russia, UMMC Ekaterinburg. To UMMC's general manager, Max Rybakov, aka Maximilian—thank you for bringing me to the team and for giving me the chance to prove myself on the court. During my difficult chapter, you went above and beyond your job as general manager and even testified at my trial. I appreciate you more than you know. Thank you for opening your family to me and becoming part of mine.

To Evgeniya "Jenya" Belyakova, my UMMC team captain: Along with Max, you testified during my trial. The way you stood up for my character meant the world to me. Also, I couldn't have asked for a better captain and teammate. You made sure the referees treated me fairly during competition. I value your friendship. Also, congratulations on getting married; I wish you well in your next chapter.

My community is part of a country I now cherish more than ever. I'm overwhelmed with gratitude for the leaders of my homeland. President Joe Biden and Vice President Kamala Harris, thank you for negotiating my freedom. You promised to do everything in your power to bring me home, and you lived up to your word. I also appreciate your ongoing efforts to reunite all U.S. hostages with their families. Thank you as well to your administration, including Secretary of State Antony Blinken and Joshua Geltzer and David Cotter of the National Security Council. In addition, I am grateful to the many public servants who raised their voices on my behalf: Congressman Greg Stanton, Congresswoman Sheila Jackson Lee, and Congressman Colin Allred; Senators Mark Kelly and Ron Wyden; and Governor Katie Hobbs.

To Ambassador Roger Carstens, head of the Office of the Special Presidential Envoy for Hostage Affairs (SPEHA): My freedom was made possible by your relentless efforts behind the scenes. Thank you for your months of advocacy, and for being a lifeline for my wife and Houston family. Thank you, too, for your kindness and calm during the prisoner swap and on the flight home. I'm also grateful for the tremendous efforts of the entire SPEHA team, including Fletcher R. Schoen, Carolee B. Walker, and Ken Kosakowski.

Special thanks to Governor Bill Richardson, who spent his last months battling to bring me home. I am forever grateful for his service and legacy; may he rest in peace. I'm also thankful to Mickey Bergman, vice president and executive director of the Richardson Center for Global Engagement. Your partnership was pivotal in my release.

To my Disney family, thank you for believing in my story from the start. I am particularly grateful to Dana Walden, Debra OConnell, Brian Lockhart, Marsha Cooke, Burke Magnus, Tara Nadolny, and Chantre Camack.

The We Are BG team relied on the support of many esteemed thinkers, leaders, and civil rights legends. Among them: Reverend Jesse L. Jackson, founder of the Rainbow PUSH Coalition; Reverend Al Sharpton, founder of the National Action Network; Rachel Noerdlinger, communications advisor to the National Action Network; political strategist Karen Finney; the leaders of the forty-four civil rights organizations who signed a letter petitioning the White House for my release; Fiona Hill, Russian historian and senior fellow at the Brookings Institution; Dr. Danielle Gilbert, political science professor and expert on hostage diplomacy; and Rhea Triñanes and Mike de la Rocha of Revolve Impact.

Thank you to the members of the media who shined a light on my case—and particularly to the Black women in media who organized around me and generously supported my wife both on camera and off. I'm grateful to Angela Rye, Gayle King, Robin Roberts, April Ryan, Joy-Ann Reid, Abby Phillip, Roxane Gay, Jotaka Eaddy, Tiffany Cross, T. J. Quinn, and the women of *The View*—Whoopi Goldberg, Joy Behar, Sunny

Hostin, Sara Haines, and Alyssa Farah Griffin. Thanks as well to *Glamour* and its Women of the Year Awards team.

No one better understands the fight to bring home hostages than the loved ones of those detained. My wife and I depended on the support of the Bring Our Families Home (BOFH) Campaign and each of the families it represents; Neda Sharghi; the team at the James W. Foley Legacy Foundation (JWFLF); and the families of Trevor Reed and Paul Whelan. Thank you for standing by us as we continue to stand with all Americans who are wrongfully detained.

Thank you to the hundreds who sent me letters during my detainment, and to the thousands who've supported me over the years. I may not know your name, but I consider you part of my village. Love has no borders, light has no boundaries. Let's all share more of both.

TO MY SON—

I pray that you learn from my hard times so that you can have a life with a little less pain in it. I love you.

A NOTE ABOUT THE AUTHORS

Brittney Griner is one of the most decorated and influential athletes of her generation—an NCAA champion, a WNBA champion, a two-time Olympic gold medalist, and a winner of the Best Female Athlete ESPY Award. In the 2013 WNBA draft, the Phoenix Mercury selected Griner as the number one overall pick. She was named the WNBA Rookie of the Year that season before helping lead the Mercury to the 2014 WNBA Championship. She's a member of the W25, the WNBA's 2021 list of the top 25 players of all time. A nine-time WNBA all-star, Griner is the first openly gay American professional athlete to sign a major shoe and apparel deal with Nike.

As an ardent supporter of LGBTQ+ causes, Griner has worked with the It Gets Better Project and other organizations inspiring hope for youth facing harassment and bullying. Griner—a Houston native and the proud daughter of a military veteran and retired law enforcement officer—has also partnered with organizations serving veterans and people experiencing homelessness. One such organization is the Phoenix Rescue Mission, where her annual BG Heart and Sole Shoe Drive provides footwear and personal-care items for hundreds. In recognition of her advocacy work, Griner received the WNBA Cares Community Assist Award in 2023 and was honored on *Out* magazine's "Out 100" list the same year. *Time* magazine confirmed Griner's stature and global impact, naming her one of the "100 Most Influential People of 2023."

While traveling to play her tenth season of overseas professional basketball in Russia in 2022, Griner was wrongfully detained for ten months. Thousands rallied to bring Griner home through the We Are BG campaign. During the crusade, Griner joined forces with Bring Our Families Home (BOFH), a campaign to raise awareness and urge action on behalf of all wrongfully detained American hostages. She continues to actively support that cause. She is also collaborating with Disney and ESPN Films on a documentary chronicling her detainment in Russia, along with a scripted series in development with ABC.

Michelle Burford served as Brittney Griner's collaborative writer. She is a number one *New York Times* best-selling author who has partnered with icons such as Cicely Tyson, Alicia Keys, Robin Roberts, and Simone Biles. She is also a founding editor of *O, The Oprah Magazine* and a former *Essence* magazine editor. A native of Phoenix, she lives in New York City.

A NOTE ON THE TYPE

This book was set in Janson, a typeface long thought to have been made by the Dutchman Anton Janson, who was a practicing typefounder in Leipzig during the years 1668–1687. However, it has been conclusively demonstrated that these types are actually the work of Nicholas Kis (1650–1702), a Hungarian, who most probably learned his trade from the master Dutch typefounder Dirk Voskens. The type is an excellent example of the influential and sturdy Dutch types that prevailed in England up to the time William Caslon (1692–1766) developed his own incomparable designs from them.

Composed by North Market Street Graphics,
Lancaster, Pennsylvania

Printed and bound by Friesens Corporation, Canada

Designed by Casey Hampton